Advance Praise for *High Quality Leadership: Practical Guidelines to Becoming a More Effective Manager* **by Erwin Rausch and John B. Washbush**

"Noted author and consultant Erwin Rausch continues to produce cutting-edge materials to facilitate the personal and professional growth of managers and those who aspire to be managers. His 3Cs model and accompanying guidelines approach to teaching management and leadership are fresh, innovative, and responsive to the needs of modern managers and contemporary organizations. This book provides aspiring, novice, and experienced managers valuable and practical strategies to enhance their effectiveness."

> – Jeffrey A. Mello
> Associate Professor Management
> Golden Gate University, San Francisco, CA

"This book contains a lifetime of experience on the insights of becoming a competent manager. Over the years, my goal has been to be a competent manager and gain the trust and respect of my staff. This book would have saved me a lot of time and effort in achieving this goal. It is an excellent book for every manager in every organization."

> – John N. Miri, Esq.
> Trial Court Administrator
> Union County Superior Court, Elizabeth, New Jersey

"*High Quality Leadership* provides a basic, practical overview of key managerial decision points that will be very useful to first time managers."

> – Nancy Monaghan
> Workforce Development Manager
> Alberta Personnel Administration Office

"These guidelines would have been useful to me during my years as a practicing manager. I can see how they could have improved some choices I made . . . the series of questions, presented in three sets of increasing complexity, assist the practicing manager to thoroughly analyze decision situations and other managerial tasks. By comparing these guidelines and question sets with actual situations, the manager can identify critical considerations which may otherwise be missed."

– Timothy W. Edlund, DBA, PE
Associate Professor of Strategic Management
The Graves School, Morgan State University

"This is a good book, particularly for those who are starting to lead...it brings the simple tools for management science to bear on the job of leading others. The scenario and simulation techniques bring the abstract to the real world of leading people properly . . . with enthusiasm and empathy."

– Jerry Shore, Chairman
Park Electrochemical Corporation

"This book offers clear, concise, and practical advice to any manager wishing to improve the performance of his or her organization. I highly recommend *High Quality Leadership* to anyone seeking valuable insights into the managerial process."

– John Malar, Director
Cranford (NJ) Public Library

"This book provides a very useful and compelling guide on how to...achieve high levels of organizational and individual effectiveness. Even if you already consider yourself an effective manager and/or leader, this book can help you become even better. It is worth the investment in making it part of your behavioral repertoire and your professional library."

– Joe LeBoeuf, Ph.D.
LTC, United States Army
Academy Professor, United States Military Academy

High Quality Leadership

Practical Guidelines to Becoming a More Effective Manager

Also available from ASQ Quality Press

Value Leadership: Winning Competitive Advantage in the Information Age
Michael C. Harris

A Review of Managing Quality and Primer for the Certified Quality Manager Exam
Thomas J. Cartin and Donald J. Jacoby

Goldratt's Theory of Constraints: A Systems Approach to Continuous Improvement
H. William Dettmer

Insights to Performance Excellence 1998: An Inside Look at the 1998 Baldrige Award Criteria
Mark L. Blazey

Leading the Way to Competitive Excellence: The Harris Mountaintop Case Study
William A. Levinson, editor

Understanding and Applying Value-Added Assessment: Eliminating Business Process Waste
William E. Trischler

Quality Quotes
Hélio Gomes

The Reward and Recognition Process in Total Quality Management
Stephen B. Knouse

Staffing the New Workplace: Selecting and Promoting for Quality Improvement
Ronald B. Morgan and Jack E. Smith

The Change Agents' Handbook: A Survival Guide for Quality Improvement Champions
David W. Hutton

Let's Work Smarter, Not Harder: How to Engage Your Entire Organization in the Execution of Change
Michael Caravatta

To request a complimentary catalog of ASQ Quality Press publications, call 800-248-1946.

High Quality Leadership

Practical Guidelines to Becoming a More Effective Manager

Erwin Rausch
and
John B. Washbush

American Society for Quality

ASQ™

Quality Press
611 East Wisconsin Avenue
Milwaukee, Wisconsin 53202

High Quality Leadership: A Practical Guideline to Becoming a More Effective Manager
Erwin Rausch and John B. Washbush

Library of Congress Cataloging-in-Publication Data

Rausch, Erwin, 1923–
   High quality leadership : practical guidelines to becoming a more
effective manager / Erwin Rausch and John B. Washbush.
     p.   cm.
   Includes bibliographical references and index.
   ISBN 0–87389-395-6 (alk. paper)
    1. Leadership. 2. Management. 3. Leadership—Case studies.
   4. Management—Case studies. I. Washbush, John B. II. Title.
   HD57.7.R38 1998
   658.4′092—dc21   98–13521
                                        CIP

10 9 8 7 6 5 4 3 2 1

ISBN 0–87389–395–6

ASQ Mission: To facilitate continuous improvement and increase customer satisfaction by
identifying, communicating, and promoting the use of quality principles, concepts, and
technologies; and thereby be recognized throughout the world as the leading authority on, and
champion for, quality.

Attention: Schools and Corporations
ASQ Quality Press books, audiotapes, videotapes, and software are available at quantity
discounts with bulk purchases for business, education, or instructional use. For information,
please contact ASQ Quality Press at 800-248-1946, or write to ASQ Quality Press, P.O. Box 3005,
Milwaukee, WI 53201-3005

For a free copy of the ASQ Quality Press Publications Catalog, including ASQ membership
information, call 800-248-1946.

Printed in the United States of America

♾ Printed on acid-free paper

American Society for Quality

Quality Press
611 East Wisconsin Avenue
Milwaukee, Wisconsin 53202

Contents

Preface

Introduction

If you manage anything, are preparing for managerial responsibilities as a college student, or if you seek to take a managerial career track, this book can be of use to you. It does not matter whether your career is in business, government, health care, retail, engineering, or transportation, just to name a few. It addresses decisions on matters which, directly or indirectly, involve people. If you are or expect to be a manager with a small or a large staff, this book will not only help you make better managerial decisions, it will also help you become a better leader. If you are on a professional track where you manage a function, but do not or will not have anyone reporting to you, your work still has impact on people. Your decisions will bring better results if you consider the thoughts and concepts discussed here.

Even if your management responsibilities are at home, managing family affairs, many sections of this book can be valuable. They address key issues pertaining to planning, decision making, and interpersonal relations, and they often do it from a different perspective than is done elsewhere.

You will find that this book looks at the world from a realistic perspective. When it presents theory it does so with *teeth*—with direct guides to application. While it is not deliberately inspirational, it does, subtly, send the message that you can reach any reasonable goal you set for yourself, provided you persevere in gradually enhancing your decision-making competence. *Gradually* is the key word. The approach suggested here allows you to apply a few simple rules immediately. Then, as you practice them, you will naturally want to know more about them. Thus, you will gain deeper and deeper insight into the kinds of decision-making skills that make for greater success in anything you do.

How to Get the Most from This Book

Even though this book quickly gets to the point in each section, you are not likely to read it straight through. In fact, you would be doing yourself a great disservice if you struggled to finish it in one sitting. You will get much more from it if you take it in little bites.

Much of what is discussed here will take on added meaning when you glance through a chapter the second time, or if you continue reading after a pause of a few days or even weeks.

Pages marked Additional Insights contain useful information which expands the discussion, but is not central to the basic thrust. That thrust is to help you become acquainted with the 3Cs model guidelines (sometimes referred to as the 3Cs guideline questions), and to show how you can best apply them to your own work. Some Additional Insights sections provide expansion of the model itself, while others relate background information such as theories, and still others suggest procedures to use.

You have the same options that you have with any book—to skim sections and to select the segments you want to read. In that respect, it might be useful for you to be aware that, after some introductory discussions, Chapter 1 presents the skeleton of the 3Cs model and the 3Cs guideline questions, which are the core of the message of this book, at the basic, simplest level. Chapter 1 then illustrates the use of the questions in two scenarios (example situations), with analyses and conclusions.

Chapters 2 and 3 present the same 3Cs guidelines in more detailed and comprehensive versions, respectively. There are three illustrative scenarios in each chapter, one for each of the 3Cs. Analyses and conclusions follow each scenario. These chapters provide increasing structure to the use of the guidelines. They offer specific suggestions on the types of issues that might be considered when adapting the respective guideline to a specific situation.

Finally, Chapter 4 provides the complete 3Cs model on which the guidelines are based. There was the question, during preparation of this book, whether the subject of Chapter 4 is more appropriate where it is, early in the book or possibly as the second chapter or as an appendix. The decision to leave it at the end was based on three considerations:

- Almost the entire benefit of the book, in helping managers become better leaders and enhancing their decisions through consideration of the 3Cs guidelines, can be obtained without reading Chapter 4.

- Placing the chapter early in the book would expose readers to a heavy load of conceptual material that might be demotivating for many.

- Nevertheless, the content of the chapter is quite valuable. It offers additional conceptual foundation for the 3Cs questions and thus closes the circle that was started with the simple guidelines in Chapter 1. The subject should therefore not be relegated to an Appendix.

All literature references are in the back, just before the index.

The Book's History

Like most books, this volume has a long history. In fact, it has three histories—one for the concepts, which give this book a foundation that is based solidly on the literature pertaining to management, leadership, interpersonal relations, and learning. A second history can be told about the guidelines which provide the bridge between theory and practice, and a third one for the travails of the author. The first two are summarized in this preface. The third one can be summed up with a few lines, slightly modified, from a famous poem:

> First across the gulf we cast
> Kite born threads, till lines are passed
> And then we build the bridge, at last.

> *John B. O'Reilly, A Builder's Lesson*

No need to waste your time with detail. Suffice it to say that much of the theoretical foundations can be found in *Balancing the Needs of People and Organizations: The Linking Elements Concept*, a book on the 3Cs model of management, which Erwin wrote with great expectations in the late 1970s. It was good to us (not the royal 'us' or the first person plural, but those of us who reaped the benefits); several large organizations built their management development programs on it and it sold a satisfactory number of copies. It did not, however, meet our expectations.

That is the reason for this book. It is much more reader friendly because it has boiled complex issues down to their essential core concepts and organized them in an appealing architecture, with scenarios and analyses of the scenarios, to illustrate the practical application of the concepts. It also provides brief capsules of useful information in separate sections (called Additional Insights) which are at the end of each chapter and that can be skipped without losing a beat from the flow of the discussion. Most importantly, the book provides a formula with guidelines for making better management and leadership decisions you can apply immediately.

Guidelines can be important for readers and learners at all stages in their lives, especially while studying management and leadership. As Ernest Stark of Bellevue University has phrased it:

> Adult learners usually crave perspective on the change in knowledge and understanding, which is required of them during leadership training and development. They seek insight into the relative importance of the material they are asked to absorb and guidance on how to integrate it into their existing knowledge base. Beyond the integration of knowledge, they exhibit a parallel need to discover how to turn such knowledge to practical purposes.

Especially for the benefit of readers who are knowledgeable in what the academic world refers to as *organizational behavior*, it is important to point out that this book does not bring any new formal research results. In fact, there is little that is *new* in the way of theory. The strength of this book lies in the way it shapes conclusions, from past research and existing theories, into a practical model with useful "starter" guidelines for decisions. These guidelines can then be shaped by you as you gain practice with guidelines and experience in working with them. The book presents a progressive arrangement of these guidelines, from simple to thorough and comprehensive. This, the authors hope, will lead to easier use, development of sound habits, and to ever greater competence.

Contributions of This Book

To avoid false modesty, we are, however, listing the significant conceptual contributions by the authors which are important foundations for this book, in addition to the idea of nonprescriptive guidelines that users can adapt to their personal style or use as a foundation for guidelines of their own. These contributions are:

- The comprehensive model of management/leadership which rests on the organization's need, and the need of its members, for Control, Competence (of all stakeholders), and Climate (Rausch 1978)

- The emphasis on the two separate aspects of every managerial decision—the functional (often technical) and the management/leadership considerations (Rausch and Washbush 1996)

- The distinction between goals and action steps, which can have a great impact on the outcomes of managerial/ leadership decisions (Rausch 1978)

- The application of the distinction between importance and urgency to goal selection and priority setting which was previously published in various titles on time management and others (Didactic Systems 1977; the National Fire Protection Association 1977; the Bureau of National Affairs 1978, 1985). Stephen Covey has since made the concept famous in *The Seven Habits of Highly Effective People* (1989) and in *First Things First* (1994), probably without awareness of our prior publications which had only relatively limited exposure.

- The separation of needs, in Maslow's Hierarchy, into those which can be satisfied with psychological rewards and those which require tangible rewards (Rausch 1977, 1978, 1985). This distinction emphasizes the great many ways in which managers/leaders can show appreciation for contributions of staff members, the steady but mundane as well as the outstanding ones.

Three less-significant contributions by the authors may also deserve brief mention here:

- The definition of *fairness* in performance appraisal, which was discussed in detail in *Win-Win Performance Management/Appraisal* (Rausch 1985)

- The idea that all who are involved in a conflict can appoint themselves "Manager of Conflict" and thereby contribute more effectively to its resolution (not previously published)

- The importance of using a wide range of approaches for showing appreciation for steady nonspectacular contributions by staff members, not only for those that are outstanding (Didactic Systems 1996)

Differential definitions of management and leadership have deliberately been avoided. As Chapter 1, Additional Insights A, (Management Leadership Theories: Origins, Growth, and Atrophy) points out, all definitions of these terms are highly subjective (Stogdill 1974; Bennis and Nanus 1985). Chapter 1 Additional Insights B and C, furthermore, discuss leadership and the related motivation theories so the reader who feels the need for definitions can draw on the discussions there or on the references provided. To stay away from the many controversies that swirl around all the subjective definitions, we discuss skills and briefly mention traits that distinguish effective leaders from others. The benefits of the ideas presented in this book do not seem to require that a sharp line be drawn between *management* and *leadership.*

The guidelines in this book have proven their worth in many hundreds of cases. Managers, in various private and public management development programs, were asked to use them for reviewing decisions or plans. Almost without exception, each manager made some change, sometimes a small one, sometimes a significant one, after considering just the basic form of the guidelines.

If you apply these simple, initial guidelines to one or two of your decisions, they will stimulate you to dig deeper. Then you will know more about the concepts on which they are founded and be able to apply them with greater confidence and to more complex situations. You are encouraged to modify the guidelines so they fit well into the way you make decisions.

Beyond serving as quality checks for decisions and plans before they are implemented, the guidelines also provide structure and focus for preparing reports and proposals to management. They help to ensure that all bases are touched.

The guidelines can also be useful when answering questions, and especially essay questions in examinations such as those for ASQ Certified Manager, certification programs of other societies, and even for some professional licenses. On the ASQ Quality Manager certification, for instance, they could provide foundation for answers to questions pertaining to the Body of Knowledge segments on Project Management, Human Resource Management, Training and Education, in elements of Organizations and Their Functions, and of Customer Satisfaction and Focus. Guidelines questions could also be useful in sharpening the written answers to the open-ended questions in the Constructed-Response segment of the tests.

Acknowledgments

In light of the three histories, to give full due to all those who have contributed effort, time, thought, and advice would bring a substantial increase in the size of the book. I have therefore attempted to credit those who have been of greatest help, and I must ask for understanding from the many others whose contributions are not specifically mentioned here.

First, I think I should mention those few among the first university professors (names withheld) whom I had approached for comments, who were helpful far beyond their intent, when they treated me like a graduate student: "There is nothing new in what you are saying, Erwin." (As if I had claimed to present something new rather than something that makes it easier and more enjoyable to learn the same stuff.) "Have you read such-and-such book by so-and-so?" Even though I glanced at, or read, those suggested titles with which I had not been acquainted, rarely were they relevant or contributed something of substance. Still, they helped me greatly by alerting me to the many obstacles I had to prepare for, and that was critical in overcoming those that did present themselves.

Almost all other academics I had the pleasure to meet were most directly helpful. By far the most important is, of course, John Washbush, the coauthor, who has given generously of his time and wisdom in his many written contributions and his numerous editorial comments.

Then there is our computer guru, Seth Savitsky, whose discipline in managing the attempt to make the ideas even more readily available in a sophisticated program for PCs has often forced better structure and coordination of thoughts.

I also have to mention Joseph A. Wolfe of Tulsa University, who helped me get started in presenting papers at academic conferences, where I met my coauthors and contributors to various papers and presentations, and where I faced the critiques so essential to honing of ideas.

The contributions by Ernest Stark of Bellevue University have to be gratefully acknowledged. His detailed knowledge of management education and the specific insights he shared during preparation of several papers which we jointly presented at academic conventions have been most helpful.

Susan Halfhill and Dahlia Bradshaw Lynn made similar contributions as researchers on a student survey pertaining to the use of guidelines in teaching of management courses, in their participation with workshops at academic conferences, and in their contributions to a paper on the research project being submitted for publication in a scholarly journal.

The editors of MCB University Press' *Total Quality Review* and later *Total Quality Magazine*, March L. Jacques and John Peters, as editors are wont to do, forced greater thought discipline than I, at first, had willingly devoted to many ideas. MCB University Press' internet presence, at http://www.mcb.co.uk also deserves mention here. It leads to a plethora of articles on management, many of which have contributed to my personal development and thus, indirectly, to this book. It also provided the venue, at http://www.mcb.co.uk/confhome.htm, for a virtual conference which I convened on New Approaches to Management Education and Development. Preparations for the conference and comments of the panel members also proved helpful.

Equally if not more helpful was Roger Holloway, the manager of ASQ Quality Press, without whose help this book may never have been written in so reader-friendly a format; and Jeanne Bohn, the book's editor, whose suggestions and encouragements and liaison with reviewers were a source of strengths along the path. The reviews of Thomas Kubiak, who has extensive book-review background, and those of L. David Weller, who graciously permitted the use of their names, contributed a number of suggestions that significantly added further to reader friendliness.

Library research is an essential element in all serious writing, and here the help of the reference librarians at the Cranford Public Library was invaluable. Though operating within the confines of the limited resources available in a community library, they and Bonnie Goldstein and Jill Riley, in particular, were able to access databases and library stacks in collections all over the state. That made searches far easier, and so much less time-consuming than could have been done without their help.

Much credit goes to academic colleagues (though not an academic myself, I hope that I may use this appellation) who participated either as "speakers" in the internet conference, as researchers in the student survey research project, or as copresenters. These colleagues include David Anderson, Robert Boozer, Timothy W. Edlund, Janet Kelly, David Lemak, Jeff Mello, Paul Miesing, Joseph A. Raelin, Jerry G. Stevenson, James A. Wilson, and Blue Wooldridge, in addition to Susan Halfhill, Dahlia Bradshaw Lynn, and Ernest Stark, who were previously mentioned.

The members of three more groups also deserve specific mention for the way they helped to shape and sharpen ideas. They are:

1. The coauthors of, and contributors to, related books, simulations, and magazine or journal articles. Though one book has yet to be published, their thoughts also helped to sharpen fuzzy thinking that existed on some of the issues covered here. They include Michelle Bernstein, Harry Carter, Arnold Drake, Arthur Kiamie, Joanna Kozoll, Robert Laudicina, Harvey Lieberman, Elliott Mininberg, Richard Nichols, John Pourdehnad, George Rausch, Bernard Scholz, and Nathan Weiss.

2. The professors and practitioners who attended the workshops, symposia, or presentations of papers which my coauthors and/or I gave at various academic conferences, and who added further refinements to the ideas presented there.

3. The many hundreds of attendees at seminars on the 3Cs management model, whose questions and challenges provided the crucible in which ideas were sharpened, honed, and at the same time made more digestible.

And finally, though obviously not last, I have to thank my wife and my daughter. My wife, for the patience with which she has read manuscripts, not once, not twice, but sometimes innumerable times, and whose down-to-earth comments were often painful, but unfailingly valuable. My daughter, for the assistance she has given me, and continues to give, to bring the ideas in this book to the attention of those who might benefit from them.

Erwin Rausch

The authors welcome comments and questions. These should be addressed to Erwin Rausch, PO Box 457, Cranford NJ 07016, USA; e-mail: didacticra@aol.com; Tel: 908-789-2194; Fax: 908-789-0038

Three Simple Questions That Can Help You Be a Better Manager and Leader, Immediately

(The Basic Guidelines)

New occasions teach new duties;
Time makes ancient good uncouth;
They must upward still, and onward,
Who would keep abreast of Truth;
Lo, before us gleam her campfires!
We ourselves must Pilgrims be,
Launch our Mayflower, and steer boldly
through the desperate winter sea,
Nor attempt the Future's portal
with the Past's now worn-down key.

The Present Crisis, James Russell Lowell
December 1844 (slightly modified)

Introduction

A little knowledge can be a dangerous thing, they say, and that's often true. Fortunately, not always. It can also be very helpful, especially if it's 'right on.'

For instance, in management and leadership, knowledge and use of a few carefully chosen guidelines can help you stand out as a competent manager/leader.*

They can bring a lifeline when you have to make a tough decision, the way a small, steep, rocky hill can bring a glimpse of the village's church steeple and show the direction in which to head for someone who is lost in a forest. More detailed guidelines can bring even more help, like the view from a hunter's tower, which shows a section of a stream that leads to the village. The hill takes some climbing, and the tower even more, but they sure beat spending the night in the forest.

This book presents such critical glimpses on core issues in management/leadership decision making. It can bring what Aristotle couldn't give to Pharaoh—a royal road to learning. Its formula is easy to apply immediately. With use and additional learning, there are ever greater benefits.

After only a cursory reading of one chapter and a glance at the others, this book can become a valuable reference when you face sticky situations. The increasingly detailed questions (often with possible answers) that the book presents are certain to stimulate ideas that will help you develop effective solutions.

Furthermore, chances are high that you will find at least one useful insight, and possibly several, wherever you read, whether it be one of the scenarios, a scenario analysis or conclusion, or one of the Additional Insights that are at the end of the chapters.

---

*The terms *manager/leader* and *management/leadership* are used here because:

- Competent managers should also be competent leaders, as supervisors, as managers of functions without staff, and in unstructured groups such as meetings of peers.
- Most skills, though not necessarily traits, are common to both management and leadership.
- Managers therefore need to gain thorough knowledge about both functions and acquire the skills of management and those of leadership that can be learned.

The 3Cs Guideline Questions

As you read on, you will explore three guideline questions (the 3Cs guidelines) with many layers of meaning. They are in three progressively more detailed forms: basic, intermediate, and comprehensive. When combined with frequent use, common sense, and some experience, even the simplest set can show the way to sound management and leadership decisions at work and in other organizations where you may be active—and to better decisions in your personal affairs.

The basic set of the initial guideline questions is very general. Still, it will make you critically review decisions that you are about to make, and point to ways in which you might be able to improve them. There is one question each for Control,* Competence, and Climate in an organization:

Basic Control Question: Are Things Going Right?

What else needs to be done to ensure effective Control and coordination, so that the decision which we are considering will lead toward the outcome we seek, and so we'll know when we have to modify our implementation, or plan, because we are not getting the results we want? In other words, how can we gain better control, or coordination, over this process of "getting there"?

Basic Competence Question: Does Everyone Know What to Do, and Can They Do It?

What else needs to be done so that all those who will be involved in implementing the decision, and those who will otherwise be affected (all the stakeholders), have the necessary Competencies

---

*There are some negative connotations associated with the word *Control* in certain environments. They usually concern the use of the word to mean tight control by higher levels in an organization, including what sometimes is referred to as *snoopervision*. The meaning of the word, as used here, is appropriate control, with a high degree of participation and with most decision authority at the lowest level where adequate information and competence is available.

to ensure effective progress, and satisfying use of the product or service?**

Basic Climate Question:*** How Will the Stakeholders React?

What else needs to be done so that the reaction of the various groups and individuals who have to implement the decision or plan, and those who will be affected by it (all the stakeholders), will be in favor of it or at least have as positive a view as possible so there will be a favorable Climate?

Interpretation of this basic set of questions relies solely on your personal experience and current knowledge. It does not provide the detailed specifics, and with it, the increasing confidence in your decisions that you'll get from the ideas in the more detailed and comprehensive sets.

The guidelines pertain mostly to matters which do not regularly show up on the *things to do* lists of managers/leaders. They involve the kinds of things that are easily overlooked because they do not ring bells or otherwise make themselves visible on a regular day. If ignored, however, they can lead to nasty crises, usually after damage has occurred. For the competent manager/leader who tries to anticipate future problems, the 3Cs guidelines can be of great help.

**The phrase *and satisfying use of the product or service?* may require explanation since it may not be obvious. It refers to the need for users to understand how to use a product or obtain the full advantage of a service. This need is especially acute with complex equipment or computer programs, and even banking services, where the manuals and brochures, intended to convey the information that will make users competent, are often inadequate for the intended purpose.

***There is also a need to clarify the use of the word *Climate* in relation to the word *culture* when referring to climate or culture in an organization. The word *Climate* is used here as defined—the extent to which the organization's management considers the satisfaction of stakeholders in decisions. The word *culture* is used in a broader sense, not specific to any one decision, and it represents all aspects of an organization's environment—the way the organization resolves the requirement to balance its characteristics and needs with those of the stakeholders.

IMPORTANT NOTE WITH RESPECT TO CULTURE: It may seem, at first, that the guidelines recommended here are appropriate only for some of the Western cultures. That is probably an inaccurate assumption. A manager who has to work with people from other cultures, or who works in another part of the world, no matter where, or how different the culture from ours, can apply the suggested guidelines appropriately. Participation in decision making and in developing norms will do much to automatically adjust the manager's decisions to another culture, as will the climate guidelines.

Furthermore, throughout this book, it is stressed that the USE of guidelines for the leadership component of management is where the reader will find the greatest benefits from the thoughts expressed here, not from the suggested guidelines themselves. It is consistently recommended that the 3Cs guidelines can be used as a starting point but, if they are used at all, that they should be adapted to the managers'/leaders' environment and personal style.

The Management/Leadership Model

The guidelines suggested and illustrated here with realistic situations, are based on the sound, comprehensive management/leadership *model* (the 3Cs model) that is solidly based on the research and writings of management scholars (see Chapter 1, Additional Insights A, Management/Leadership Theories: origins, growth and atrophy; Additional Insights B, Leadership Theories; and Additional Insights C, Motivation Theories). A skeleton diagram, in Figure 1.1, and the associated discussion provide a brief overview of the model. A more detailed discussion can be found

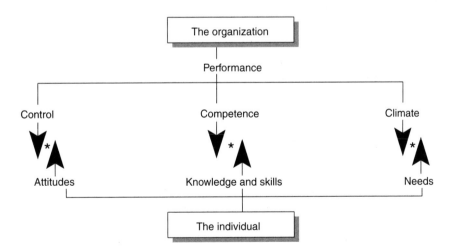

Figure 1.1 Diagram of the 3Cs of management or the Linking elements concept. Asterisks (*) indicate the skills (Linking Elements) a manager must apply to facilitate alignment between the needs and characteristics of the organization and the individuals.

in Chapter 4. The model has been used widely in management development programs, in such diverse organizations as the American Management Association, U.S. Air, Cabrini Hospitals, U.S. Federal Prison System, U.S. Federal Office of Personnel Management, U.S. Army, U.S. Navy, Government of Alberta, General Electric, Girl Scouts, and JC Penney. The entire model, or portions of it, has been published in various books and publications (Rausch 1978, 1980, 1985; Heyel 1982; Associates, Office of Military Leadership 1976; Didactic Systems 1977; Jones and Lieberman 1978). In a special edition, the model is required foundation for the fire officer exam in many states (Rausch 1977; Rausch & Carter 1989).

The model identifies the 3Cs on the top half of the diagram: Control, Competence, and Climate. They spell out the characteristics and needs of an effective organization. In effect, they define the arena where a manager's/leader's decisions are made.

- **Control** concerns the definition, communication, and coordination of direction to ensure that it is clear and understood and that warnings are raised quickly when progress is unsatisfactory. Control, as used in the 3Cs model, is not control by the manager, but rather control by the organizational unit *as a result of appropriate participation* in all relevant decisions and plans, as suggested by the model.

- **Competence** concerns the knowledge, skills, and abilities (KSAs) for the functions, including management/leadership and other stakeholder competence.

- **Climate** concerns the environment in which staff members and other stakeholders can find the maximum possible satisfaction from participating or being affected.

At the same time, the bottom half of the diagram details what staff members bring to the work scene; that is, their attitudes toward the organization's control policies and procedures, their competencies, and their needs.

It is the manager's/leader's job to bring the best possible alignment between the characteristics and needs of the organization and those of the people in the organization. The goal is to reduce, or eliminate, the gaps between the opposing arrows in the diagram.

This book can help you gradually build your knowledge and skills for doing that, through sharpened management and leadership decision making. Later it can serve as a convenient reference on all related skills as you endeavor to gain greater competence.

You may have been led to think that management and leadership require different skills and different guidelines, or that management and leadership skills apply only to positions with supervisory responsibilities. Neither is true. Decision skills, though not the personal traits, are almost the same for sound management and for effective leadership. The guidelines that will make you a good manager are almost certain to make you a better leader at the same time. They apply at all organizational levels, and even to managers of functions without direct reports since, almost without exception, management of functions affects people— the stakeholders.

Beyond decision making, the main difference between a good manager who is also a good leader and one who is not lies with personal characteristics. Some of these traits can be acquired. Most, for better or for worse, are part of your nature. There is no use fretting about them, however. If you accept at least some of the guidelines suggested here initially as a starting point, and then gradually shape them to fit your personal style, you will have won most of the battle. You can then concentrate on also acquiring those traits of more effective leaders which you do not have already.

The Critical Importance of the Distinction Between Functional (Technical)* and Management/Leadership Considerations in Almost Every Decision

While it is easy to see that management and leadership is decision making, it is not widely recognized that there are two sides to every such decision.

---

*The word *technical* will be used as a synonym for *functional* throughout the book to prevent excessive repetition of the word *functional*. For the purposes here there is validity to such use, even though there are some significant distinctions between the dictionary explanations of the meaning of the two words. It is hoped that the reader will accept this usage.

In your work, you are a professional in some field. You are familiar with the technical (functional) aspects of your function. You are comfortable with that knowledge whether it is in operations, customer service, marketing, or accounting and whether it pertains to the organization's activity, such as manufacturing, retail, health care, or even government, including, of course, the quality considerations in all of these. You probably have studied the function in school, and most of your experience, even as a manager, has concentrated on it. In every decision, you apply that technical knowledge. This book, however, does *not* pertain to that side of your decisions.

It covers the other side of your decisions—the management and leadership considerations which should, but often do not, get the same amount of thought and attention. It's about those aspects of your decisions which help you see to it that your priorities are on the right things, and that these things get done right, hopefully the first time.

Here the book talks about guidelines for those aspects of decisions, and of skills, that are relevant no matter what the field, or the position, in which you work. It also speaks to you in your roles as parent and as a responsible member of the other organizations—religious, recreational, or fraternal—to which you may belong. In short, it can help you make better decisions everywhere.

Applying the Foundation for Guideline Questions: (The 3Cs Model)

If you accept that it is the manager's/leader's responsibility to see to it that the right things get done right, then you also have to accept that people will be affected.

When people are involved in the implementation of a decision, or affected by it, it is almost always desirable to consider their reaction. Because they have a stake in the work or in the outcome, we use the name *stakeholders* for them, including the staff members of the organization in your unit and in others, as well as the customers, clients, suppliers, neighbors, and so on.

In effect, you will get the best results if, as manager/leader, you constantly strive to align their needs and characteristics with those of the organizational unit, or of the task. The three keys to such an alignment are the 3Cs from Figure 1.1: paying close attention to achieving appropriate Control (including effective coordination), ensuring thorough Competence, and creating and maintaining a satisfying Climate.

Now that might not sound like it brings much in the way of new insights, but there may be more depth than appears on first sight. Let's see what a few specific situations might reveal.

Four Examples

1. In our first example, the department manager thinks that his people know what to do and that they work out problems with each other. That is certainly true in most cases, especially when it comes to routine work. Once in a while, though, projects have to be handled that require new work arrangements. The department manager thinks that the staff members should work out what needs to be done; he says that he does not want to interfere in their work—they know what to do and they should do it. The result is that there is friction when new projects are started; some things get delayed because people can't agree on how they should be done, and sometimes quality problems result. Everyone blames everyone else in those situations, people are frustrated, and morale suffers. The manager thinks he is doing right, because he does not look over the shoulders of staff members and treats them like professionals. Still, he overlooks two of his responsibilities: to assure sound coordination, and to see to it that potentially damaging conflicts are prevented or resolved.

The conclusion from this example is that better alignment between the organization's and the people's needs could be achieved if the manager followed guidelines that clarify his role in appropriate coordination, a major element of control. The same can be said about more astute attention to the needs of people, with greater attention to guidelines that would bring a more satisfying climate.

2. Another organization designs and distributes computer programs for specialized applications. Once a new user becomes thoroughly familiar with them, they are excellent and save considerable time over alternate ways of doing that particular work.

The problem is with the quality of communications with customers through the Users' Manual and the Help files. Most users, even very computer-literate people, have great difficulty finding the information they need. The result? A larger staff in the customer support function, more telephone lines, a longer wait for customers who call in for help, and so on. All of these quality problems could be avoided with better analysis of their learning needs—greater management attention to the guidelines that concern Competence—not only competence of staff members who prepare manuals and Help files, but in this case customer, and distributor competence.

As this example shows, the quality needs of customers and the needs of the organization for lower costs could both be satisfied with greater knowledge, skills, and abilities (KSAs) for developing better manuals. Thinking about the 3Cs, but especially Competence, and even Climate, or following guidelines pertaining to all 3Cs elements, can avoid annoying and possibly serious problems.

3. In another organization, production of a new product started recently. There were some early indications that one aspect of the design may lead to low reliability when the product is used under certain conditions. Only very careful attention to related production tasks could prevent the quality problem. This was, of course, pointed out to the relevant people in the production process.

Soon a fairly large number of complaints came in from the field. Investigation showed that special attention to the critical tasks sometimes lapsed when a regular staff member on that critical operation was absent and replacement personnel had to be used.

Though this problem may be less pervasive than the one in the previous example, it still points to the critical importance of ensuring staff competence. At the same time this case hints at the need for adequate control so that something important does not slip between the cracks and so that a problem is detected quickly, and remedied, when it does arise. Had there been adequate training for replacement staff and safeguards against inadequate attention to the critical tasks, the quality problem may not have occurred or would have been identified and possibly corrected before there were field complaints.

4. This final example concerns an organizational unit with about 200 staff members, including 20 with supervisory responsibilities. During a recent downsizing the unit was not hit as hard as some others because its work is critical, highly professional, and more in demand, here and elsewhere, than most other functions. Still, despite favorable pay and good benefits even before the downsizing, and more apparent since then, people in most departments are dissatisfied.

Management is aware of these negative feelings and concerned that they are one of the reasons for the limited success of the recently started quality improvement program. In trying to eliminate the dissatisfactions, it has relied almost exclusively on repeated assurances that the organization's problems were in the past, and that the future looks bright. Because staff members do not trust management, these statements are taken with a grain of salt. Management has not done much to reduce the widespread insecure feelings. Many staff members are looking for new positions and some of the most competent have already left.

It is not hard to see what's wrong here. The needs of people are not being met. It is also fairly clear that management is lacking knowledge, skills, and abilities (KSAs) in communications and leadership. However, the differences in the climates of the departments hint at considerable variation in management/leadership knowledge, skills, and abilities of the staff members with supervisory responsibilities, below the top level. Some are better able to insulate their people from the causes of dissatisfactions than others, and better able to align their needs and characteristics with those of the organization. In the subunits where the dissatisfactions are less pronounced, the supervisors do things differently than in the others. You could think of them as following guidelines better, or following better guidelines.

It is conceivable that the unsatisfactory climate and the inadequate management communications competence contributed to the need for downsizing.

These examples demonstrate, and dramatize, the 3Cs: the fundamental requirements for effective functioning of any organization.

Please note that, though the three requirements of the 3Cs model— Control, Competence, and Climate—are stated as three distinct entities, the actions necessary to achieve each one, often impact on one or both of the others.

- Control, which involves coordination, has a powerful impact on climate because knowledge of the extent to which one's organization has control over the direction in which it is moving, and the level of friction created by the quality of coordination, affect work satisfaction and thus the climate.

- Control affects competence because it determines the extent to which competence strengths are used and competence weaknesses are reduced.

- Competence affects Control because effectiveness depends on the extent to which people can do what they are expected to do.

- Competence affects Climate because stress, and feelings about work in general, are influenced by how competent people feel.

- It goes without saying that anything done to affect Climate, in turn, affects both Control and Competence.

The Three Basic 3Cs Guideline Questions

Looking back at the four situations, it is not hard to draw some basic, initial guidelines from them.

As you have already seen, the three guidelines are nothing else but three questions about the three fundamental requirements (Control, Competence, and Climate). They leave it up to you to decide how to apply them in your specific situation.

Do not look back at the guideline questions now. First, read on.

Even though the questions are general and nonspecific, they can be powerful if you treat them seriously. Try them. Without looking at the guideline questions, think of an important decision, or plan. It doesn't matter whether it concerns something in the past or something that addresses a current challenge.

Can't think of one? Then think about something significant that you would like to accomplish at work. You don't have to have people reporting to you. It can concern a project that is almost solely your responsibility.

If you are thinking about a challenge from the past, remind yourself of the steps you took to resolve it. If it is something new, lay out a course of action that you think is a pretty good one (or even a very good one).

Only after you've done all that, slowly and carefully ask yourself the three guideline questions which are repeated below. Give considerable thought to each one.

If they work with you the way they have worked, almost without fail, with hundreds of managers and situations, you will make some change in your plan—possibly a small one, maybe a big one. That is the point. Even in this basic form, without discussion of all the issues on which they are based, the questions will have helped you improve on your decision.

Basic Control Question: Are Things Going Right?

What else needs to be done to ensure effective Control and coordination, so that the decision which we are considering will lead toward the outcome we seek, and so we'll know when we have to modify our implementation, or plan, because we are not getting the results we want? In other words, how can we gain better control, or coordination, over this process of *getting there?*

Basic Competence Question: Does Everyone Know What to Do, and Can They Do It?

What else needs to be done so that all those who will be involved in implementing the decision, and those who will otherwise be affected (all the stakeholders), have the necessary Competencies to ensure effective progress and satisfying use of the product or service?

Basic Climate Question: How Will the Stakeholders React?

What else needs to be done so that the reaction of the various groups and individuals who have to implement the decision or plan, and those who will be affected by it (all the stakeholders), will be in favor of it or at least have as positive a view as possible so there will be a favorable Climate?

Well, what change or changes should you make in the way you approached, or plan to approach, your personal challenge?

If you couldn't think of any changes, there are two likely possibilities.

1. You are an outstanding decision maker and very knowledgeable in management and leadership. You had therefore considered, thoroughly, all the issues which the 3Cs guideline questions raise. For you, this book can only bring reinforcement and possibly sharper perspectives on things with which you are already familiar, or

2. You have not considered all the possible issues which may affect your decision. One or the other may have prompted you to make a change, as you will see when you explore the application of the guidelines in this and later chapters.

THE SCENARIOS

The scenarios in the remainder of the chapter and their analyses that follow will demonstrate the application of the guideline questions.

SCENARIO 1.1

Jean's Challenge: Staffing the Extended Hours*

Focus: All 3Cs guidelines, introductory example

---

*This story was first published in *TQM Magazine* V9/1, Jan/Feb 1997, pp. 83–85, MCB University Press, with different analysis and conclusions.

Abstract: Jean, the manager of the packing and shipping departments, has to solve the problem presented by the company's policy to ship all orders received up to 5:00 PM on the same day. Sometimes there are not enough people on duty after 5:00 PM to get all orders out.

❖ ❖ ❖ ❖ ❖ ❖

The Scenario

"You know, Bev, if I could only get better teamwork between my two groups, I'd get John off my back." Jean referred to the Marketing Manager who had told her that customer complaints about delayed service were hurting business. "He hasn't got it easy because we do delay some customer orders, especially those that come late in the day. And it seems that's happening more frequently nowadays. I really have to do something. What do you think, Bev? You know the situation, and my people."

Over lunch, Jean and Beverly often talk business. Their personalities clicked from the moment, several years ago, when Jean was hired to head up the packing and shipping departments. Both now have young children and talking about them can be relaxing fun. But they are also both very conscientious and their different opinions on how to manage and lead adds a spicy edge to their lunch conversations. Each respects the other's opinions and they feel that their differences help them come up with better solutions when a challenge faces either one of them.

"I don't know," Beverly replied, "if someone calls in an order late in the day, is it reasonable for them to expect shipment the same day?"

"Our catalog says that orders received before 5pm will go out the same day; the post office is open 'til six. We have arrangements with UPS and the air carriers to pick up between six and seven." Jean stopped, with a pensive look.

"That's why you have that skeleton crew with regular hours 'til six, and at least one person 'til seven, right? But, I guess you run into the problem, sometimes, where someone is out and no one wants to stay. I can understand that; they all have families and want to get home. Still, it probably wouldn't be too hard on them to commit to taking turns, being 'on-call' for such emergencies, even if they'd average one a week. Or, does it happen more often? Do you always get the orders out if no one is absent?" Hey, did you hear me? Jean had that far away look in her eyes that made Beverly wonder whether she had paid attention.

"I was thinking that maybe I should call them all together to talk about this."

"What, all 20 of them? I wouldn't do that. It might lead to conflicts. Let's first see what we come up with."

"Yeah, that's what I started to think, but I guess you are right. What were you saying? I didn't hear it all. Oh, yes, you asked whether we had the problem sometimes when the late crew are all in. We do, but not too often. That's another headache—when I see it coming I go around to everybody and try to get more people to stay. Sometimes I'm OK and sometimes it seems like there's nothing I can do except stay myself—and I've had to do that more often than I like. What else did you say?"

"I don't know anymore—oh, yes, what about a rotating 'on-call' system to stay later?"

"That's one possibility, certainly. I was first thinking of trying to get more of them to take a later shift, you know, report later and stay later. I don't know whether I could find anyone, though. It would be nice if I could hire some people but we have so little turnover. It'll be a long time before I can add someone for that later shift."

"You probably should first do that—see whether some of your regular people will take later hours. If not, try the on-call idea. It wouldn't be a firm commitment, and I like things that can be tried before they become permanent. Let's also look at what else you could do." Beverly is careful—she does not want to make a strong suggestion—just stimulate ideas and kick them around to see what they may bring.

"I haven't been able to think of anything. If we can't come up with anything better, I'll first see whether some of my people are available—maybe the situation has changed for some of them. Then I'll bounce the on-call idea around. That way I'll see how they feel about it. But I'd like to have more things to suggest if they don't like it."

"I understand you have to be prepared. That's why we should kick it around some more. Whatever you decide to do, you probably should explore it, confidentially, with the supervisors in your two sections. But if nothing better comes up, I'd go for the on-call idea, myself. Hey, wait a second, Jean! Do you think you could find some people who live nearby who would be available on a call-in basis, to make a few extra bucks once in a while? If you had several, you probably would always be able to get someone."

"We tried that once; it didn't work so good. We had several people, but when we really needed someone, we couldn't get 'em. Still, we could try that again, in conjunction with the 'on-call' rotation. Oh, well. Let me call them all together, state the problem, and tell them that we've got to solve it. They'll probably come up with something. I can mention the on-call system and challenge them to find something better, or improve on it. What do you think?" Jean looked at Beverly, the question mark all over her face.

"Looks to me like you got your bases covered. Only I am not sure that you need all your people to resolve this—might it not be better to discuss it with the supervisors, let them talk to some of their people, and then make the decision tentatively with the supervisors? They can then get feedback from all their people to the draft of a written memo. If something worthwhile comes up, you can modify the memo. That should make them all as happy as possible. Now, just so I understand what you are planning to do, why don't you tell me."

"I guess it's clean; I like what you are saying and will do it just that way."

A week later, when Jean and Beverly were at lunch again, they got around to the same subject.

"Tell me more specifically what you did, Jean. I am curious, because I haven't heard any repercussions."

"Well, as I told you, I let the supervisors handle it. They liked the idea of voluntary on-call with an ad for local part-timers who might be available. Two responded but we haven't had to use them yet, so we don't know how that'll work. Anyhow, it seems no one had any suggestions, so I wrote out a memo which merely stated the on-call system to which they had agreed. It clarified the specifics on how they are to put their names on the list, what to do when too many people want one date and not enough another one, that there are to be three names for each date, that it is their responsibility to find a substitute if something comes up when they won't be able to make it as planned, or when an emergency arises, etc. We bounced it off on the crews and everything's OK. So far it's worked well."

"Great." Beverly is pleased that she had been able to help. Still Jean's explanation brought up a question. "Jean, do the people from both your sections take their turns? I mean, do the packers also put their names on the list?"

"Of course. There is always work in both sections, though usually more in shipping. Without help from the packers, each one of the shippers would have to reserve an on-call day at least once a week."

"Do the packers know what to do when they have to fill in for shippers, or the other way 'round?"

"I forgot to tell you that there has to be at least one person from each section on the list for each date. I've also asked Quality to look at our plans and to make suggestions."

"Well, that should help. I hope it'll continue to work well. What else is new, Jean?"

❖ ❖ ❖ ❖ ❖ ❖

Analysis: Jean's Challenge—Staffing the Extended Hours

A fairly realistic situation. A problem, discussion, involvement of the affected people. Seemingly handled well, the way competent managers would likely handle the situation.

Let's see what the basic guidelines might ask, from the management/leadership perspective.

How about asking yourself the guideline questions now? It will be more meaningful for you if you hold off with reading the story's conclusions until after you have thought about any improvements on Jean's plan, which the guidelines might suggest. Think about it, jot down a few thoughts, then read on.

Let's do the analysis with the use of the guideline questions, slightly abbreviated, one at a time.

1. How effective is Control on the project? Will the plan bring the expected results? Will communications be thorough? Will it quickly be obvious when changes in the plan will be needed to ensure high-quality implementation? What could be done better?

   If Jean were aware of this guideline, and used it, she might have asked herself one or more questions such as these:

   - Should a supervisor stay awhile, the first few times when on-call staff members work on tasks with which they may not be fully familiar?

   - What special instructions, if any, should that supervisor receive?

   - Should she set goals with the supervisors on the maximum number of errors that should not be exceeded?

   - What new performance and quality records should be kept, and what standards should be set so the records can be compared with them?

   - Would there be a need for additional coordination procedures between packing and shipping, or between the supervisors, to ensure smooth operation with on-call people who normally report to the other supervisor, or who are not familiar with the way the after-5:00 PM tasks differ from the regular daytime work?

   - What should be communicated verbally, and what in writing?

   - To what extent do regular daytime staff members share the work norms of the later shift, with respect to keeping busy when they may be alone in the area, checking their work, and so on.

2. Will the needed Competence be there? What could be done to make sure? What could be done better in that respect?

   With respect to this guideline question, if Jean were aware of it, and used it, one or more questions like these might have come to her mind:

   - What steps, if any, should be taken to make sure that the staff members who may have to work in the other section than their own will have all the competencies to be fully effective?

   - Do the supervisors know how to look for potential problems or do they need some coaching in that area?

   - Do the supervisors know how to work with, and to coach, staff members from the other section (packing supervisor with shipping staff, or vice versa)?

   - What qualifications should be checked with potential call-in people before they go on the list for actual call-in?

   - What training should be given to potential call-in people before they are actually called in?

3. What about Climate? How will the stakeholders see the organization, the organizational unit, the project, and the issues?

   In addition to any questions Jean might have asked herself, she also might have thought of one or more questions, such as those that follow, if she were aware of this guideline, and used it.

   - How strong might any hidden negative feelings be about the on-call system? (Keeping in mind that those who do want to get the chance to earn the extra money from working later apparently have frequent opportunities now, without an on-call system. If anything, the system, as described, might reduce the likelihood that they will be called on when there is a need. On the other hand, there could be some positive fallout if on-call people are asked only after volunteers have been given a chance to serve.)

- Was the process that was used for making the decision a very sound one that should make everyone feel confident that management seeks their input when decisions are made that affect them?

- What could be done to ensure that the on-call system will add the least possible amount of stress to staff members?

- What psychological rewards could be used to bring pleasant moments to staff members as reward for accepting the on-call system?

- How can the late hours of on-call people be made more pleasant?

- What can be done so not-totally-routine contributions of staff members during the late hours are noticed and receive special recognition?

❖ ❖ ❖ ❖ ❖ ❖

Conclusions: Jean's Challenge—Staffing the Extended Hours

Had Jean and Beverly asked the 3Cs guideline questions, chances are that they would have also asked some of the more specific questions listed above. Jean would have somewhat better implementation, and she would have felt more secure that she had done almost everything right.

Before you continue reading, refer back to the personal challenge you analyzed with the 3Cs guideline questions just before you started to read about Jean's Challenge. Would you make some additional changes in the steps you took to resolve a challenge from the past, or in the course of action for a current challenge?

Once you have finished those thoughts, you will decide whether you should read on. You can, of course, do just that, and you will undoubtedly find it useful and interesting. On the other hand, you might prefer to do less reading and get to the specific message of this chapter. If you do, you will find it in the Conceptual Summary at the end of this chapter.

SCENARIO 1.2

───────────────────────

**Steve's and Sally's Challenge:
Planning for More Efficient Operations**

Focus: All 3Cs guidelines, introductory example

Abstract: Steve, the MIS manager, and Sally, the data input supervisor, are preparing to install optical scanners that will reduce the workload and require layoffs.

❖ ❖ ❖ ❖ ❖ ❖

The Scenario

"We've really got to get cracking with the operating and capital budgets." Steve got right to the point, even before Sally had time to sit down in the comfortable chair next to the little coffee table in his office. "Did you get all the figures on the scanners and programming costs, and were you able to finish the forecast?"

"I certainly did." There was a hint of pride in Sally's tone. She continued, more hesitantly. "But, I am also quite concerned. We'll save some money alright, but the impact on our people, that's another story."

"What do you mean? I thought that our initial estimates showed that we would not have to cut the staff—that attrition would take up most of the slack and the growing workload would take care of the rest. Is that no longer true?"

"I'm afraid not. We may have been a little too conservative in estimating how many hours we will save with the scanners and the efficient program the consultant has shown us. I don't know whether I told you, but the other evening I went through a bunch of incoming mail and made some specific, realistic assumptions about the time it will take to scan the forms, and how many would have to be entered manually. The good news is that, unless the people who will respond to our mailings with the new forms mess up more extensively than I think they will, we'll be quite a bit more efficient than we had expected. The bad news is that we may have to lay off more people than we thought.

I've also checked informally with Personnel. They don't think that they can place any of my people in other departments, though they'll try. They did tell me about the severance packages they can offer to anyone who'll be laid off. They will tell people about that, and about any job openings for which they could apply. All that's useful but it doesn't really do much—it would have been great if they knew of jobs they could offer. We've got to look at the staff and see who'll get hit. It's sad."

"Well, if that's what you think, let's talk about it. First, though, do you have the budget figures?"

"I have the capital budget requirements for this entire thing: equipment, programming, piloting and debugging costs, and form design. It also includes our regular equipment replacement needs. Printing will be in the Public Relations and Marketing budgets. As far as our operating budget is concerned, I thought I would prepare that after I knew whether you want to move ahead full blast, or take a gradual approach."

"It's probably best to move as quickly as possible, considering the transition needs. Let's get it over with, so the agony will be short and so there will be no lingering concerns about job security by the staff that remains."

"I think you are right, Steve. I was leaning toward that myself. Ok. I'll have the operating budget figures for you in a week or less."

"That'll be fine. Now let me see what you did with the capital budget."

Steve was satisfied with what Sally showed him. "This looks fine. Thanks. I'll submit it as you've presented it here.

Now, one more thought, before you go. It might be useful if you gave some thought to the way this reorganization will roll out. Could you think about it and then give me an outline of the steps you would take?"

"Certainly. When would you like that?"

"Probably soon. Do you think that word is out about this new equipment and that it may mean a staff cutback?"

"You know that everything gets out around here. I've already had a few people ask me whether there's some truth to the rumors about a layoff. It's hard to answer this question. So far I've said that the possibility does exist but that nobody knows at this point—no decisions have been made."

"If that's the case we better move quickly so we can calm the apprehensions that must be building. Get Personnel's suggestions on what and how we should communicate now. Also, can you let me have the plan with the budget in about a week, so we can get approval and move swiftly?"

"OK, I'll try."

A week later, Steve and Sally reviewed her operations budget, which Steve also found satisfactory. Then Steve took a quick look at her plan, which listed the following steps to be taken as soon as approval of the capital budget could be obtained. Sally said that she would add dates as soon as Steve had approved the steps.

1. Order one scanner.

2. Finalize the forms jointly with Marketing and Public Relations.

3. Authorize the consultant to proceed with development of the program.

4. Jointly with Personnel, prepare and issue more specific communications than the vague statements to be made now about the tentative plans to staff members who are in positions that might be affected.

5. Arrange with Public Relations and Marketing to make a pilot mailing, as soon as the forms are ready, and to prepare for a second one soon thereafter.

6. Process the returns from the first pilot mailing without any new equipment, entering the data into the database by hand, as was done previously with the old forms; concurrently estimate the time savings that scanners will bring.

7. As soon as the scanner and the new program are installed, test the program, with duplicate entries from the first pilot mailing and compare with the manual entries.

8. Revise and debug as necessary.

9. Use the scanner on the returns from the second pilot mailing and make any final adjustments that may be necessary.

10. Arrange with Public Relations and Marketing to proceed with the new forms on all future mailings.

11. Purchase and install additional scanners.

12. Concurrently

    a. Make staff separation decisions, with priorities so actual separations will be coordinated with staff needs.

    b. Train those staff members who will work on the new system.

    c. Arrange with Personnel for staged separation interviews with staff members who will no longer be needed, as the old returns dwindle and increasing proportion of returns come in on the new forms.

13. Start full operations with the new system.

Steve seemed satisfied. "Ok, before we take a closer look at the plan, let's talk about what we are going to tell your people. Have you had any more questions?"

"Not really. Word must have gotten around that I don't have much to say at this time."

"What did Personnel suggest that we do?"

"They weren't as much help as I thought they'd be. They said it's more up to us. In general they feel that honesty is the best policy, but they are also concerned that people will get even more anxious if we give too much detail. What we have to watch is that morale doesn't suffer. They think it's important that we show that we care and that we'll do all we can for the affected individuals if there should be a need to reduce the staff. They asked that, if we send people to them, we should make it clear that they can only talk about transition help, because they know even less than we do about a staff cut, whether one will actually be necessary, when it might occur, and how deep it might be."

"If we get all your people together and do just that, who should tell them?"

"I think that you should do it. If possible, your boss George should be there, to show that higher levels of management are also concerned about reducing any hardship on individuals."

"Sounds good. Let me try to convince George to say a few words, after I give my little talk, to reinforce that point. Now let's look at the steps in your plan more closely."

Steve only had three questions: Who would coordinate with Public Relations and Marketing? How would Sally make sure that the people who will make the entries from the pilot mailing returns, and those who would use the scanners, would be able to work efficiently so the comparisons would be valid? Would it be useful to have Quality Assurance review the procedures and set up monitoring records and quality standards?

Sally assured him that she would work with the other departments herself, that the two staff members who would be needed for the pilots would be comfortable with the new tasks before working on the actual returns, and that she would call for help from Quality. In addition, Steve wanted to review the forms before they were to be used, and he asked Sally to give him a verbal update once a week so he would be able to answer any questions that might be put to him.

He then promised to get approval to proceed, in conjunction with the budget, and to give Sally the go-ahead signal as soon as he could.

❖ ❖ ❖ ❖ ❖ ❖

Analysis: Steve and Sally's Challenge: Planning for More Efficient Operations

This is not a rare situation—a technological opportunity which unfortunately carries pain for people in its wake—and was handled well by Steve and Sally, the way competent managers would likely deal with it.

Let's see what changes Steve might have suggested had he asked the basic guideline questions.

Again, should you think about any changes you would recommend if you were in Steve's shoes, based on the guideline questions? The book's conclusions will be more meaningful, if you do. Then read on.

The functional (technical) decisions here are straightforward. Ordering equipment, designing forms, working with a consultant on the programming, printing, and pilots mailings are all functional tasks. They require functional expertise, but the management/leadership issues in those decisions are minor and are usually routine, unless something is not going according to plan.

Let's look at what issues the guideline questions might bring to the surface. Steve and Sally may have considered some of them, but there is no evidence in the story that they did.

1. How effective is Control on the project? Will the plan bring the expected results? Will communications be thorough? Will it quickly be obvious when changes in the plan will be needed to ensure high-quality implementation? What could be done better?

   Issues which this guideline might raise for Steve and Sally:

   - With Sally as the primary coordinator with other departments, what other coordination challenges, if any, might arise?

   - What intradepartment coordination challenges might arise?

   - What interunit communications, other than with Public Relations and Marketing, need to be considered?

   - Should Sally set goals when each step in the plan will be completed, based on a date when Steve brings approval?

   - Should Sally set goals on the productivity and quality of the data entry with scanners?

   - Should Steve review the dates to see where he could provide support that could speed up the process before the goals are finalized, and how could he be of help in setting and achieving the productivity and quality goals?

- What monitoring is needed to ensure high quality of data entry of returns accepted by the scanners and of those which are rejected by them?

- What can be done to ensure that positive work norms survive the trauma of the reorganization?

2. Will the needed Competence be there? What could be done to make sure? What could be done better in that respect?

   Issues which this guideline might raise for Steve and Sally:

   - How adequate is the training plan for those staff members who will work on the new system?

   - How can we ensure that staff is trained thoroughly on any changes that might result from program bugs that were not caught until full operation?

   - Who will do the training, and what can be done to ensure that person is not only knowledgeable in the procedures but also competent in training techniques?

   - What follow-up should be done before staff members begin to work on the scanning operations to ensure that training was effective?

   - What additional training will the programmers need so they can effectively integrate the consultant's output into the system and check it out so they discover any potential problems prior to use of the program?

3. What about Climate? How will the stakeholders see the organization, the organizational unit, the project, and the issues?

   In addition to whatever questions Steve asked himself, he might also have asked himself and Sally one or more questions similar to the ones below if he were aware of this guideline and used it.

Issues which this guideline might raise for Steve and Sally:

- What are their respective responsibilities with respect to what could or should be done, by whom, when, and how, to make sure that any negative impact of the reorganization on staff members of other departments will be as little as possible?

- What could or should be done to ensure minimum negative impact from the content and timing of communications with staff members—those who will be laid off, those who might be laid off, and those whose jobs appear to be safe? (It must be kept in mind that telling someone that his or her job is secure will translate into insecure feelings by anyone who does not get that message. Promises to keep that information confidential are notoriously unreliable.)

- What, if anything, can be done to encourage Personnel to try harder to find positions for displaced staff members?

- What can be done so not-totally-routine contributions of staff members during and after the transition are noticed and receive special recognition?

- What can be done so the transition is made as stress-free as possible for staff members who are retained?

❖ ❖ ❖ ❖ ❖ ❖

Conclusions: Steve and Sally's Challenge: Planning for More Efficient Operations

Asking the 3Cs guideline questions in this situation would probably have raised some or most of the issues discussed. The outcome would certainly have helped to bring some improvements in the plan, or at least some clarifications.

In a more general sense, asking the Climate guideline question for instance, would lead to reviews, on any major decision, about what should be communicated within the department. It would also bring an analysis of what the department manager should do to ensure that there will be appropriate communications to other departments and possibly to others outside the organization.

Asking the 3Cs questions, and especially the Climate guideline question, when making family and other personal affairs decisions may also bring benefits by preventing disappointments and even hard feelings.

Before you continue reading, refer back to the personal challenge you analyzed with the 3Cs guideline questions just before you started to read about Jean's Challenge. Based on the broader perspective that this analysis has given you, would you make some additional changes in the steps you took to resolve a challenge from the past or in the course of action for a current challenge?

A Conceptual Summary

Each one of the 3Cs guideline questions is meant to stimulate thinking about what could be done to improve on a decision or plan that has to be implemented. The discussion below can help you expand the meaning of the questions as you use them.

Now that you have had a chance to see how useful it could be to ask the questions, it may be an appropriate time to review some of the issues that could come to mind as you apply the basic level of the questions to your situations.

For your convenience, the 3Cs guideline questions are restated below, again in abbreviated form, at the beginning of each discussion segment.

The Control Guideline Question

How effective is Control on the project? Will the plan bring the expected results? Will communications be thorough? Will it quickly be obvious when changes in the plan will be needed to ensure high-quality implementation? What could be done better?

To achieve effective Control, several elements are likely to contribute:

1. *Sound goals* (please note that despite some controversy on the definition of the two words, *goals* and *objectives,* they will be used interchangeably here for the purposes of this book). Goals define what is to be accomplished by the organizational unit and the individual during the coming period, such as production quantity, quality level, budgets, and so on. Goals should be set with appropriate participation, and be supported by steps most likely to achieve them.

   There should be only a limited number of goals on which staff members should work at any one time. For that reason, organizational and individual goals should concern some significant improvement, or ensure progress on a major project. All staff members have to understand, of course, that everything not covered by goals shall be done at least as well as in the past.

   Please note that the specifics of what is to be accomplished with a goal are part of the *functional* aspect of the goal decision or plan—it depends on the business of the organizational unit. The *managerial/leadership* aspects concern the how of the process, which will lead to achievement of the goal—participation, coordination, communications, competencies, and so on—in short, all the considerations involved in the 3Cs guidelines.

2. *Effective coordination and communication* that ensure full awareness by each organizational unit and each person of what is to be achieved and what their respective roles are.

3. *An appropriate set of values,* or norms, for morality and diversity, work ethic, quality, cooperation, and behavior limits, which are understood by everyone and to which staff members adhere (mostly voluntarily—see Chapter 4, Additional Insights L, Positive Discipline and Counseling).

4. *A system for effective and timely monitoring of performance and progress* as an early warning system.

Three points need reinforcing here. They affect all actions to achieve full satisfaction of the 3Cs characteristics of an effective organization. There needs to be:

- Appropriate participation in all types of decisions (not too much, not too little, not too soon, and not too late) by those who should be involved (see Chapter 1, Additional Insights D, Participation in Decision Making and Planning).

- A sound system of communications with all stakeholders, on all matters important to them, by all segments of the organization. People want to be kept informed and feel that they are appreciated, which means that they are entitled to know what is going on (see Chapter 2, Additional Insights H, Communications Theories, Techniques and Skills).

- An awareness of the intense interrelationships between the 3Cs requirements for an effective organization: that actions taken to strengthen Control affect the strength of Competence and Climate, for better or for worse. The same comprehensive impact is true of actions to improve Competence, or Climate, respectively.

The Competence Guideline Question

Will the needed Competence be there? What could be done to make sure? What could be done better in that respect?

Competence will be enhanced with consideration of the following:

1. *Effective selection of new staff members* to ensure that the raw material is there on which to build a high-competence team or organizational unit. This does not mean that new recruits should have all the skills they will use on their jobs, but that they are willing and able to learn quickly, and that they have the positive attitudes to make them valuable additions to the staff.

2. Review of *knowledge, skills, and abilities (KSAs) strengths and weaknesses of existing staff members* so the organizational

unit can take greatest advantage of the strengths through work assignments and even promotions, and so the appropriate steps can be taken to reduce or eliminate competence weaknesses.

3. Review of *KSA weaknesses of people outside the organizational unit* to identify needs for effective cooperation on the project or use of the product or service.

4. Review of *managerial/leadership KSAs* of staff members with supervisory responsibilities.

The Climate Guideline Question

What about Climate? How will the stakeholders see the organization, the organizational unit, the project, and the issues?

For Climate, the guideline should raise all the issues that can contribute to staff member satisfaction, especially the many steps that staff members with managerial/leadership responsibilities can take to increase job satisfaction and reduce stress.

1. *Psychological rewards* for performance, not only for outstanding achievements but also for the many small, but steady, ways in which reliable, friendly, positively motivated staff members contribute to the success of the organizational unit.

2. *Stress reduction* through realistic deadlines which may, however, demand consistent high-level effort, and through effective communications on matters that are of considerable concern or interest to staff members. These include important developments affecting the organization and the unit, and especially matters directly impacting on job security, compensation, and benefits.

3. *Counseling* on career opportunities and on personal problems that may, or may not, affect performance

4. Tangible rewards, distributed fairly and equitably, including raises, bonuses, special awards, developmental work assignments, and promotions.

What Does It All Mean and Where to from Here?

Even at this most general level of guidelines, there is a fairly large number of issues to consider. That should not come as a surprise. After all, management/leadership is a comprehensive discipline and profession, with a rich literature and extensive research findings.

However, and this is the good news, you do not necessarily have to be highly knowledgeable to be a competent manager/ leader. Sound judgment, honed with experience, will go a long way. Using the basic guidelines, or guidelines which you have developed yourself, consistently, even if you do not consider all the issues discussed above, will help you make better decisions. Just *ask the questions suggested by this book, or equivalent questions that you develop yourself, before you implement.* That, by itself, will prevent many errors or oversights.

In addition to the basic reason mentioned above, there are several other powerful arguments in favor of decision making with guidelines (the 3Cs guidelines or others).

1. By creating a structure for participation in decision making and planning, guidelines can ensure that the special knowledge and the views of several people can be used to enhance any decision in which they are invited to comment. With the spreading use of PC networks, these insights and views can be focused on a specific decision or plan without one of the major drawbacks of participation—the need for lengthy meetings or the emergence of conflicts.

2. By providing a framework for easily recording the use of the guidelines, a record and audit trail can allow review of decisions or plans just prior to implementation.

3. Decisions of new managers/leaders can be monitored for coaching purposes.

4. If an organization decided on encouraging the regular use of guidelines, it could make that a requirement for consideration in promotion decisions, thus signaling to all staff members that it would be in their interest to develop their decision-making KSAs with the use of the 3Cs guidelines or their own.

Chapters 2 and 3 present the same guidelines as this chapter in the form of more detailed questions, with additional situation examples and more structured analyses.

As you read what is of interest to you, keep in mind that the book can serve you as a foundation for planning self-development, as a reference resource, and as a basis for gradually creating your own guidelines. While the guidelines suggested here may be fine for your needs, you can modify them or even develop your own. In any case, guideline questions can help you cope more effectively with the challenges you face as manager and leader.

Additional Insights A

Management Theory and Concepts: Origins and Pathways

The problem is to organize
This monumental enterprise
So that, to see that all are boarded,
Both need, and reality are rewarded.

Principles of Economic Policy, Chapter 10
Kenneth Boulding (adapted)

Introduction

This Additional Insight traces the evolution of management theories and thus provides a foundation for the concepts discussed in this book.

In the Beginning

It all started toward the end of the industrial revolution, as many organizations and businesses grew to considerable size. Frederick Taylor, an American engineer who is often seen as the father of what is called either *management science* or *scientific management*, along with others, began to study worker productivity. The objective was to find optimal ways to design the jobs of production workers and to determine how those workers might best be selected, trained, paid, and supervised. The effort led to standard costing, method study, time-and-motion study, worker performance standards, and other measurement techniques. In an indirect way, Taylor is also the father of total quality management (TQM) concepts which evolved from the *value engineering* approach that was popular during the 1950s.

Soon, question arose about the ways in which managers and supervisors contributed to productivity. Here, Henry Fayol, a French mining engineer, led the way. He depicted the manager's function as a cycle of planning (defining ends and means); organizing (providing for the necessary equipment, resources, and

1   Insights A Continued

people); commanding (supervising subordinates); coordinating (ensuring that equipment, resources and people are effectively interacting); controlling (ensuring that outcomes are consistent with plans); and back to planning. The inclusion of *commanding* sounds strange to us today, but in the early part of the twentieth century it was expected that a manager issued orders (commanded). In a similar vein, today we do not speak of *subordinates* as was the practice well into the 1950s, but refer to people who report to a manager as staff members or associates.

Looking at the manager

Most modern management books continue to be organized around versions of Fayol's cycle. However, while planning and organizing have usually remained, some of the other terms have been replaced by the various writers with words like *executing, implementing, staffing, leading,* and *follow-up.* In a way, these words reflect more current views of the functions of managers.

Fayol also defined a number of *Principles of Management,* including *division of labor* and *unity of command* (the principle that one person should report to only one manager or supervisor). These concepts, too, have been modified, or partially replaced.

World War II and the emergence of the Cold War era stimulated development of the managerial uses of quantitative decision analysis methods, statistical inference, and computer technology. Techniques such as linear programming, probability-based decision analysis, game theory, dynamic programming, and simulation are direct descendants of this period. The modern digital computer continues to make powerful techniques such as these readily available to managers at all levels of organizations, and the development of modern computer information systems and software tools are, in a way, also results of management science.

A shift in direction

On a different track, a management theory branch came by accident from a famous attempt to determine how working conditions affected productivity. At Western Electric Company's

Hawthorne plant in Chicago during the late 1920s, among other experiments, six young women were detached from a department with hundreds of assemblers. In their separated room they were under close observation and given friendly attention. Their work environment was altered, first favorably with longer breaks and other changes such as better lighting, and then made less and less desirable. At one point, rest periods were eliminated entirely. Through it all, work output increased.

During the extensive Hawthorne experiments, the various aspects of human behavior in the work environment were studied in depth for the first time. Topics included group formation and development (formally and informally), behavioral influences on productivity, communications, and the sources of morale.

As interpreted by Elton Mayo (1933), these studies heralded the beginning of the human relations theory of management, often referred to as the *behavioral sciences in management*. Today there are two primary branches of this body of theory: leadership, and motivation.

The impact of motivation and leadership theories on management education and development reached a peak during the 1950s and 1960s when the most significant, broad-gauged research was performed. Since then, the efforts of scholars and other researchers have concentrated on correcting or adjusting for inadequacies in the original theories and to introduce other ideas, some of which are highly subjective and even controversial. In effect, what has happened since then is a fractionalization of behavioral theories, with overlaps and internal contradictions. Only sporadically have there been significant attempts to create bridges between these theories and practical applications and uses. Total quality management is one of the most successful attempts of such a bridge.

Disappointments

Unfortunately, this field of studies continues to offer more questions than answers, and is full of competing and conflicting models and theories. As Moorhead and Griffin (1992, xix) have phrased it so aptly:

Insights A Continued

The field of organizational behavior, still in its infancy as a science, remains full of competing and conflicting models and theories. There are few laws or absolute principles that dictate proper conduct for organizational members or predict with certainty their behaviors. The role of human resources in the long-term viability of any business or not-for-profit enterprise is nevertheless recognized as enormously significant. Other resources—financial, informational, and material—are also essential, but only human resources are virtually boundless in their potential impact (positive or negative) on the organization.

Leadership theories, in particular, are having a hard time. In *Handbook of Leadership: A Survey of Theory and Research,* Stogdill (1974) noted that there are as many definitions of leadership as there are persons who have attempted to define the concept. In *Leadership: Strategies for Taking Charge,* Bennis and Nanus (1985) referred to leadership as the most studied and least understood topic of any in the social sciences. Colleges and universities offer a plethora of courses and workshops on the topic of leadership, undaunted by the challenge of teaching that which cannot be defined and is not yet well understood. Unfortunately, managers who participate in such courses often emerge with a frustrating sense that leadership is akin to the abominable snowman, whose footprints are everywhere but who is nowhere to be seen.

The question of whether or not a discipline of management has developed continues to occupy the concern of both academics and practitioners. Surely if such a discipline exists there should be available to all of us a common definition of management and a body of consistent literature. This, unfortunately, is not the case. Many have argued for understanding management as a general concept rooted in organizational theory, as understanding human behavior in organizations, as problem-solving, as decision making, and as a social process. None of these approaches can stand alone. The distinguished management scholar Harold Koontz (1980), after a lifetime of study, lamented the existence of a continuing *Management Theory Jungle* composed of these schools of thought: empirical (case study), interpersonal behavior, group behavior, cooperative social system, sociotechnical systems, decision theory, systems, mathematical (management science), contingency (situational), managerial roles, and operational (management function). Koontz even commented that the situation had actually deteriorated in the 20 years since his earlier review of the state of the art.

Part of the reason for lack of progress may be that there is not much of a comprehensive nature that new research is likely to uncover. Also, there might be the pressure of more rewarding ideas to concentrate on. During the 1980s and 1990s, in addition to continuing growth of computer-related concepts, attention shifted to issues that would help businesses overcome the increasingly fierce domestic and foreign competitive pressures and assist government agencies to cope with the ever more severe budget cuts. These issues addressed organizational culture and organizational strategies—quality improvement which brought total quality management and quality circles; productivity which led to reengineering, restructuring, and mergers, with their almost inevitable downsizing; increasing concentration on global marketing; and the most recent, interest in organizational learning.

Conclusion

This is the situation today. The many and frequently bewildering theories often confuse more than clarify and do not provide practical guidelines for decisions and action, especially those that concern the leadership aspects of management. The search for such answers continues to lead us to seek solace in those who promise easy answers to complex realities. So we tried focusing on topics such as time management (Lakein 1973), one-minute management (Blanchard and Johnson 1982), habits of effective people (Covey 1989), transformation, and total quality. While none of these are irrelevant, they seem to have their day, deliver less than they promise, and lead us to start the search for insight all over again.

1   Insights A Continued

All, however, bring useful insights that can help in some situations, but they fail to concentrate on the practical application of what we have learned from the theories, by providing answers to two questions: What does management/leadership mean to me? How can I best manage and lead in a given situation? To answer these questions you need something that is important at every managerial level—a comprehensive approach that fits *all* decisions and enhances managerial competence as well as leadership competence.

Attempts to develop programs which address the practical needs of managers are discussed in Chapter 4 (Additional Insights N, Management Development Programs: Hopes, Disappointments, and Status).

1 Additional Insights B

Leadership Theories

If you can talk with crowds and keep your virtue,
Or walk with Kings—nor lose the common touch,
If neither foes nor loving friends can hurt you,
If all men count with you, but none too much;

If, Rudyard Kipling

Introduction

The following will be briefly discussed in this Additional Insights section:

- Trait Theory
- Behavioral Theories
- Contingency Theories
- Other Theories

The theories discussed here are not meant to be exhaustive—they represent a listing of thoughts which have had major impacts on the thinking of others. When appropriate, one or very few names are associated here with each theory or group of theories. In most cases, others have contributed to the respective theories as we know them today. However, the researchers or thinkers who are listed have either originated the concept, have provided a thorough overview, or are most often considered to have made the most important contributions.

Leadership is widely seen as the ability to influence the behavior of others (usually toward the achievement of some end result). In this regard, power and authority are, of course, important elements of leadership. However, these external influences aside, theories discussed here address primarily the personal characteristics, behaviors, and even perceptions of followers, which are believed to make some leaders more successful than others. The

1 **Insights B Continued**

complexities of the issues involved led to a very large number of theories. Brief highlights are given below.

Trait Theory

Trait theory (Ghiselli 1963; Stogdill 1974) emphasizes the importance of personal characteristics and traits of leaders in shaping the quality of their leadership. These traits include physical, mental, and cultural attributes, including charisma, decisiveness, intelligence, self-confidence, and energy, all of which make some leaders more successful than others.

Behavioral Theories

Behavioral theories address the question of whether or not there is some identifying behavior of leaders which can make them more effective. There are a number of such theories. The two-dimensional theories (task vs. relationship), discussed below, are the most widely known:

1. One theory (based on studies at Ohio State University; Fleishman, Harris, and Burtt 1955) states that leaders initiate structure, such as assigning group members to tasks, and that they expect that standards are met. They also show "consideration" for their staff members, such as respect for their ideas, concern for developing trust, and interest in their work satisfaction. The most effective leader, according to this theory, usually is one who can balance these two aspects of leadership, though there are some problems which such a leader faces.

2. Other behavioral theories, based on studies at the University of Michigan (Likert 1961; Kahn and Katz 1960) use two different dimensions, *employee orientation* and *production orientation,* as measures of leader effectiveness. These studies found that groups with leaders who have high employee orientation perform best.

1 Insights B Continued

3. A third type of behavioral theory is based on the managerial (or leadership) grid model (Blake and Srygley-Mouton 1964), which groups the behaviors of managers/leaders into *concern for people* and *concern for production*. According to studies by two researchers, Blake and Mouton, the leaders whose style combines high concern for both dimensions, led the most productive teams.

Contingency Theories

There are many contingency theories which attempt to look at leadership characteristics and skills from the perspective of the needs of the situation in which the leader has to act. The most widely known of these are the autocratic-democratic continuum model, leadership-participation theory, the Hersey-Blanchard situational model, Fiedler's contingency theory, and the path-goal theory.

1. The Tannenbaum and Schmidt autocratic-democratic continuum model (Tannenbaum and Schmidt 1958) holds that a leader can choose from many possible combinations of autocratic control and authority for decisions by followers. The model depicts these combinations ranging from complete control by the manager/leader over decisions to the other extreme where the members of the staff have wide freedom in determining what should be done. According to this model, the most effective leaders are those who have the best batting average in choosing the most appropriate mix between *boss-centered* leadership and *subordinate-centered* leadership (the terms actually used originally by the authors in 1958).

2. Leadership-participation theory (Vroom and Yetton 1973), though focused primarily on decision making, is a refinement of the autocratic-democratic continuum model. It selects five points from the many possible ones along the continuum. A leader should choose the measure of

Insights B Continued

other attributes of a commanding presence, an engaging personality, possibly something akin to the ability to see and articulate a vision or at least direction, and so on. These are all matters that we cannot change or that take a lot of effort and a long time to change.

Most of the behaviors, however, are based on the competence to develop a climate in which followers can gain trust and confidence in the leader and in the direction in which he or she is leading the organization. This competence is a bundle of skills that can be learned fairly easily and that can effectively link the organization's characteristics and needs to those of its stakeholders.

Guidelines drawn from a sound, integrated, comprehensive model of the leadership component of management can provide a practical approach to applying the lessons that the theories convey. They can serve as foundation for learning and honing the skills that can make a manager as inspiring a leader as his or her traits permit. The 3Cs concept (the Linking Elements) appears to be the best currently available model for such guidelines.

It is important to note here that the 3Cs model of management/leadership, on which the guidelines in this book are based, incorporates the critical elements of both leadership and motivation theories. The questions the guidelines ask are central to the leadership and motivation issues that are discussed from various perspectives in the theories. That is why greater knowledge of the conceptual/theoretical foundations of the guidelines can make them more useful.

1 Additional Insights C

Motivation Theories

We don't want someone to motivate us,
but we want a motivational climate
where we can find enjoyment and
growth in our work.

Anonymous

Introduction

The following will be briefly discussed in this Additional Insights section:

- Hierarchy of Needs (Maslow 1954)
- Theory X and Theory Y (McGregor 1960)
- Motivation-Hygiene (Herzberg 1959, 1968)
- Other Theories

As with the leadership theories, the following list is not meant to be an exhaustive one—just those theories that have had major impacts on the thinking of others. Only one name is associated here with each theory. In most cases, others have contributed to the respective theory as we know it today. However, the name is that of the person who either originated the concept or is most often considered to have made the most important contribution.

As was pointed out previously, there is much overlap between leadership and motivation theories. This is, of course, understandable since follower motivation is a primary, if not the overarching, objective of leadership.

Hierarchy of Needs (Maslow 1954)

The most widely known work was done by Abraham Maslow, who depicted human needs in a five-level pyramid, with basic

1 Insights C Continued

physiological needs (survival needs such as food and shelter) at the base, safety and security (protection of the survival needs for the future) at the next level, belonging and social activity at the third level, esteem and status at the fourth, and self-realization and fulfillment at the peak. Maslow's statement that satisfaction of lower-level needs is a prerequisite for motivation by higher-level needs has been widely criticized and much empirical evidence has shown serious flaws in that statement.

Theory X and Theory Y (McGregor 1960)

McGregor's scheme of two management assumptions is almost as widely known as Maslow's hierarchy. It has less operational impact because it merely describes two managerial styles:

- Theory X, which is based on the assumption that managers have to exercise tight control over every aspect of the productive process because "workers" are naturally inclined to work as little as possible, to shirk responsibility, and so on.

- Theory Y, which holds that people do not have an inherent dislike of work and that management's role is to arrange organizational conditions and methods of operation so that people can achieve their own goals best by devoting effort toward organizational objectives.

There is evidence that, by and large, organizations which display a Theory Y style are more productive and have more positively motivated staffs.

Motivation–Hygiene (Herzberg 1959, 1968)

At about the same time as McGregor's work, Frederick Herzberg and his group from Case Western Reserve University surveyed professional employees and came to the conclusion that there were factors in the work environment which did not motivate people but which, when absent, had a detrimental effect. He called them *dissatisfaction avoiders,* or hygiene factors. They included salary, fringe benefits, even working conditions such as breaks. On the other hand, the survey showed that the nature of the work itself—achievement, responsibility, recognition, and advancement—were the factors that motivated people. 'Job Enrichment' programs in which jobs were restructured to bring more intrinsic rewards, which were popular during the 1970's, were the result of this work.

Other Theories

Taking off from Maslow, McGregor, and Herzberg were many other theories, some of which were quite popular for a number of years. They include:

1. Three needs theory, which emphasized achievement, power, and affiliation as the key influences on motivation (McClelland 1961).

2. Expectancy theory (Vroom 1964), in which the level of motivation is determined by the expectation of the employee that he or she will be able to successfully complete the task, combined with the expectation of the psychological and/or tangible benefits which such success will bring.

3. Equity theory (Adams 1965) is based on the fact that almost everyone wants to be treated fairly, especially in relation to others. Motivation, lack of it, or demotivation results from this comparison.

4. ERG (existence, relatedness, and growth) (Alderfer 1969) is a modification of the Maslow hierarchy. In a rough sense, *existence* is equivalent to Maslow's physiological and safety/security needs, *relatedness* is similar to social and esteem needs, and there is great similarity between *growth* and self-realization.

5. Another modification of Maslow's hierarchy is described by Rausch (1978, 1985). It separates all but the top (self-realization and fulfillment) and bottom (basic physiological) needs into two components: those that can best be satisfied

Insights C Continued

with psychological rewards and those that require tangible rewards. For instance, there are esteem needs that the supervisor can satisfy in various ways without spending money, and there are others which, for some people, can only be satisfied with things that cost money.

6. Cognitive evaluation theory (Deci 1975) suggests that there are close links between psychological rewards of the work itself (intrinsic motivators) and tangible rewards (extrinsic motivators), with significant implications on compensation strategies.

7. Reinforcement theory (Steers and Porter 1979; Skinner 1968) is based on widely researched psychological theories that confirm the ability of recognition or other psychological rewards (positive reinforcement) for certain behavior to encourage repetition of that behavior.

8. Goal setting theory (Locke and Latham 1990; Locke 1994) suggests that setting goals for, or with, staff members has strong motivational impact.

There are other motivation theories which are less widely discussed in the literature. Furthermore, there is considerable overlap with leadership theories since it is obvious that effective leadership has a strong motivational component in encouraging followers to support the leader's goals.

It is important to note here, as was also stated in Additional Insights B, that the 3Cs model of management/leadership, on which the guidelines in this book are based, incorporates the critical elements of both leadership and motivation theories. The questions which the guidelines ask are central to the leadership and motivation issues that are discussed from various perspectives in the theories. That is the reason why greater knowledge of the conceptual/theoretical foundations of the guidelines can make them more useful.

Figure 1.2 shows a graphic comparison of four of the theories with Maslow in order of their similarity to the hierarchy (Rausch 1978; Alderfer 1969; McGregor 1960; Herzberg 1959).

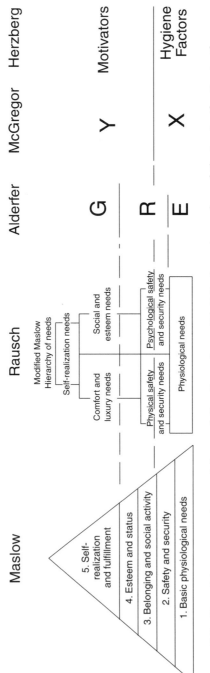

Figure 1.2 Graphic comparison of four of the theories with Maslow, in order of their similarity to the hierarchy. Used with permission.

Insights C Continued

Conclusions from the Motivation Theories

The conclusions from the motivation theories are quite similar to those of the leadership theories. Leadership behaviors that motivate followers inspire them to trust their leader and to have confidence in his or her ability to provide all the components of a satisfying work-life. These are skills which stretch from identifying successful direction, to developing a satisfying climate, to ensuring that followers have confidence in their respective abilities to contribute effectively to the total effort.

The skills for creating and sustaining a motivational climate are essentially the same as those that achieve high quality leadership. The 3Cs concept (the Linking Elements) appears to be the best currently available model for guidelines to develop these skills.

Additional Insights D

Participation in Decision Making and Planning

> It's not my place to run the train,
> the whistle I can't blow,
> It's not my place to say how far
> the train's allowed to go.
> It's not my place to shoot off steam,
> or even clang the bell,
> But let the bloody thing jump the track,
> and see who catches hell.
>
> *Anonymous*

Introduction

After the introduction, the following guidelines will be briefly discussed in this Additional Insights section:

- Overall participation guideline
- Specific Guidelines for:
  1. Selection of decision participants
  2. Level/extent of participation
  3. Technical and acceptance quality
  4. Work-maturity of participants
  5. Other elements of the situation

Appropriate participation, (allowing the right amount of authority—not too much, not too little, with the right people, at the right time, and so on) has a major impact on all 3Cs (Control, Competence, and Climate). It is so critical an element of effective management/leadership that it deserves exceptionally careful attention.

Insights D Continued

Sharing of decision making has a far greater impact on organizational performance than is commonly assumed, for many reasons. Obviously, appropriate participation brings better decisions because it focuses the expertise of several minds on the issues. It creates a more motivating climate, more open communications, and usually a higher level of mutual trust. At the same time it satisfies the expectations of people that their views are, at least, considered.

It is often difficult to see whether or not a manager practices appropriate participation. Take the example of a fire. The battalion chief arrives first, moments before the first two fire engines. He already knows who they are from his two-way radio contacts. The building is heavily involved, with fire pouring out of windows on the first and second floors. Two people are framed in third floor windows, screaming for help. On the radio the chief gives these orders: "John, there are two people on the third floor. Do not hook up (the water hoses). Get these people out." Then he continues: "Bill, hook up and protect John."

Was this participative decision making or was it a set of autocratic orders from a "boss"?

Even though the example refers to a crisis situation where most people would consider "orders" to be appropriate, it could be either, depending on the relationship. If John heard that he has to get these people out or there will be unpleasant consequences, or if either man felt that the assignment should have been reversed and they were reluctant to point that out, then there was little or no participation.

On the other hand, it is possible that John interpreted the message as: "Do your best to rescue these people, I know the task couldn't be in better hands." Furthermore, if both knew that even though this was a crisis situation they could make a quick plea for changing, even reversing the assignments and be given full consideration for their point of view, then this was highly participative decision making, displaying very strong mutual trust.

Participation, then, is like a book—it cannot be judged by the cover or, like beauty, can be skin deep, but usually is not. The mutual trust that is built up from many instances of appropriate participation is the key to this most important management/ leadership skill.

Participation in planning and decision making is not a yes-or-no issue. Instead, it is a series of continuums:

- Who should be invited to participate? (from no one to everyone)

- How much weight should the views of staff members be given? (from the slightest consideration to letting their views be the controlling issue)

- When should the staff members be brought into the decision-making process? (at the very beginning or only after limits for their participation have been set)

- Who should be informed of progress toward the decision or plan, and how and when? (from no one to everyone)

A number of factors should be taken into consideration to make this decision. These are discussed in the form of guidelines which follow.

Overall Participation Guideline

Before making any significant decision, ask yourself whom to involve, how much authority to grant that person or group, and when they should participate. Your criterion should be the way in which participation will bring the highest level of success.

If you want more detail, you could think in terms of five subordinate guidelines:

1. Selection of decision participants   Who should participate actively and when, who should be kept informed of what is happening, and who should merely be informed after the decision has been made? This selection has to be made on the basis of the relevant considerations in items 2 through 5. It should also consider to what extent individuals may feel that they should be involved in the decision-making process.

Insights D Continued

2. Level/extent of participation How much of a voice should participants have in the decision? (See Tannenbaum and Schmidt's autocratic-democratic continuum, and Vroom and Yetton leadership-participation theory in Additional Insights B, Leadership Theories.) This question also involves when each person should participate and covers the whole range of possibilities, from requesting opinions only after the decision has been made tentatively to full participation in almost every step of the process, starting right from the beginning. One guiding principle should be to vest the primary decision authority at the lowest level where adequate information and competence is available.

3. Technical and acceptance quality How much technical expertise is needed for a sound decision and to what extent do people (all stakeholders) feel that they should have a voice in the decision? Determination of the alternatives to consider, and selection of the best alternative requires consideration of the expertise/knowledge that is needed (technical requirement) and the extent to which acceptance of the alternative will help successful implementation of the decision or plan (acceptance requirement). These two considerations were illustrated by Norman R. Maier of the University of Michigan in a grid (Rausch and Carter 1989, page 60, and Maier 1974). Figure 1.3.

The grid shows four spaces (quadrants): low acceptance requirement/low technical requirement, high acceptance requirement/low technical requirement, low acceptance requirement/high technical requirement, and high acceptance requirement/high technical requirement.

One important expansion of the Maier concept: acceptance requirement does not refer solely to staff members. If an alternative will impact other stakeholders, thought has to be given to the issues that would affect their acceptance and what the implications of rejection by any one group of stakeholders would mean. Sometimes consultation with representative members of these other stakeholders may be advisable.

Low acceptance requirement/low technical requirement decisions generally involve matters on which nobody really cares

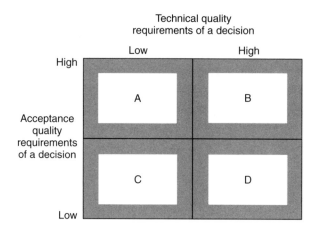

Figure 1.3 Simplified leadership and decision-making grid (based on the work of Norman Maier). Used with permission.

what will be done. Everybody wishes that somebody else would make the decision and go on with the business at hand. There are, however, not too many decisions of this type in the work environment. A manager who does not see to it that a decision in this quadrant is made quickly, either by delegating it or by making it, gives the impression of a procrastinating decision maker.

Matters with high acceptance requirement/low technical requirement might be plans to reduce absenteeism or increase the attention to certain specific quality details, reduction of waste, better customer communications, etc. Most matters involving a significant amount of effort or attention by staff members would be in this area, except for those which, in addition to acceptance, require high technical knowledge. For instance, the goal of reducing absenteeism by 20 percent does not require technical knowledge. Everybody knows what is involved. That does not mean that everybody can decide that 20 percent is the right amount of reduction to set as a goal, but everybody knows what the implications of the decision are and to what extent it will affect the people who have to implement it.

Some trivial decisions, such as whether, or how, to allocate parking spaces or change the coffee break time also lie in this quadrant.

1   Insights D Continued

In decisions with high acceptance requirement/low technical requirement, staff members or their representatives should have the primary voice.

It is obvious that any decision or plan in which people believe that they can make a useful contribution and which affects them seriously will turn out better if high levels of participation can be used. If there are differences of opinion among group members, the manager must lead the group to a joint decision which will bring the minimum resentment from individuals so that all will exert the greatest effort toward making the decision or plan successful.

Decisions and plans with low acceptance requirement/high technical requirement clearly need the involvement of people (from inside the organization and/or from outside) who have the necessary technical expertise. Often these people can recommend the decisions or plan and the manager can approve it (after confirming that the acceptance requirement is really very low), possibly without consulting staff members; all that may be necessary is to inform them in sufficient detail. Whether a decision is on the low end of acceptance requirement or near the high end makes a big difference. If in doubt, it is better to consider the decision to belong to the latter.

Finally, decisions and plans in the high acceptance requirement/high technical requirement area require the greatest skill on the part of the manager. Quickly reducing the time required to improve the reliability of a technical product may call for considerable technical knowledge to develop a realistic plan. For successful implementation, though, a high level of acceptance may be necessary. For instance, the engineering department may believe that, based on tests, a product defect can be eliminated through a combination of component redesign and special attention to a number of critical operations during assembly; or a research organization would be able to offer a highly desirable service if it could perfect a computer program and obtain the necessary data regularly within a tight deadline.

Plans related to these situations must be decided by the people who have the technical knowledge to determine what is feasible.

1 Insights D Continued

Success of the decisions and achievement of related goals, however, require implementation by several or even many people. If the decisions and goals have high acceptance among these people, then the probability that challenging goals will be achieved is much higher than if such acceptance is lukewarm or lacking. After obtaining the advice of the experts, the manager therefore should convince the other staff members that the recommended plan or decision alternative is indeed the best course of action.

4. Work-maturity of participants   To what extent can the participants be counted on to accept responsibility for their input into the decision and for their respective roles in implementation? (See Hersey-Blanchard situational leadership model in Additional Insights B, Leadership Theories.)

5. Other elements of the situation   To what extent should other aspects of the situation influence participation? These include the time and cost of participation (to the organization and to the participants), the extent to which potential participants expect or want to be involved, the likelihood of conflict, the information that is available or can be made available, the extent to which the decision is predetermined by procedures and policies, the impact of the decision on the participants, and the urgency and importance of the decision.

It is useful to appreciate the extent to which appropriate participation helps to achieve *better control.* It gives staff members greater freedom to make independent decisions, but it clearly identifies the limits. Experienced and competent staff members are given wider limits than those who are new or less competent.

By establishing and revising these limits, managers/leaders are adequately involved in the control process. Better control, when understood as a joint activity, and appropriately implemented, will also lead to higher levels of KSAs and performance, and greater work satisfaction for staff members, further strengthening effective control.

No one can make participation decisions "right" all the time. Perception of those who participate is a critical element; success is measured by "batting average" on all important considerations.

If Three Simple Questions Can Be of Help, What Can More Detailed Questions Do?

(The Intermediate Guidelines)

Introduction

This chapter begins with a closer look at the 3Cs guideline questions. It uses more detailed versions and illustrates them with three scenario examples and analyses. The scenarios will be examined more rigorously than the situations in Chapter 1.

More Detailed (Intermediate) Guideline Questions

Please note that the more detailed guidelines merely expand the basic 3Cs guideline questions with specific issues to consider.

More Detailed Control Question

What else needs to be done to ensure effective Control and coordination, so that the decision which we are considering will lead toward the outcome we seek, and so we'll know when we have to modify our implementation or plan because we are not getting the results we want? Specifically,

1. Are the goals appropriate and effectively communicated to all stakeholders?

2. Is there appropriate participation in decision making?

3. Are coordination, cooperation, and inter- and intraunit communications being stimulated?

4. Is full advantage being taken of the potential of positive discipline and performance counseling?

More Detailed Competence Question

What else needs to be done so that all those who will be involved in implementing the decision, and those who will otherwise be affected, have the necessary Competencies to ensure effective progress and satisfying use of the product or service? Specifically,

1. Are changes needed in the recruiting and selection for vacancies?

2. Are management of learning concepts applied effectively?

3. Are coaching and counseling on self-development being used to best advantage?

More Detailed Climate Question

What needs to be done, if anything, so that the reaction of the various groups and individuals who have to implement the decision/plan of this alternative, and those who will be affected by it, will be in favor of it or at least have as positive a view as possible so there will be a favorable Climate? Specifically,

1. Are policies in place to help reduce work-related stress?

2. Are appropriate psychological rewards offered and provided effectively and efficiently to bring the highest possible level of satisfaction from the creation or use of the product or service?

3. Are appropriate tangible rewards offered and provided effectively and efficiently, to bring the highest possible level of satisfaction from the creation or use of the product or service?

THE SCENARIOS

Let us see what the additions to the basic guidelines do for us in three realistic situations. Each scenario will emphasize one of the 3Cs guidelines.

SCENARIO 2.1

Goal Setting for the Organization or Unit

Focus: The Control guideline, emphasis on goal setting, and participation

Abstract: John, the MIS manager for WGT Corporation, a messenger service organization, works on reducing complaints from internal clients who feel that the department is slow in providing programming and user support services, partly because of the need for revisions in programs.

❖ ❖ ❖ ❖ ❖ ❖

The Scenario

John, the MIS manager for WGT Corporation, a messenger service organization with about 220 employees, looked around the table. All the members of his team were there: Irene, the senior programmer and statistician; George, the new programmer; Judy, who supervises the administrative assistants and data input; and Frank, who is in charge of equipment, tech support, and user training. "I see everyone's here, so let's get started. Any urgent matters we should discuss?"

There were only negative responses and John continued. "As you know, Irene and I just attended a seminar on quality in MIS management. It seems, as we suspected, our department is not the only one facing complaints. In fact, the same gripes crop up everywhere—glitches in programs, not enough tech support and training, things take too long—you name it. Still, most of the people there agreed that we can do better, and we heard a lot about what could be done. Continuous improvement was the key phrase there, and customer orientation—right Irene?" Irene nodded agreement. "Yes, and speeding up the feedback loop."

"Anyhow," John continued, "that's what I called this meeting for—to decide what we can, and should do."

George immediately raised his hand. George is bright, young, and ambitious. He has a tendency to rub some of the others the wrong way—especially Judy and Frank's staff members who complain occasionally about his brash manner, treating them like they reported to him when they ask him a question or bring a problem to him.

Without waiting to be recognized, George blurted out: "Users have to give us better definitions on what they want so we don't have to revise so much. That'll bring better relations and fewer complaints. It'll also show a lot of improvement for us."

"That's a good way to start, let's blame them . . ."

"Come on, guys, let's concentrate on the positive—what WE can do to improve." John cut Frank short, with a smile, gently admonishing him and George while focusing the group's thinking on the task.

"Well, though it hurts me to have to agree with George," Irene tried to inject a little humor, while pointing to the positive in George's remark, "he is right. Better initial definition of what's needed would certainly cut complaints and costs at the same time."

"Yeah, but that does not mean that it's all their fault." Frank added. "They only know roughly what they want, at first, and get more ideas after we show them some sort of prototype—maybe we should spend more time showing them what a program will be like before we start to really work on it."

"If that's what we are talking about, shouldn't we have someone from operations and sales here, and also from marketing and maintenance? They are our clients and they should give us input on what they think about this."

Judy's suggestion seemed to get a favorable reception.

"I agree that we have to bring them into the loop. But, should we do that now, or should we first clear our heads a little? Maybe come up with some specific things we propose to do and get their feedback on that—otherwise we may invite a free-for-all with them asking for the impossible." John wants a little more thought before the group plunges into uncharted waters. "How about getting some ideas together on a continuous improvement program, if that's what we want to do, and even look at the way we get feedback on how we are doing? What do you think?"

All nodded their heads. John walked over to the easel pad and wrote three lines:

• Continuous improvement

• Client orientation

• Faster feedback

"All right, what about continuous improvement? What should we do?"

Irene was the first to respond. "With respect to the rework, I think we will have made a great start if we take the road we talked about—I mean, to find out how we can avoid rework by helping users define more clearly what'll best satisfy their needs. But you know, John, I was a little puzzled at the seminar why they did not include customer orientation and gaining feedback quickly as part of continuous improvement."

"I agree, we can think of it that way, at least at the start. Anyhow, can we make things actionable by setting some goals as we go along?" Frank is his usual results-oriented self.

"You always have to spoil the fun, don't you?" Judy tends to lean to the light side, though she has a sharp grasp of situations. "It's much easier to talk about these things than to commit to something. Seriously, though, don't we have to know what we want to measure and how we could measure it before we can set a goal?"

"You are absolutely right." George had been quiet till now. "But that might not be as tough as it looks. With respect to rework, we could look back into our records to see what proportion of time was used for it on each project and go from there."

"I wish our records would show that. They are nowhere adequate to serve as a useful basis for comparison. No, I'm afraid that won't work. I think we will have to use something else. And besides, that rework business applies primarily to us, George, because we are the only ones who do the programming. What about the others? How could we measure improvement there?" Irene sees the broader picture, but she also has a tendency to be intimidated by obstacles.

"I agree that we can use the proportion of time on rework as one measure for improvement. Would you two, Irene and George, accept the goal to set up some sort of system to keep accurate track of time spent on rework, and also on repeat visits to clients on the same problem, from now on? It'll certainly help us figure the proportion. OK?" Even though George and Irene nodded agreement, John sensed that the meeting might take forever if they tried to actually set goals for all the many things on which continuous improvement could be considered. He tried again to clearly focus on the first steps of a plan for the future. "But, on a broader scale, can we agree that you will each come up with some ideas on what goals you can set for continuous improvement in your function, on how you can improve client orientation, and how you can stimulate faster, honest feedback? Let's discuss it when you are ready. Just give me a ring as soon as you can. Ok?"

There was no objection and John ended the meeting, pleased that, in such a short time, an important first step had been taken.

In preparation for meeting with the individual members of his team, John thought about goals that might be useful and came up with a list that he planned to discuss with them. The list included, in addition to the item on keeping track of rework time or repeat visits to clients on the same problem or request for assistance, which Irene and George had already accepted:

- Reducing rework time or repeat visits to clients every quarter

- Keeping records of all complaints

- Establishing criteria for deciding which complaints are major and which are minor

- Reducing minor and major complaints every quarter

- Calling a meeting once a month with users served during the preceding month to discuss what could have been done to provide better service

- Identifying opportunities for relevant personal development and for staff training

- Planning and implementing learning/training programs

- Identifying opportunities for cost savings

- Reducing costs every quarter

John also planned to get their ideas, of course, and to review with them what they would like included in a memo to inform all departments about the continuous improvement program being planned by MIS. The memo would invite the managers of the departments to a meeting to discuss their thoughts on the program.

When he met with Irene, Frank, Judy, and George, they offered only suggestions that folded easily into this list. When John tried to get specific dates and improvement percentages he found that getting target dates for starting records, establishing criteria, calling a monthly meeting, starting on learning programs, and identifying opportunities, were easy.

Everyone balked, however, when it came to gaining commitments on reduction of rework time, repeat visits to clients, complaints, and costs. There is no history on which to base estimates of what could be accomplished, they contended, and John had to agree.

Knowing that they were devoted, serious people, he accepted their assurances that they would do their best. After all, if specific goals were set on these matters, they would be pure guesses. What good would it do to hold the team members responsible for failing to achieve such goals, or commend them for their achievement?

Before reading the analysis, and those for the other scenarios, always take a few minutes to jot down your own comments based on your approaches to similar challenges in the past or based on your interpretation of the more detailed respective guideline question. That way you will gain most from the points in the analyses, the Conclusions, and the conceptual summary at the end of the chapter.

❖ ❖ ❖ ❖ ❖ ❖

Analysis: Goal Setting for the Organization or Unit

Please keep in mind as you read on that the important thing about management/leadership decision guidelines (3Cs guidelines or your own) is *use* with every important decision and plan. Such use acts like the handle on a pot. It acts as a simple device to gain the use of the entire device—in the case of the handle, the pot itself; in the case of guidelines, all the management/leadership concepts that are useful to you. The guidelines should, of course, be sufficiently specific for your needs and you should be able to articulate them.

With respect to the 3Cs guideline questions, the basic questions from Chapter 1 will do fine. The benefit of the more detailed questions in this chapter, and the comprehensive ones in Chapter 3, is that they suggest issues that may not come to mind when you think of the respective basic guideline. They can also help you develop a thought process that automatically expands each guideline with the kinds of issues that you may want to consider. However, and this is a key point, all the guidelines suggested in this book are best used as a foundation for developing a system of guidelines with which you will be fully comfortable.

There are many perspectives from which to comment on John's situation. All, in one way or another, relate to the 3Cs guideline questions which pertain to Control, Competence, and Climate.

Please remember that there is an intense interrelationship between these 3Cs requirements for an effective organization: actions taken to strengthen Control affect the strength of Competence and Climate, for better or for worse. The same comprehensive impact is true of actions to improve Competence or Climate, respectively.

Our purpose here is to review this scenario in light of the more detailed Control guideline question. In the restatement of that guideline, the expansion segment is separated into its components:

> What else needs to be done to ensure effective Control and coordination so that the decision which we are considering will lead toward the outcome we seek, and so we'll know when we have to modify our implementation, or plan, because we are not getting the results we want? Specifically,
>
> a. Are the goals appropriate and effectively communicated to all stakeholders?
> b. Is there appropriate participation in decision making and planning?
> c. Are coordination, cooperation, and inter- and intraunit communications being stimulated?
> d. Is full advantage being taken of the potential of positive discipline and performance counseling?

Let's take these one at a time.

    a. Are the goals appropriate and effectively communicated to all stakeholders? (see Chapter 2, Additional Insights E, Making a Goals Program Work)

Let's look at what issues the guideline questions might bring to the surface. John may have considered some of them, but there is no evidence in the story that he did.

- Goals should not be confused with actions steps. Which items on the list are really goals and which are action steps?

- Goals should be realistic and challenging. Are those items which are goals realistic and challenging?

- Are the goals communicated appropriately to all affected staff members, or will they be?

Useful goals are different from action steps. They should be arrived at participatively and they should be realistic and challenging (deciding on action steps is primarily the staff member's responsibility). There also should be only a limited number of goals on which staff members should be expected to work at any one time. For these reasons, goals for an organizational unit, as well as the goals for individuals, should focus on matters that are very important to a major project or could be expected to bring some form of departmental improvement. At the same time it has to be understood that all work that is not covered by a goal shall be done at least as well as it has always been performed.

Goals are end results that are not fully under the control of the person or team assuming responsibility for their achievement. Responsibility for setting and for achieving goals is a complex matter. If the manager and the staff member each accept their shares, realistically and appropriately, then the department is likely to have a smoothly working goals program.

Action steps are things to do in the process of working toward a goal because, by definition, they are not seriously affected by external conditions. A staff member who commits to an action step can almost always achieve it—and be held accountable.

Considering the above definition of a goal, in Scenario 2.1 John and his team's primary goal was to establish an effective continuous improvement program for the entire MIS department. Leading to that goal were the lesser goals on John's list: reduction of rework time, repeat visits to clients, complaints, costs, and possibly other goals not yet identified. On the other hand, target dates for starting records, establishing of criteria, calling of monthly meeting, starting on learning programs, and identifying opportunities for competence improvement are action steps and not goals.

It is fully understandable that the team members easily committed to action steps but had difficulty establishing specifics for the goals. Still, without specifics, working toward a goal is considered by many people, even experts, to be like shooting an arrow and declaring that the target is where it lands. Yet, without defined goals, *continuous improvement* is not much more than just a slogan.

What to do? Clearly John was not aware that, for practical purposes, a goal can effectively be defined by the action steps that are planned to achieve it. Defining action steps, with timelines, is more useful than to hang quantities and timelines onto a goal. If the action steps are fully appropriate and competently executed, the best possible outcome, including quantities, will be achieved. Specifying higher (or lower) quantities when the goal is set often does not help (see Chapter 2, Additional Insights E, Making a Goals Program Work).

For helping you ensure soundly based goals, you might want to ask yourself either question a. from the guideline on the previous pages or:

> When setting a goal, what else can be done to ensure that strategies for achieving and communicating it are considered, as well as importance and urgency of the goal,

the distinction between goals and action steps, the work load on teams and individuals, achievability and challenge, progress review milestones, and the respective responsibilities of managers and staff members?

b. Is there appropriate participation in decision making and planning?

John might have asked himself one or more questions, such as those following:

- Did I ask the appropriate people to the meeting? Who else, if anyone, should have been at this initial meeting?

- Was the meeting held at an appropriate time?

- Did I delegate appropriate authority to the members of the group?

- What plans were made for informing other stakeholders about the new program?

Appropriate participation (with the right amount of authority—not too much, not too little, with the right people, at the right time, and so on.) is so critical that it deserves careful attention (see Chapter 1, Additional Insights D, Participation in Decision Making and Planning).

For appropriate participation, you might want to ask yourself either question b. from the guideline above or:

> Who should be involved, at what level of authority, and when? Your criterion should be the way in which participation by that person, or group, will bring the highest level of success.

c. Are coordination, cooperation, and inter- and intraunit communications being stimulated?

Issues which this guideline might have raised for John:

- What else, besides the planned memo and the meeting with the department heads, should be done to ensure that there will be effective coordination procedures and full cooperation between departments and staff members?

- What conflicts might arise and how can they be blunted or prevented?

- What else should be done to ensure that there will be continuing, thorough communications *within* the department and *with other* departments?

- What else should be done, if anything, to ensure that there will be appropriate communications with other stakeholders?

We often speak of coordination and cooperation in one breath, without making a distinction between these two activities. However, there are big differences.

Good coordination (availability of all needed resources and actions taken as expected) depends primarily on sound procedures, thoroughly communicated and understood. Procedures do, of course, require monitoring and sharpening with time. They also require willingness to follow, and that is cooperation with the coordination procedures. That's probably why these two topics are so closely linked.

For coordination, you might want to ask yourself either question c. from the guideline on the previous page or:

> What needs to be done, if anything, to ensure the highest possible level of coordination through appropriate procedures and removal of any obstacles?

While coordination concerns primarily *functional* issues, cooperation involves perceptions. It depends on attitudes toward the people with whom to cooperate and on the matters for which cooperation is desired. It therefore is in the province of management/leadership. Answers to the relevant segments of guideline questions on all 3Cs may be necessary.

For cooperation, you might want to ask yourself either question c. from the guideline presented before or:

What needs to be done, if anything, to ensure the highest possible level of cooperation through early identification of cooperation problems and prevention or effective resolution of all potentially damaging conflicts?

d. Is full advantage being taken of the potential of positive discipline and performance counseling?

Issues which this guideline might have raised for John:

- What will be the impact of the new program on the staff, what behavior problems might arise, and how can they best be prevented?

- Does he need additional training in performance counseling processes?

Positive discipline is the discipline of a team that wants to "win." In sports it's almost universal, partly because of the need, and partly because such is the nature of the beast. It is also easy to see when a team "wins." Not necessarily so in organizations where the competitive element is not so direct. Yet, there the willingness of individuals to set aside their personal interests, desires, and needs, for the benefit of the team's or organization's interests, may be just as important. Underlying this willingness is the absence of conflict.

When an individual does not respond to the atmosphere of positive discipline, counseling is needed.

For positive discipline, you might want to ask yourself either question d. from the guideline above or:

What should be done, if anything, so that appropriate norms, including norms pertaining to morality and diversity, are established and maintained, and so that staff members at all levels of the organization respect and follow them?

Conclusions: Goal Setting for the Organization or Unit

1. Control

Overall, John was on the right track, whether or not he was aware of the 3Cs guideline questions on Control, Competence, and Climate. All three are likely to be favorably affected if the primary goal of continuous improvement takes meaningful shape and is indeed achieved.

John, however, was not aware of the distinction between goals and action steps. If he had been, he would not have written his list the way he did. He would have separated out the goals in his list: reduction of rework time, repeat visits to clients, complaints, costs, and possibly other goals not yet identified, and asked for action steps to accomplish them. These were the items on which agreement was difficult to reach.

If John had asked for detailed plans for the achievement of each vaguely stated goal, the chances for quickly developing a useful continuous improvement program would have been greatly enhanced. At the same time, the element of the guideline pertaining to strategies for communicating and achieving the goal would have been furthered. Similarly, with action steps added, each goal could be made both *challenging* and *achievable.*

He also did not seem to have a sound grasp on what makes a goals program successful, such as the number of goals to set, the respective responsibilities of manager and staff member in the achievement of goals, and the implications of making goals both challenging and realistic. He did understand the need to make the goals statements as specific and measurable as possible.

John acted competently on appropriate participation, apparently based on his intuition. It was a sound approach to have all the staff members who report directly to him involved right from the beginning. Seeking input from other departments before calling the meeting, as suggested, might have brought some involvement by stakeholders outside John's staff. But, he probably was wise to postpone inviting members from these other departments until after he had a better fix on an MIS plan that could be presented to them for their comments and suggestions.

The participative decision-making approach used by John practically assures that obstacles to coordination and cooperation are aired and resolved, and that intraunit communications are thorough.

John intended to communicate the new program in a memo to all other departments and to invite department heads to a meeting for discussion of the program. Obtaining input from them certainly should do much to further ensure coordination, cooperation, and inter- and intraunit communications.

Positive discipline and competent performance counseling are important aspects of effective control in an organization or of the implementation of a program or project. Both, however, affect planning only if there is a problem or challenge in an organizational unit. The story was silent on these issues.

In addition to the Control guideline question, which has been the emphasis for this scenario, Competence and Climate guidelines have to be considered. Since the other two scenarios in this chapter will emphasize those guidelines, only highlights are covered here.

2. Competence

Competence involves hiring the right people, using sound training strategies, and making effective use of coaching. In John's situation, he had two goals on his list:

- Identifying opportunities for relevant personal development and for staff training

- Planning and implementing education and training programs

From that, it seems reasonable to assume that John asked himself the critical competence question: What do we have to do, that we are not doing already, to ensure that the Competence will be there when needed?

3. Climate

Climate involves strategies for reducing work-related stress and ensuring that staff members are given appropriate psychological and tangible rewards. With respect to this guideline there is no evidence in the scenario that John specifically asked himself relevant questions. However, he did take several steps to reduce stress and provide psychological rewards. He

- showed respect for staff member comments throughout the meeting

- showed concern for the views of other departments

- showed confidence and trust when he accepted their assurances that they would do their best (by doing so, he not only gave evidence of his high regard, but he also kept stress at a low level by preventing undue pressure from targets that might possibly be difficult to achieve)

- also planned to get their ideas and to review with them what they would like included in a memo.

What is the conclusion from this short scenario? It is the same as for all other scenarios: Competent managers/leaders lead toward establishing potentially successful direction and they see to it that there is progress toward the desired results. However, with use and better understanding of the Control, Competence, and Climate guideline questions they can lead toward strategies which help their organizations get there faster, and often with less effort and the use of fewer resources because the organization works smarter.

SCENARIO 2.2

The Downsized Department Store and the Challenge to Maintain Quality of Customer Service

Focus: The Competence guideline

Abstract: Ruth Moxton, training manager for a small depart-ment store chain, has a problem: downsizing has created tensions and customer complaints. The primary cause is the lack of knowledge of salespeople who are transferred temporarily to help out in departments with greater need for floor staff.*

❖ ❖ ❖ ❖ ❖ ❖

The Scenario

Paul's phone rang. A woman introduced herself as Ruth Moxton and told him that she was the training manager for a small department store chain. Her function is to provide some management development, but primarily training of new salespeople, concentrating on activities which are common to all departments. Her problem: downsizing has created tensions. She has been asked to look into the situation and to make recommendations so the growing number of customer complaints could be brought under control. Could he help, and what would his fee be?

Paul said yes, he thought he could. Though his work had concentrated on developing training materials, and he had never really provided training systems analysis and consultation, he felt confident that he could recognize what had to be done and be able to make some useful recommendations. He asked whether it might be possible for him to see the environment and speak with some of the staff members so he could be certain that he could be of service. Such a visit would also provide an opportunity to assess the scope of the assignment so he could prepare a detailed proposal, including the services to be provided and the fee.

Ruth agreed, and a few days later she met him at the chain's store headquarters, a little more than an hour's drive from his office. After some short pleasantries, Paul suggested that they walk through the store, while Ruth brought him up-to-date on the situation.

"Management is very concerned about this. There are now fewer salespeople and they have to be more flexible so they

*This story is adapted from one published in *TQM Magazine* V8/3, May/June 1996, pp. 63–64, MCB University Press.

can adapt quickly when they are needed in another department. We also move them around when there's little work in their department and something needs to be done elsewhere, like price marking for sales. When they go to other departments to be salespeople, they have to quickly learn about current inventory, what is on sale, and how to answer specific customer questions so they can provide quality service. In my initial orientation and general training course for new salespeople, I train on store procedures, fashion principles, and answering general customer questions that apply to all departments. I also give them some basics on customer service and selling skills. But, when it comes to helping people in this kind of a situation I frankly don't know what to do."

Paul had already sensed that Ruth would be more comfort-able in front of a group of trainees than in a task that required extensive training background and analysis. Ruth continued:

"In the past, after the initial training program, we used to send new employees to the floor where they would be working. There, a more experienced salesperson would help them become acquainted with the stock and sales merchandise, latest styles, and so on. We also have follow-up training where we concentrate on sharpening customer service and selling skills. Now, in addition to that . . ."

Ruth interrupted herself as she stopped at a register where a salesperson had just finished ringing up a customer purchase. Ruth introduced Paul and then asked: "How's everything going, Laura?"

"OK, I guess. Certainly now. But management doesn't want to hear how hard it can be when we are busy, like in the evenings, especially Thursday night and on weekends. As you know, Ruth, it's not easy for someone from another department to come here and help out." Laura addressed Ruth, but looked more at Paul, possibly hoping that he might have influence with management. "There's a lot to learn. We mark sales merchandise more carefully than we did in the past. When we do that, we really need the help we sometimes get from other departments. But, when there are three or four customers standing in line to ask questions, it's a different story. You know, we lost two people in this department, and you just can't fill those shoes with temporary people. What's more, when we are busy, so usually are the other departments. If we get anyone at all, they are from entirely different areas, like shoes or cosmetics. What do they know about fashions? I'm really afraid of the holiday seasons; we might lose a lot of customers if we can't give them the service that they expect."

"That's what Paul is here for. Maybe he can come up with suggestions on what we can do so customer service will not suffer. I doubt that management will give us more people until we get some big increases in sales, but we'll see. Thanks, Laura."

With that, Ruth motioned to Paul to follow her and continued on the tour.

"As I was saying before we stopped, Paul, in addition to the training that I do, we always had one or two salespeople in each department give on-the-job training to new people, and also when we had to send in replacements for people who were out. Now people say that very little of that occurs because they are too busy as a result of the layoffs. However, the store managers believe that staff shortage is primarily an excuse. They think that the main reason is apprehension about job security if employees can quickly became competent to work effectively in any department."

"There may be some truth to that, but it seems to me that what the salespeople say about workload and lack of time, just when new people need the most help, may also be valid. So, we will probably have to find a way to satisfy the competence need while relying less on the floor staff. Do you know some people who do well when they are asked to help out in another department?"

Ruth thought for a moment. Then she pointed straight ahead. "There's Gloria in Sportswear. She is great. She is one of the few whom they all want when they ask for help."

"Great. Can I talk to her for a moment?"

"Let's see whether she is available."

As they came closer, Ruth spotted her. "Gloria, do you have a moment? I'd like to introduce you to Paul, who might be able to help us with this problem we've got—you know, the complaint that doesn't apply to you—that people who are asked to work in another department need more training."

Gloria held her hand out and Ralph shook it. "Nice to meet you. How can I help?"

"Ruth has told me that you are so quickly at home when you are asked to work somewhere else. I am curious. What do you think you do differently than other people who don't adapt that easily?"

"Well, I don't really know . . ." Gloria stopped with a pensive look on her face. "Maybe it is that I really like my work. When I help out somewhere, I ask a number of questions as soon as I get there, like what's on sale, what's in demand and out of stock, what's expected in soon. You know, the kind of questions which customers ask the most. I sometimes write some of that down, when there's too much to remember."

"Thanks, that's most helpful." After a short pause. "Can you think of something else you do that helps you get adjusted quickly?"

Gloria hesitated, searching her mind. "No, I can't think of anything else, offhand. But I do notice that, when we get help from somewhere else, we have to take the initiative— only rarely does someone ask questions."

"That's also a good point. Thanks. I really appreciate what you told us." Paul was clearly delighted. So was Ruth, as she also thanked Gloria.

"Could you tell me more about the downsizing, Ruth? What were people told, what did they get in writing, were meetings held and who ran them? You know, that kind of thing. I don't need it now, but I'd like to get any papers you can get your hands on easily, if and when you want me to go ahead."

"Sure, I can get that for you, and fill you in where there's nothing in writing." After a brief pause. "We could head back to my office, if you feel you've got enough information to prepare your proposal."

"That'll be fine. Thanks for giving me a chance to see all this."

On the way back, they walked through two more departments. In one, salespeople were busy working with merchandise, preparing for a special sale, as Ruth explained. In the other department, the only two salespeople on the floor were standing near the register, in conversation. Paul could not hear what they were talking about, but both laughed heartily.

Back in her office, Ruth thanked Paul for visiting and told him that she had liked the way he was approaching the challenge. Paul also thanked her once more, promised to prepare the proposal within the next two days, picked up his briefcase, and left.

In his proposal, Paul suggested the following steps:

- Interviews with at least five department heads and at least one store manager to gain their views of the situation, on their scheduling of people to help out in other departments, and on their needs. Emphasis would be on what they perceive to be the competence deficiencies of salespeople who are "helping out."

- Interviews with eight to 12 salespeople, giving priority to those who adapt quickly when sent to help in another department. Whenever possible, there would be at least two from a department. The primary purpose of the interviews would be to identify what the salespeople believe that people from other departments should know quickly when they come to help out.

- Identification of urgent learning needs when someone is scheduled to work in another department, based on the information to be obtained during the interviews.

- Review of the initial training program to ensure that it includes competencies commonly required for rapid effectiveness when helping out in other departments, and recommendations for possible changes.

- Preparation of a draft *Competence Profile* for all salespeople.

- Preparation of a draft outline of a training program for department heads in completing the Competence Profile with each sales staff member reporting to them, in identification of competence strengths and weaknesses, in providing recognition for strengths, and in coaching to eliminate the weaknesses.

- Preparation of a plan on when and how to communicate the contemplated program to all staff members, prior to implementation, so that there would be opportunities for them to offer suggestions on any changes they might consider desirable.

- A meeting with whomever Ruth deems appropriate, to review the draft Competence Profile, the department-head training program, and the communications plan so that their comments could be used to make whatever revisions would be desirable.

- Revisions to the drafts, addition of milestones to be achieved, and implementation.

❖ ❖ ❖ ❖ ❖ ❖

Analysis: The Downsized Department Store and the Challenge to Maintain Quality of Customer Service

There are as many perspectives from which to comment on Paul's situation, as there were for John's. All, in one way or another, relate to the 3Cs guideline questions which pertain to Control, Competence, and Climate.

Our purpose here is to review the scenario with emphasis on the more detailed Competence guideline question. In the restatement of that guideline, the expansion segment is separated into its three components:

> What else needs to be done, so that all those who will be involved in implementing the decision, and those who will otherwise be affected, have the necessary Competencies to ensure effective progress and satisfying use of the product or service? Specifically,
>
> a. Are changes needed in recruiting and selection?
> b. Are management of learning concepts applied effectively?
> c. Are coaching and counseling on self-development being used to their best advantage?

Let's take these one at a time.

a. Are changes needed in recruiting and selection?

Paul is a staff development professional. Still, if he were aware of this aspect of the guideline question, he might have asked himself to what extent the criteria for hiring new salespeople consider flexibility in adapting to new situations. He might then have included a recommendation related to this aspect of competence.

Many organizations understandably look at specific technical competencies, work history, and experience as the primary criteria for selecting new staff members. In light of the rapidity of technological change and reorganizations, it might be useful to give the ability to learn quickly and to change or adapt equally high priority.

For recruiting and selecting, you might want to ask yourself question a. from the guideline on the previous page or:

> What, if anything, should be done to ensure that the recruiting and selection process is efficient and effective in filling vacant positions with highly qualified, flexible, and motivated candidates who will quickly be fully functional?

b. Are management of learning concepts applied effectively?

Paul clearly knew what he was doing here. He considered identification of learning needs, various delivery methods for information, and skill development, including training programs, self-development (using the Competence Profiles), and coaching.

Management of learning is different from teaching, primarily in perspective. Teaching is the passage of information and conveying of skills, from one who knows and can do, to those who need to know and do. Management of learning is providing assistance to people as they strive to acquire competence. The difference is in the emphasis—in teaching it is on the learning content. In management of learning it is on the learner and on the process of acquiring competence. It starts with identification of learning needs, proceeds from there to selection of methods and materials to provide the needed competence, and ends with follow-up to ensure that full competence has been or will be reached.

For management of learning you might want to ask yourself either question b. from the guideline above or:

> What can be done, if anything, to help staff members, including those with managerial functions, take greater responsibility for their own competence development, and that all necessary and desirable support and developmental opportunities are provided to them efficiently and effectively?

c. Are coaching and counseling on self-development, being used to best advantage?

Here, too, Paul knew what he was doing. He supported participative identification of learning needs, with coaching as needed, and he recommended a training program for department heads to enhance their coaching competence.

Coaching can be an essential element in management of learning. Staff members can acquire knowledge from an instructor's presentation from reading materials and by asking questions. Skills, however, require much more. They need demonstrations and, in addition, they need practice and feedback. Coaching provides these skill-learning steps, after helping the learner identify competence (skill and foundation knowledge) deficiencies.

For coaching you might want to ask yourself either question c. from the guideline above or:

> What else can be done, if anything, to ensure that I, and other managerial staff members, are skilled in coaching?

❖ ❖ ❖ ❖ ❖ ❖

Conclusions: The Downsized Department Store and the Challenge to Maintain Quality of Customer Service

1. Competence

Ensuring competence requires much more than training. It demands that every manager/leader must also be a *Manager of Learning.* Emphasis is on *learning, which means on the learners*—what knowledge and skills they should acquire and what is done so they will retain and be able to apply them when needed. That implies that these needs are jointly identified by the learners and the managers of learning, that learning materials and other support are provided, and that follow-up, including recognition, is arranged. All this needs to be in an ongoing cycle until full competence has been reached to apply what has been learned.

In the work environment, emphasis on learning rather than on teaching is of special importance. It is so wasteful and demotivating to learners when they have to attend training on matters that they know or can already do. Learning should emphasize and concentrate on what they, as individuals, have to learn or practice.

Managers/leaders who also want to be effective managers of learning help their staff members identify what they need to learn to become more competent, and then help them learn. This means that they have to arrange for attendance at fully appropriate programs, suggest self-study and practice steps, and provide feedback on learning progress. They also have to do some direct coaching (including on-the-job-instruction), and provide appropriate recognition. Paul correctly involves the department managers, helping them develop as effective managers of learning.

In addition to the Competence guideline question discussed above, Control and Climate guidelines have to be considered. Since the other two scenarios in this chapter emphasize those guidelines, only highlights are covered here.

2. Control

With respect to Control, while no goals are specifically spelled out at this stage of the project, it appears that Paul's plan includes the setting of goals, particularly competence development goals, for each salesperson. Implied in the preparation of the plan, and in the milestones to be included in the implementation program, is also the likelihood that a goal might be set on the total program.

His inclusion of a communications plan appears to be intended to ensure that there is thorough communication of the goal and the specific actions intended to achieve it. If so, the plan provides the procedures which should also lead to good coordination. The participatory approach to the development of the entire program should help to bring full cooperation and reduce or eliminate apprehensions.

3. Climate

With respect to Climate, Paul has set the stage to reduce work-related stress to a minimum. However, if he were aware of this guideline, he might have asked questions about the psychological and tangible rewards available to use in conjunction with the program. He might also have included methods and skill development for providing psychological rewards as part of the department head training program. These rewards would be in addition to satisfactions which staff members would gain from identifying competence strengths during the review of the profile.

If there was tacit resistance based on job security concerns, Paul's approach should go a long way toward surfacing the concerns and addressing them. Trust is the essential ingredient in this. Yet trust is something that few organizations know how to establish and maintain, or reestablish after an adversity. It rests on two foundations: (1) the perceptions of employees about the openness and honesty of those to whom they report, and (2) how fair the organization is in protecting people. That adverse developments can occur is understood; however, people expect an organization to help them ameliorate their tangible and psychological impact. Many managers cannot influence overall organization policies that impact on trust, but they can do much with respect to their own units. Paul's program would bring higher trust levels in departments where it would permanently improve communications between management and staff.

What is the conclusion from the scenario? It is the same as for all other scenarios: even managers/leaders who are only reasonably competent lead toward establishing potentially successful direction and they see to it that there is progress toward the desired results. However, with use and better understanding of the Control, Competence, and Climate guideline questions, they can lead toward strategies which help their organizations get there faster, and often with less effort and the use of fewer resources because the organization works smarter.

SCENARIO 2.3

The Case of an Insufficiently Appreciated Staff Member

Focus: The Climate guideline, emphasis on recognition for staff member contributions

Abstract: George is confronted by Raol, a staff member who feels that George fails to show appreciation for the effort and quality of work of staff members.*

❖ ❖ ❖ ❖ ❖ ❖

The Scenario

"Hey, I knock myself out for you, even stay late to finish this lousy job, and all you can say is 'That's fine, put it on my desk, thanks.' You didn't even look up. Don't you believe in giving a guy credit once in a while?"

George is startled by the unexpected outburst from a staff member who was usually quite reserved. "I do appreciate what you did, Raol, and I know that I can count on you when the chips are down. But I am busy with Tim right now." George is forcing a smile. "I'll look at your papers as soon as I can get back to my office and I'll talk to you then. OK?"

The defensive answer didn't seem to satisfy Raol. He just mumbled an abrupt "OK," nodded, and walked away.

A while later, after looking at the tables and the chart which were on his desk, George stopped at Raol's cubicle. In a deliberately loud voice, so others in the facing and adjoining units could hear, he attempted to calm the ruffled feathers. "That was a fine job you left on my desk, Raol, especially the chart—I know the rep will love it. I've already passed it on to her. Thanks. I knew you would come through on time."

"I appreciate what you are saying, George, thanks. Still, everyone feels you don't fully realize how good a crew you've got. Like today, one has to get annoyed before you say 'thanks'. Isn't that right, Sally?" Raol, only partially

---

*This story is adapted from one published in *TQM Magazine* V9/4, July/August 1997, MCB University Press.

satisfied, turned and looked for support from his coworker at the desk behind him.

Sally had first listened to George, but when Raol began his challenge, she had turned her attention back to her work. Now, she lifted her head and hesitated. Then, without looking at George, she said softly, "I guess there is something to what Raol says, George. You are fair and a nice guy. I think that we'd rather work for you than for some of the others we have known. I'm sure that you are right when you say that you appreciate good work. It's just that you don't show it, so we really don't know for sure whether you see how much we do for you and the company."

"You've both given me something to think about. Thanks." George's words had a sincere ring.

Returning to his office, George did think about the way he apparently was perceived. He was not completely surprised. His relations with his staff were solid and he knew he could count on them whenever a special need came up. Still, he knew that he was not the most outgoing of the managers. Not like Jerry, for instance, who had such an easy way about him—and his people always referred to him admiringly.

Could he do something so his group would also feel more satisfied with their work? He couldn't do it Jerry's way. That would not be genuine, and he smiled as he remembered a short saying he had heard the week before. What was it again? He tried to remember. 'Be what you is because if you be what you ain't, you ain't what you is.' That's it! The first try got it right.

So, what can he do, and still be himself? Maybe the library could be of some help.

George did look at the literature, and after considerable digging, he came up with the following points:

1. Research reported on in the literature (Maslow 1954; Herzberg 1959, 1968; Alderfer 1969; McClelland 1961; and so on) has repeatedly indicated that appropriate,

honest, and regular positive feedback and recognition are likely to stimulate an accomplishment-oriented motivational climate.

2. Nobody wants someone else to motivate him or her; still people respond favorably when they like the work. Response to awards and occasional recognition is, therefore, often short-lived. However, a climate of trust and confidence in the organization and the manager/leader, where individual staff members can find satisfaction in their work, is likely to bring greater personal motivation to achieve.

3. Most organizations have some form of formal recognition process which grants tangible rewards regularly for meeting targets that can be quantified factually, such as sales, production, and reject goals. Recognition is provided through *incentive* systems, some of which are almost analogous to the *piece work* systems from the early part of the century. Tangible awards are also given for longevity, attendance, quality achievements, overall performance, and other accomplishments.

   Tangible awards, like special bonuses, travel, or merchandise, other than those that are tied directly to quotas or goals, are usually awarded only once or twice a year.

4. There is nothing in the literature about organizations with systematic approaches to bringing continuing, frequent psychological recognition to employees. Hardly any are organized to ensure that employees with steady, reasonable, but not outstanding contributions are given positive feedback and thanks for their efforts. Even the language ignores such expressions of appreciation.*

Recognition, though a widely used word, implies an audience and hints at an outstanding accomplishment. There is no single word that conveys the expression of appreciation for all contributions, including the nonspectacular but consistent ones which are at the core of this discussion.

5. There is extensive data on tangible rewards available from the publications in the *incentives* industry, which can be tapped for data on volume of incentive awards.

   Very little, if any, data is available on the way organizations provide psychological rewards, and even less on the way they are organized to gain full potential benefit from greater satisfaction of this potent human need.

From these points he concluded:

1. An organizational culture which provides frequent sincere signs of appreciation for employee contributions is dependent on supervisor and manager competence in *identifying nonspectacular* contributions.

2. An organizational culture which provides frequent sincere signs of appreciation for employee contributions is also dependent on supervisor and manager competence in *using the many different ways in which appreciation and thanks can be expressed.*

3. A great many signs of appreciation are needed to balance the crescendo of negative signs that are present in even the best work environments, from unavoidable errors, accidents, malfunctioning processes and equipment, various types of conflicts, complaints, and so on. Still, few organizations provide training to managers/leaders to help them contribute significantly to the overall volume of satisfying moments for staff members.

4. Top management support and modeling is not widespread. Where it is, there is more effort devoted to *recognition.*

5. Raol may be more aggressive than most staff members, but the feelings he expressed are widespread.

"So much for the conclusions," George thought. "Now what? Knowing what should be done does not make it happen."

Over the next few weeks, the challenge rarely left his mind. Slowly he began to build an approach. First he spent a few minutes every day thinking about things which his staff had done the day before. That was helpful.

To his surprise, the list kept growing, and it also became more specific. He started, of course, with the obvious: quantity and quality of work, working longer hours, spending less time during breaks, regular attendance, meeting deadlines, skill in handling nonroutine assignments, maintaining appropriate work-area appearance, participating constructively in meetings, following procedures, courtesy and calmness when speaking with clients, willingness to learn new routines or tasks, etc.

He started to notice staff member behavior that was not as directly related to overall responsibilities and the tasks at hand, but rather contributed in different ways—not letting conflicts erupt but settling them, helping to maintain a friendly and cheerful atmosphere, assisting others who had questions or difficulties with a task (especially when a new program was introduced), maintaining nonroutine records, finding things that had been misplaced, and so on. The list never seemed to end.*

He continued to add to the list, but he also wanted to make practical use of it. He wondered how he could say thanks, repeatedly, and not have it appear to be routine.

Here too he decided to make a list, but this one was not so easy. In fact, he struggled, and though he was finally able to come up with a fairly long list, it did not grow like the other one. He realized that his overall goal was to make every staff member feel important. He also realized that he

---

*For more information on how to identify opportunities for providing signs of appreciation, and for ways to show appreciation, see *Providing Recognition, a Handbook of Ideas,* Didactic Systems, 1974, and *ASP - The Achievement Stimulating Process, A Handbook for Managers/Leaders,* Didactic Systems, 1996.

would have to develop habits so he could be sincere and not be perceived as manipulative.

These are the things he began to practice, usually verbally, sometimes with informal notes:

- Listening carefully and not interrupting a staff member who wants to say something or make a suggestion

- Spending a few moments, whenever a staff member hands in an assignment, for a quick review and to provide immediate feedback (and, if a postponement is necessary, to let the staff member know that he will get back to them soon—and keep the promise)

- Telling a staff member that he considers a specific accomplishment to be important

- Indicating awareness of an accomplishment that came to his attention without the staff member's knowledge

- Offering help with an assignment

- Asking for an explanation of how a difficult task was accomplished

- Distinguishing *thanks* from routine acknowledgements by doing them deliberately in a different place or time, such as his office, in front of other staff members, or employees from other departments, informally, or even formally in front of some or all members of the team, and so on.

- Asking for ideas and suggestions

- Asking for an employee's opinion on an idea, or ideas and suggestions from others

- Promptly providing information on occurrences affecting the team

- Arranging for the manager of another department to provide any of these items

- Arranging for customers or members of the public, with whom a staff member may be in regular contact, to provide any of these items

- Arranging for a higher-level manager to provide any of these items

- Taking a staff member into his confidence on an event or a decision not yet public

- Promptly implementing a staff member's suggestion or idea

- Consulting with staff members on decisions where they have the knowledge or experience to contribute

- Including a staff member in the list of those to whom he delegates management/leadership tasks that the staff member can perform, such as leading a meeting in his absence or taking his place at an interdepartmental meeting when he cannot attend

- Initiating career counseling and responding effectively to questions on career opportunities

- Giving full consideration to staff members during the selection of candidates for vacant positions

- Helping employees acquire skills that might be useful for positions up the career ladder (through developmental assignments or a training program)

❖ ❖ ❖ ❖ ❖ ❖

Analysis: The Case of an Insufficiently Appreciated Staff Member

As in the previous scenarios, there are many perspectives from which to comment on the situation. All, in one way or another, relate to the 3Cs guideline questions which pertain to Control, Competence, and Climate.

Our purpose here is to review the scenario in light of the more detailed Climate guideline question. In the restatement of that guideline, the expansion segment is separated into its components:

What else needs to be done so that the reaction of the various groups and individuals who have to implement the decision or plan, and those who will be affected by it, will be in favor of it or at least have as positive a view as possible so there will be a favorable Climate? Specifically,

a. Are policies in place to help reduce work-related stress?

b. Are appropriate psychological rewards offered and provided effectively and efficiently to bring the highest possible level of satisfaction from the creation or use of the product or service?

c. Are appropriate tangible rewards offered and provided effectively and efficiently to bring the highest possible level of satisfaction from the creation or use of the product or service?

Let's take these one at a time.

a. Are policies in place to help reduce work-related stress?

Identification of staff member contributions, and the actions George is planning to show his awareness of them, can reduce work-related stress significantly by showing his high regard for all staff members who are helping the department achieve its goals.

If he were aware of this guideline, George might have asked himself, in conjunction with any thoughts he had on the issue, what else could be done to further reduce any undesirable work-related stress (within the limits imposed by ensuring that the department's progress is fully supported by each staff member).

Like conflict, not all work-related stress is detrimental. Healthy competition is stressful. Still, up to the limit that an individual can tolerate, it can be quite beneficial. The key here is the limit. Really effective leaders have sensors in place to ensure that they become aware when stress levels are at or beyond the individual's limit and thus detract from the satisfaction that the staff member gains from the work.

How can you develop better sensors? Ask yourself whether your communications are sufficiently open so people will confide in you and enlist, formally or informally, the help of other staff members who may alert you to staff members who are overly stressed.

b. Are appropriate psychological rewards offered and provided effectively and efficiently to bring the highest possible level of satisfaction from the creation and/or use of the product or service?

For most managers/leaders such as John, the appropriate psychological rewards are the most meaningful opportunities, but also the most daunting challenges. George is addressing these challenges in a very effective way, by identifying the types of staff member contributions that should or could be noticed, and by planning to provide ways to show appreciation for them.

In effect, he asked the two critical questions: What (for what contributions), and how and when?

George's thinking, and the steps he is taking, paint a fairly comprehensive picture of the issues in providing appropriate psychological rewards. The Climate guideline itself and especially question b. above beg the issue whenever you use it.

c. Are appropriate tangible rewards offered and provided effectively and efficiently, to bring the highest possible level of satisfaction from the creation or use of the product/service?

This is one segment of the guideline questions that is often on the minds of managers/leaders, and therefore does not need special attention here.

Being heavily occupied with psychological issues in the aftermath of the confrontation with Raol, George did not seem to have given any thought to tangible rewards. If he had, he would undoubtedly have realized that he should seek answers to questions such as:

- Are there some tangible rewards I can use that would not run counter to any organizational policy, that would not be seen as favoritism, and that would not set an undesirable precedent, such as inviting one or several employees for lunch at a good restaurant, or a plaque, or certificates, or merchandise gifts?

- Might it be possible, and wise, to set up a voucher system with clear criteria, which would allow staff members to earn points toward a travel or merchandise award?

- How could he effectively integrate performance assessment into his renewed attention for providing signs of appreciation for staff member contributions?

Like most managers, George has little impact on the tangible rewards that are being offered. However, George and managers at all levels can ensure that staff members and users of the organization's products or services obtain the greatest satisfaction. With respect to the users, the answer is simple: quality is the big item. For staff members, on the other hand, this is most difficult. Not only is it necessary to consider those staff members who receive tangible rewards (whether it be a compensation increase, a bonus, or a special award), but it is also important to consider the impact on the other staff members who do not. What they hear about the rewards given to others, from whom, and when, can make a big difference in how they regard their manager as a leader (see Chapter 1, Additional Insights C, Motivation Theories).

For tangible rewards you might want to ask yourself either question c. (on the previous page) or:

> What should be done to ensure that all other staff members with management/leadership responsibilities are aware of the tangible rewards which they can give staff members? What are the criteria which staff members have to meet to be eligible? Are they sensitive to whether they are basing decisions pertaining to tangible rewards on performance evaluations within the limits of the organization's policies and procedures? Are they skilled in

distributing tangible rewards in ways that will have the highest possible motivational impact on all staff members, not only on those who receive the reward?

❖ ❖ ❖ ❖ ❖ ❖

Conclusions: The Case of an Insufficiently Appreciated Staff Member

1. Climate

George had full control over the nontangible signs of appreciation that he gives. He also could exercise considerable control over those that come from the higher-level managers since they are not likely to refuse a request to say something positive to members of his team.

Gaining help from other departments should also not be difficult if he is willing to initiate such a relationship. Other departments are likely to reciprocate if he and some members of his team show appreciation for achievements which favorably impact his team. If he wanted to be even more certain of cooperation, he could reach an informal agreement with managers of other departments.

Gaining help from customers, clients, or other members of the public is not as easy, of course, but it can sometimes be stimulated. Either orally, in writing on routine mail, or as a separate message, word can go out that says, in effect: "When something is not what you expected, let *me* know; when everything is OK, let the person know with whom you have been in contact." If sent frequently, a message like this fosters some results, though this source of recognition for staff members is not likely to be consistent or have great impact.

In addition to the Climate guideline question which has been the basis for the analysis, Control and Competence guidelines have to be considered. Since the other two scenarios in this chapter emphasize those guidelines, a brief statement suffices here.

2. Control

The scenario itself is mute on issues directly connected with Control. Nevertheless, the steps George is taking will undoubtedly be helpful. Effective, practical control is strengthened by listening, by greater empathy with staff member views and feelings when reviewing projects, by greater attention to ideas and suggestions, and by asking for opinions. These managerial behaviors bring opportunities to discuss more alternatives than would otherwise be considered, and thus further enhance the department's de facto control over its progress.

3. Competence

Better communications also have the effect of increasing George's awareness of the way staff members approach their responsibilities. They thus give George deeper insight into staff member competencies and open the door to taking advantage of strengths and to coaching to reduce or eliminate weaknesses.

What is the conclusion from the scenario? It is the same as for all other scenarios: Even managers/leaders who do not use guidelines and who are not acquainted with the 3Cs lead toward establishing potentially successful direction and they see to it that there is progress toward the desired results. However, use of the Control, Competence, and Climate guideline questions (asking them with every important decision and plan), can get their organizations there faster, and often with less effort and the use of fewer resources because the organization works smarter.

You undoubtedly thought, as you read the analyses and conclusions from each case, that they contained little that is new to you, and that you probably would have considered many of the thoughts discussed. However, and this is the crucial point: *there probably were one, or a few, thoughts that you might not have considered. It is these thoughts that might have helped you make a somewhat better decision. The more you practice guideline thinking, along the lines suggested here, or along your own adaptations, the more likely that the management/leadership aspects of your decisions will be more thorough and more comprehensive.*

2 Additional Insights E

Making a Goals Program (or Management by Objectives) Work*

(Though there are various definitions for the words *goals* and *objectives* in the literature, the words are used interchangeably in this book.)

> Our policy, to be effective,
> Must chase a suitable objective,
> So our economy should be
> Both Growing, Stable, Just and Free.
> The Dog would surely be a Dunce
> Who tried to chase four things at once,
>
> *Principles of Economic Policy, Chapter 1*
> *Kenneth Boulding (Adapted)*
>
> As you ramble on through Life, brother,
> Whatever be your Goal,
> Keep your Eye upon the Donut
> And not upon the Hole
>
> *Cover of Mayfair,*
> *New York Coffee Shops Menu*

Introduction

After the introduction, this section discusses the characteristics of effective goals. It is these characteristics that differentiate goals which are used primarily to satisfy procedural requirements from those that actually help to improve organizational performance.

---

*For a thorough discussion of the issues that make a goals program successful, see *Balancing Needs of People and Organizations—The Linking Elements Concept (Rausch 1978, 1985), and How to make a goals program successful,* Training and Development Journal (Rausch 1980).

2 Insights E Continued

Goals exist at all levels of an organization, whether all staff members, some, or none know them, and whether or not they are part of the management and leadership system. In some organizations they are only ideas in the minds of some managers, or words. In others they are paper tigers, used primarily to communicate lofty ideals and dreams. Many organizations have some sort of formal goals program that is either successful, limps along partly ignored, or partly used to satisfy procedural requirements.

There are different types of goals. Long-range goals (including mission statements for an organization) are implemented with shorter-range goals. Some organizations even differentiate between strategic goals and tactical (operational) goals, which support them. Successful use depends on how well goals are set, communicated, understood, and respected.

At the highest organizational level, the long-range goals are often referred to as *vision,* an important element of effective leadership. Vision is meaningless, however, unless it is shared and accepted.

While vision is usually considered to be the province of top management, one can talk about vision at the level of a small department. There it is likely to be the goal of the department's manager/leader to make the unit a highly effective one. In reality, this vision shows itself in the form of specific long-term and short-term goals, in conformance with the goals at higher levels in the organization.

Whether originated by you as the department manager or based on suggestions by staff members, goals most likely concern functional issues (pertaining to sales, marketing, health care, operations, agency work, quality, investments, finance, and so on). How the specifics are to be decided, what subsidiary goals are to be set, and how the goals are to be implemented are the issues of concern from the management/leadership perspective.

Goals are decisions. It is therefore important to keep the 3Cs management/leadership issues of Control, Competence, and Climate in mind. This is particularly relevant because the functional aspects are usually dominant and have a tendency to overshadow all other considerations.

Insights E Continued

The idea of working toward goals seems deceptively simple, yet much is involved. Specifically, the following questions should be answered if the goals program is to be successful:

1. Are the goals of high quality, which means:
   - Are the unit's goals in line with the larger organization's goals?
   - Do they address matters that are important, rather than those that are urgent?
   - Are they both challenging and realistic (achievable)?
   - Is it possible to determine whether they were achieved or not?
   - Are they *true* goals or are they action steps?
   - Are they for a meaningful time span?

2. Are the goals being communicated effectively to all stakeholders?

3. Are there an appropriate number of goals for the organizational unit and for each staff member, considering staff abilities and workload?

4. Is there appropriate participation by stakeholders in the setting of the goals?

5. Have you, the manager/leader, accepted your respective share of responsibility for achievement of the goals?

6. Do goals address not only the functional achievements but also the management/leadership aspects of Control, Competence, and Climate?

7. Is the award/reward system of the organization coordinated with goal performance?

Let's look at these requirements for successfully managing with goals one at a time.

2 Insights E Continued

Are the goals in line with the larger organization's goals?

Goals of an organizational unit are of good quality only if they are in line with and contribute to the larger organization's goals.

Do they address matters that are important, rather than those that are urgent?

Goals are useful only if they focus on achievements pertaining to a major project or to some significant improvement. If goals are set on trivial matters, they are not likely to earn the respect of the staff, nor do they help to separate important matters from unimportant ones. One of the significant benefits of goals is that they can assure that the matters on which they are set receive their proper share of attention in relation to more urgent ones.

The relative importance and urgency of something to be achieved, can help determine whether it deserves a goal (see Chapter 4, Additional Insights M, Time Management and Delegation). Considering the four possible combinations of these two considerations, surprisingly, it is not the important and urgent matters that deserve to be considered for goals—they automatically receive maximum immediate attention and it is too late to set goals on them. Matters that are *important and not urgent are the best candidates for goals.* Goals bring with them timeposts for action steps and thus can ensure that these matters do not get pushed aside for other urgent ones until they reach crisis stage. At that point it may be too late to deal with them most effectively—but being both urgent and important then, they will certainly receive maximum attention, the way battling the biting alligators always has priority over draining the swamp.

Are they both challenging and realistic (achievable)?

According to much of what has been published on the subject, goals can have a high motivational impact on the organizational unit as well as on individuals if they are challenging and realistic. Realistic means that they are believed to be achievable. In practice it does not necessarily work out that way, partly because there is a contradiction here: realistic and achievable means that the goal can be reached. Yet, the challenging criterion means that even with maximum effort it may not be achieved, because matters beyond the control of the individual and of the organizational unit will prevent the goal from being fully satisfied.

All goals are predictions of what can be achieved with diligence and maximum reasonable effort. To determine what the goal will require in the way of budget and time, and any quantities that may be involved, requires some form of forecasting. Therefore, if a goal is to be set both challenging and fully realistic, and those who set the goal are very good at their craft and at forecasting, then there is likely to be a greater than 50/50 chance that slightly less will be achieved (because of the challenging aspect), and a smaller than 50/50 chance that the actual outcome will be better than the goal. Perfect achievement of a goal (in the sense of exact budget, quantity, quality, completion time, and any other conditions are met) occurs most rarely.

From the perspective of the Control guideline, the best goals are indeed those that are challenging and realistic/achievable. To determine what will make a goal realistic, it is necessary to lay out the steps that could be taken to achieve the goal. A goal that is set without a review of the alternative steps to reach it (plan alternatives) is more of a guess than a serious effort to provide meaningful direction for the team or staff.

For practical purposes, it may often be better not to insist that a staff member provide specifics for a goal, as was the case in Scenario 2.1. Instead it can temporarily be defined by the action steps that are planned to achieve it. Often this alternative is more useful than specifics such as quantities, quality, and timelines, at least in the interim, until the view is clearer and specific attributes of the goal can be set. If the action steps are fully appropriate and competently executed, the best possible outcome will be achieved.

Is it possible to determine whether they were achieved or not?

Often goals are too vaguely stated to be useful. However, a goals program that provides long-term goals as general guidance and

2   Insights E Continued

supports them with short-term goals needs to have the specifics (dates, budgets, quantities, quality specifications, and so on) incorporated only in the short-term goals.

Are they true goals or are they action steps?

From a decision point of view, it is important to consider whether the steps that have to be taken to achieve the goal are totally under the control of the person, team, or organization who has accepted responsibility for achieving it. The question you have to ask yourself is, "If that person/team/organization wants to achieve the goal, can anything other than an emergency or another major, totally unforeseeable event stand in the way?"

If the desired end result can definitely be achieved with competent action and adequate effort, possibly with some extra effort, then it is not a goal. It is merely a task or project, requiring one or a series of action steps possibly directed toward a goal. An end result is a goal only if there are circumstances beyond the control of the individual/team/organization (such as the case with sales quotas) which may help or hinder its achievement.

You have entirely different tasks and responsibilities with respect to goals and action steps. With a goal you have to consider all the issues involved in making a goals program successful. With a task or project you do what you do with other day-to-day activities: you agree on a completion date and then follow up.

Sometimes it will not be clear whether an expected result should be treated as a goal or as an action step. If in doubt, the particular performance element can be labeled as action step, especially if it does not involve such matters as sales, quality, or output. Then, if the action step has not been completed or major obstacles have developed, it can always be changed to a goal and treated accordingly, possibly by developing an action plan.

Are they for a meaningful time span?

Setting goals properly requires considerable time and effort, and involves timelines for the supporting action steps. It is therefore impractical to set them on urgent matters that have to be done in

2   **Insights E Continued**

a few days—these matters require immediate attention and setting milestones is usually not practical.

Are the goals being communicated effectively to all stakeholders?

Timely communications in appropriate forms with all stakeholders are of utmost importance in helping to ensure that everyone knows what is to be achieved and when, and what the respective roles of staff members are. Only with that knowledge can there be full coordination and cooperation (see Scenario 2.1). Sound communications contribute to a motivational climate for goal achievement and are important to ensure that stress related to the *challenging* aspect of goals is held within reasonable limits.

Are there an appropriate number of goals for the organizational unit and for each staff member, considering staff abilities and workload?

An individual and a team can work on only a limited number of goals. By setting goals only on those end results which are most important to the organizational unit, the special attention which goals engender will focus on a limited number of matters. The current and anticipated workload, of course, as well as the individual staff member or team abilities, also influence the number of goals.

Is there appropriate participation by stakeholders in the setting of the goals?

Participation-in-decision-making concepts have to be kept in mind throughout the goal-setting process, and even during assignment of tasks or projects. Without appropriate participation, there is a less motivational climate and the image of the manager as an effective leader is reduced (see Chapter 1, Additional Insights D, Participation in Decision Making and Planning).

Have you, the manager/leader, accepted your respective share of responsibility for achievement of the goals?

It is not hard to see why goal setting has heavy impact on the Climate, as well as on Control. Goals can easily involve political

2 Insights E Continued

strategies. In an organization that has established a climate favorable to achievement, and where communications are open, it is likely to be safe for an organizational unit, as well as for an individual, to set and to shoot for challenging, ambitious goals. However, if the climate is such that negative consequences can result from failure to fully achieve a goal, then there is strong incentive for goal setters to gain acceptance of conservative, less challenging goals.

To ensure that the goals program adds to a positive climate, you, as the manager/leader, have to be involved and be satisfied with the methods your staff uses to work toward accomplishment of their goals. You have to provide any support that may be needed and, most important of all, you have to be prepared to accept your full share of responsibility for the outcome of the strategies.

Do goals address not only the functional achievements but also the management/leadership aspects of Control, Competence, and Climate?

To help ensure that goals will be achieved, staff members must be competent for all aspects of their respective responsibilities. Goals should therefore consider any competence needs that may exist and include whatever competence development may be necessary.

The same is true of staff member satisfaction with the goals program. By accepting your share of responsibilities, and by making most effective use of the organization's reward system, you can help ensure that the Climate guideline is satisfied.

Is the award/reward system of the organization coordinated with goal performance?

It is highly desirable, of course, for people to be rewarded fairly, if not generously. Psychological rewards play as important a role as do tangible rewards (see Chapter 3, Additional Insights K1, Performance Evaluation and K2, Providing Recognition).

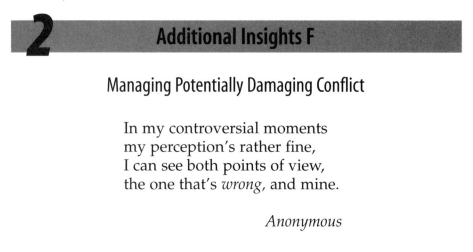

2 Additional Insights F

Managing Potentially Damaging Conflict

In my controversial moments
my perception's rather fine,
I can see both points of view,
the one that's *wrong*, and mine.

Anonymous

Introduction

After the introduction, the following topics will be discussed in this section:

- Everyone can be a conflict manager

- Conflict management steps

- The five groups of solutions

- Third parties

- Conclusion

Preventing and resolving potentially damaging conflicts can be beneficial, way beyond the issues involved. Organizations and individuals who are able to prevent or settle such conflicts benefit greatly in trust and confidence, in loyalty, and in respect.

Not all conflict is damaging, of course. Healthy competition is conflict. Up to the limit that an individual can tolerate it effectively, it can be quite beneficial.

The presence of conflict beyond competition, whether it is based on conflict of interest, conflict of goals, dissatisfaction (often not recognized as conflict), or personality clashes affects all 3Cs management/leadership areas: Control, Competence, and Climate. Control benefits from the best possible cooperation, brought by the absence of conflict. Competence is enhanced because everyone learns, from the resolution of conflicts, about the many

2   Insights F Continued

different perspectives on the issues that are in dispute. Climate, of course, will be much better when there are no simmering or unresolved conflicts. As manager/leader, one of your personal goals should be to ensure that conflicts will not find fertile ground in your organizational unit.

While some types of conflict are not damaging, unresolved disagreement about what to do is likely to be just that—at the least it takes time and attention away from more important things. At worst, it brings an escalating spiral of frustration, mistrust, serious discord, refusal to cooperate, punitive actions, and retribution.

To manage discord, this spiral must be broken or prevented—the earlier the better. Not all damaging conflict, unfortunately, can be prevented or resolved. The toughest types of disputes to resolve are usually based on a complex set of circumstances, including irreconcilable conflict of interest between the parties and many psychological factors such as pride, feelings of security, self-esteem, and hate. Such conflict, when even compromise is not in the cards, sometimes cannot be resolved. It must be played out to the end, where one side wins and the other loses. The major obstacle often lies in the commitment, of at least one party, to 'winning' on his or her terms. That type of conflict (except when it is part of a game or sport) requires early intervention since it can set the escalating spiral in motion.

For you the potentially most productive strategy is to ensure that every member of your staff knows how to be a *conflict manager* and is willing to accept that role whenever a conflict threatens or arises. That may require a meeting, with each group of five to 10 staff members, to explain the concept, and refresher meetings to develop habits.

Everyone Can Be a Conflict Manager

What is involved?

Anyone and everyone can be a manager of conflict. One does not need a position of authority. One needs to understand conflict and then just appoint oneself. There can be as many managers of conflict in a dispute as there are people involved in it. If all your staff members take this role in every conflict in which they are involved, all will have their eyes on winning the war, not winning sectional battles. They will be aware that the enemy is not the antagonist in a specific disagreement. It is the stress, trouble, strained relationships, unsatisfactory climate, and losses that follow in the wake of poorly resolved conflicts.

In this sense, a war is completely over only if or when a dispute is resolved in such a way that both sides *win*. Ideally that happens when all parties are as satisfied as they would have been if they had *won* the way they originally wanted to win. Often it does not take so creative a solution to end a war. A satisfactory compromise is usually adequate.

Staff members who appoint themselves as managers of conflict in which they are involved can do so at any time. They need not, and probably should not, tell anyone that they have assumed that role. Every conflict can use at least one manager on each side. The more conflict managers, the better. Those involved in the dispute who also understand conflict well enough to have appointed themselves conflict managers will welcome the decisions of others to also do so as they become aware of them.

What managers of conflict do is to bring leadership to help achieve a rational, unemotional search for the best outcome, one that satisfies the *perceptions* of *both* parties that it is the best solution in their respective short-term and long-term interests. The emphasis in the search is on perceptions, since people and groups often do not know or may even misunderstand their own best interest. Resolving conflict must deal with exposing the reality, so each party can gain a realistic perspective of its best interest.

Keeping the eye on both the issues on the table and on the process of conflict resolution at the same time is not necessarily easy to do, especially in the heat of battle. Short sections from two poems are so much to the point here they deserve quoting:

> If you can keep your head when all about you
> Are losing theirs and blaming it on you,

Insights F Continued

If you can trust yourself, when all men doubt you,
But make allowance for their doubting too;

If, Rudyard Kipling

In the world's broad field of battle,
In the bivouac of Life,
Be not like dumb, driven cattle!
Be a hero in the strife!

A Psalm of Life, Henry W. Longfellow

Conflict Management Steps

To resolve disagreements, conflict managers help the parties proceed through several steps. Communications skills are central to these steps:

1. Preventing or reducing undesirable emotions

2. Identifying the central issues in the conflict

3. Identifying possible solutions

4. Choosing the best solution, with consideration for the views of the parties and others who are seriously affected

5. Implementing the best solution, including communicating it to those who are affected by but not parties to the dispute

6. Follow-up to monitor how well the outcome has helped to completely end the dispute

The steps are the same, whether the conflict is between two individuals, a group and an individual, or two groups.

These steps are, of course, not the only approach that can be used. In their best-selling book, *Getting to Yes* (1981), Roger Fisher and William Ury, of the Program on Negotiations at the Harvard Law School, suggest a different, somewhat more elaborate

2 Insights F Continued

approach. That book, and a follow-up volume by William Ury entitled *Getting Past No* (1991), present a very useful perspective.

Step 3, identifying possible solutions or outcomes (ways to settle the conflict), deserves more explanation here. In this step conflict managers suggest, or respond to, very specific possible solutions offered by the parties. If these do not lead to a closing of the gap between the parties, competent conflict managers may suggest other alternatives from one of the five groups listed below. Four, except the first, are always available. The first one, the creative win-win type of settlement, is not always within reach but it is the one that conflict managers should focus on throughout. One can never tell when such a solution might pop up unexpectedly.

The Five Groups of Solutions

These five groups are:

1. *Creative solution:* a win-win outcome that leaves both parties as satisfied, or almost as satisfied, than if they had *won* the way they wanted to win.

2. *Compromise:* gives each party somewhat less than they had hoped to get, but enough so they consider the outcome to be fair and reasonable.

3. *Postponement of the discussion:* depending on the situation, sometimes brings a temporary win for one party, if time is in its favor. Frequently, however, postponement is neutral and brings cooler heads and solutions that are better all around.

4. *Concession by one party:* usually a loss for that party in the short term; it can turn into a win-win over the long run, especially if the good will it generates brings reciprocal actions that lead to increasing mutual respect and support.

5. *Use of authority:* may feel like a win at least for the short run, whether the party using it is in a position of authority or not. Over the long run, the benefits of using authority are not as clear; that's why it should be used most cautiously.

2 Insights F Continued

There are, however, instances when a party to a conflict, or a conflict manager, has to use position authority or authority as parent. In the case of parents it often works to the long-run benefit of both parties. The same can happen in a work environment. Using authority is also the best thing to do in the rare instances when one side wants the responsibility for the outcome to be solely on the other side.

When either conflict party is not in a position of authority over the other party, authority can still be used in a conflict. One side can refuse to listen, to agree to a course of action, to rightfully or wrongfully withhold an object or service wanted by the other party, to demand a postponement of the discussion when such a postponement benefits their side, or just refuse to cooperate with further attempts to resolve the problem. These are all uses of authority and the party who uses it can *win*, for the moment at least. Though steps like these can give a temporary advantage, they can also trigger retaliation from the adversary.

Third Parties

You may want to consider bringing in a third party when you are aware of a dispute that is not resolving well or is festering. Such a third party can be either an arbitrator or a mediator.* The third party could be a volunteer neutral person or group, a person with higher-level responsibilities for all or some of the issues, or a professional mediator or arbitrator.

---

*Mediators are impartial persons, or panels, without authority to impose a settlement; the function of mediators is to help the parties come to a mutually satisfactory outcome of the dispute. Sometimes mediators have been given the authority to recommend a resolution, as is the case with fact-finding panels who are sometimes appointed by municipal, state, and even federal authorities, primarily in labor disputes.

Arbitrators, by contrast, specify a settlement, like judges, or with specific limitations. Arbitrators may sit alone or as panels. Their authority derives from a contract, from other agreement between the parties, from policies of the organization to which the parties belong, or from governmental regulation. Arbitration eliminates the need to take a dispute to court. A special case of arbitration is the situation where a manager makes the decision on an issue on which members of the staff cannot agree.

2 Insights F Continued

Conclusion

Ensuring that all staff members understand how to be managers of conflict, and creating a climate in which they want to apply this skill, will help ensure that most conflicts will have a happy ending. Conflict management skills also lead to preventing future conflicts by bringing consideration of issues that might carry the seeds of new conflicts in the wake of the resolved ones, such as:

- The long-range impact of the solution. Bitter experiences have shown, time and again, that short-term gain may lead to long-term loss, and vice versa.

- The effect of the settlement on preventing future conflict.

- The outcome's likely impact on individuals and groups who are not parties to the dispute.

2   Additional Insights G1

Learning Theories and Management of Learning

And then the whining schoolboy, with his satchel
And shining morning face,
Creeping like snail unwillingly to school.

As You Like It, Act II, William Shakespeare

The topic of this Additional Insights is so closely related to that of the next one (G2, Coaching and On-the-Job Instruction) that both share the G designation.

After the introduction, the following topics will be discussed in this section:

- Relevant theories of learning
- Conclusions from theories
- Management of Learning

Introduction

Why a section on these topics in a book on management and leadership? The answer is both obvious and rarely considered—managers and leaders are also managers of learning if they want to ensure that their organizations will always have the necessary competencies. Even more so if their organizations are to be learning organizations (Senge 1990), considered to be the new imperative of success.

To assess an organization's competence and to develop the plans for overcoming any shortcomings, a basic awareness of relevant theories can be useful, and an understanding of management of learning is essential.

2 Insights G1 Continued

Relevant Theories of Learning

Theories based on research on human learning have, understandably, concentrated on determining the validity of various hypotheses which attempted to identify what constitutes learning. To a large extent it has been assumed that, once this knowledge is available, instructional strategies could be developed that would bring the most effective learning. Most of this work was, at first, conducted with animals and children.

Implications of theories, for the design of learning programs, especially for adults, were addressed only tangentially, concentrating mostly on relatively simple concepts appropriate for the grade-school level. Research into learning of highly complex skills, as are needed for professional topics, have been left to the professional societies themselves. Members of the Management Education and Development Division of the Academy of Management have done the most extensive work in this area, much of it concentrating on environmental factors and on transfer of learning.

The critical issue in management of learning, one that does not seem to receive adequate priority in staff development programs, is the arrangement of information so that it will have most meaning to learners. This is especially true in the critical nontechnical competencies, where there may be the greatest need. These include management and leadership development, interpersonal skills enhancement, conflict resolution, and client and customer relations programs. Technical competence enhancement, by contrast, usually is based on reasonably sound arrangement of information.

Several issues support the position that topic arrangement is of great importance and that guidelines can provide structure for such an organization of information:

> At an early date, Bloom (1956, 35) expressed it most clearly: "Our general understanding of learning theory would seem to indicate that knowledge which is organized and related is better learned and retained than knowledge which is specific and isolated. By this we mean that learning a large number of isolated specifics is

Insights G1 Continued

quite difficult simply because of the multiplicity of items to be remembered. Further, they cannot be retained very well if they are kept in such isolation." Guidelines and the structure to support each one clearly provide such organization of knowledge.

The stimulus-response concept (Skinner 1968) suggests that sound foundation can encourage additional learning and discovery of new concepts. For example, the need to prepare a plan, or to make an important decision, can act as a stimulus to the recall of guidelines (the response), especially the basic, easy-to-remember ones. Gradually, they, in turn, act as stimuli for the more detailed, more complex responses (the recall of relevant, more detailed guidelines and the concepts supporting them).

Among the cognitive theorists, Bruner (1966) suggests a spiral curriculum which presents the simplest concepts at earlier stages and revisits them at progressively more advanced conceptual levels. This concept is used for expanding knowledge of the issues behind each one of the basic 3Cs guidelines.

Early research by the integrative theorist Gagne (1968) confirmed the benefits of presenting material with simple concepts first. Later, Gagne (1977) spoke of the need of prerequisites, organized in learning hierarchies.

Bass and Vaughan (1966, 31) expressed it this way: "To sum up, the ease of learning will depend upon how well the material lends itself to perceptual organization so that it can be connected with previously learned responses."

A simple tongue-in-cheek sequence provides an even more dramatic summary. It concerns the predicament which even the most competent instructors face:

- They will know *only a portion* of the *complete,* currently available knowledge about a specific subject.

- Faced with limited time available for training, they decide to present that portion of their own knowledge which they consider to be most important

- As a result of delays, communications gaps, and learner attention problems, *what reaches individual learners is far less,* and different for each one, than that to which they were exposed.

- What each learner *remembers* after a period of a few weeks, months, or even later is still less, just a small fraction of the instructor's message—and not necessarily the most important points.

Does this mean that development is a hopeless task? Not really. It does dramatize, however, what most trainers know, yet fail to give adequate weight in their training plans and schedules: that it is far more important *how* and *what* of the subject is presented, than how *much* is covered.

Conclusions from Theories

With respect to adult competence development, Malcolm Knowles (Knowles 1968, 1990) has suggested five principles. All, in one way or another, point to the creation of a motivational climate. That, in effect, becomes an umbrella principle for the other five.

If it had to be summed up in one sentence or so, adult learning is a matter of motivating the learners to accept responsibility for the outcome of the learning—the broader knowledge or the enhanced skill. More so than with students in school where the instructor often has considerable authority, directing adult learners to learn is nearly impossible, however. Motivation is not a button which can be pushed or a handle which can be turned. A climate has to be created in which the learner can find the desire to achieve greater knowledge or higher levels of skill. Creating such a climate requires that trainers understand the nature of the adult learner—the characteristics that distinguish them from other

2 Insights G1 Continued

learners. Knowledge of these characteristics can help managers of learning select and/or design training/learning experiences that are meaningful to learners and thereby stimulate them to seek more learning.

There are five major characteristics that reflect the nature of the adult learner:

1. They are motivated by previous experience and knowledge.

2. Their orientation is life-centered; learning must be perceived as relevant.

3. They want learning to be self-directed.

4. They are likely to be more skeptical and apprehensive than students in school.

5. Differences between individuals increase with age.

Adults are motivated by previous experience and knowledge

Adults are motivated to learn by their previously experienced needs and by interests that learning will satisfy. They want the manager of learning to be aware of previous knowledge they possess and to adjust the program accordingly.

Orientation is life-centered; learning must be perceived as relevant

The adult's orientation to learning is life-centered. Therefore, the focus for organizing adult learning should be on life situations, not subject. When working with adults, it is of great importance, however, to ensure that learners see a principle or theory as relevant to their needs and/or work. As much as possible, opportunities for learners to quickly apply new knowledge, and new skills, to the job should therefore be provided whenever possible.

Adults want learning to be self-directed

Adults have a deep need to be self-directing. They want to know why they should learn a specific subject and they want to be consulted about how much they should learn about it. Therefore, competence development should be a process of mutual decision making.

Adults are more skeptical and apprehensive

Adult learners are skeptical. They need to know that the new learning is correct in a conceptual sense, and that the new information is adequate to cope with the situations to which it applies.

Adult learners are also apprehensive about learning and about their ability to learn because they are no longer in the routine of learning and because they often have more at stake if they should fail to learn adequately and quickly.

Differences between individuals increase with age

Competence development, as well as education, must make optimal provision for differences in thinking patterns, speed, and ability to grasp complex concepts and the amount of material a learner can handle at one time. When a learner feels that the material is too simple, he or she may lose interest. If not enough material is provided, the learner may procrastinate or not consider it important enough to devote the necessary effort. If the material is too much or too difficult, then the learner is likely to give up trying to master it.

There are also principles which apply to adult learners as well as to other learners. They include:

Encouragement and support are important

Providing encouragement and support is very important for overcoming apprehension and for stimulating motivation when managing learning. This is at least as true of adults as it is true for learners in general.

Reinforcement aids retention

Very little that is learned only once is retained and used; all important points have to be reinforced, sometimes repeatedly.

2   Insights G1 Continued

There is a close relationship between reinforcement and encouragement. Competence sharpening and even acquisition of knowledge are reinforced when encouragement follows immediately after correct or appropriate application.

Recognition, such as praise, approval, other encouragement, and attention, is usually effective in stimulating learners to continue. Large rewards are not more effective than small ones; regular, periodic, rather than continuous reinforcement is considered to be the most efficient way to provide reinforcement.

For the same reasons it is also very important to reward only appropriate behavior and to avoid confusing the learner by giving recognition for inappropriate action.

Careful organization of material helps to bring understanding; a conceptual framework can be helpful

Organization of the material to be presented, so that it flows logically from simple thoughts to more complex ones, aids understanding and retention. Simple or foundation concepts should be presented first. Reminder devices like a conceptual framework should be used whenever possible.

A conceptual framework is basically a picture or format of certain related things or ideas that help a learner remember information, a concept, or a set of related concepts. A conceptual framework could be provided by an acronym, a refresher booklet, a picture, pictures, diagrams, a simple table, or a list of steps.

Prompt feedback is essential to learning and retention

Feedback is a two-way street. While the manager of learning needs feedback from learners, to know how they are progressing, learners need feedback even more. Feedback must refer to specific behaviors so the learners can make decisions about additional study or practice that may be needed.

Management of Learning

Management of learning strives to shift the responsibility for acquiring competence to the learners. Curiosity and motivation to learn are stimulated by presenting only that portion of the material which learners can readily absorb, and presenting it in an interesting, stimulating format so learners will reach out for more information and greater competence.

Basically the concept is simple. As with the management/ leadership guidelines, there's nothing new—just a number of questions that go to the heart of the challenge:

- What does the learner need to learn?

- What goals will achieve the most improvement in competence?

- What learning experiences will be most effective in reaching the goals?

- When and how should the experiences be delivered?

- How can progress best be measured and ensured?

1. What does the learner need to learn? An organization that firmly stands behind a policy of competence development can benefit from encouraging the use of knowledge/skill profiles for identifying competence strengths and deficiencies. A knowledge/skill profile is a list of topics that defines the knowledge and skills—the competencies—required by a position, or by a major segment/function of a position. Each line on the profile represents either

- A limited amount of knowledge that can be learned from a short presentation or discussion, by studying a small book or manual, several chapters, or several articles; or

- A skill that can be enhanced with a limited amount of practice.

Most lines are likely to represent both, some knowledge and a skill. To be most useful, they are developed jointly by the person

2 Insights G1 Continued

charged with assisting the learner (the manager or a coach) and the learner. Learners know better what they know and can do, and the manager or coach knows more about the competencies that have to be acquired.

Beyond serving as a tool that can provide step-by-step guidance in analyzing strengths and weaknesses, a knowledge/skill profile can serve as a foundation for setting goals and priorities, and also for recommending learning assignments.

2. What goals will achieve the most improvement in competence? Little needs to be said about learning goals. They are no different than other goals and all the relevant points from Additional Insights E, Making a Goals Program (or Management by Objectives) Work, apply.

3. What learning experiences will be most effective in reaching the goals? An organization attempting to enhance competence has available a wide range of information and competence delivery systems, to be used singly or in combination, as the situation requires. With modern technology, more such choices exist than ever before. These delivery systems include (many are available with and without multimedia support):

1. Traditional classes
   - Lectures
   - Case studies
   - Simulations
   - Role-plays
   - Field assignments between classes
2. Traditional self-study with appropriate materials
3. Learning-topic discussion and hypothetical or real decision-making sessions at meetings, with reflection or other evaluations of learning

2 Insights G1 Continued

4. Distance instruction (learning) on electronic networks or with individual PC programs

- Lectures

- Case studies

- Simulations

- Supervised individual work-projects

5. *Action Learning* techniques where learning is drawn from work projects

6. Developmental work assignments

7. Supervised cooperative team work-projects

8. Coaching

- Traditional on-the-job instruction

An extensive literature exists for all these methods. Space here does not permit discussion of any, except the last two, which are critical to manager/leader responsibilities at all organizational levels in pursuit of satisfaction of the competence guideline (see Additional Insight G2)

4. When and how should the experiences be delivered? Many factors influence the when and how and not all are related to learning effectiveness. Availability of facilities, learners, instructors or facilitators, all can be major determinants of timing, and even greatly affect the types of experiences that are scheduled.

There are, of course, also principles that apply. Among these are:

1. Characteristics and needs of learners, such as those listed above need to be taken into consideration

2. Sequence of topics to satisfy the theories of learning also referred to above, is, of course, of great importance

2   Insights G1 Continued

3. The delivery of learning experiences is also affected by the need to follow the four steps of a satisfying learning experience (Rausch 1978):

   - Exposure to new knowledge (acquisition)

   - Demonstration (to show how the new knowledge can be applied)

   - Personal application (gaining skill in applying new knowledge), and

   - Feedback/correction (to achieve greater retention and sharpen skills)

4. Spacing of learning and practice—it is better to allow some time between several exposures and practice, than to schedule long sessions of acquisition and practice since there is a need for new competencies to sink in and be absorbed, before they will be retained effectively.

5. How can progress best be measured and ensured? This is a very complex issue with many factors influencing effectiveness of measurement and learning achievement.

Many different techniques can, and are, used to measure learning, including tests, self-evaluation by the learner, observation during simulated and on-the-job application, and task performance. A good discussion of evaluation of learning can be found in Kirkpatrick (1994) *Evaluating Training Programs: The Four Levels* and in the educational psychology and evaluation literature.

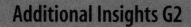

2 Additional Insights G2

Coaching and On-the-Job Instruction

Introduction

Many managers do not appreciate the importance of coaching to meet their total respective responsibilities. Yet, without effective coaching, staff members, and especially staff members in management/leadership positions, will not necessarily move aggressively toward enhancing their competencies.

At lower managerial levels, coaching responsibilities may even include direct on-the-job instruction.

Coaching and on-the-job instruction, in effect, apply the management of learning questions very specifically to one person.

The differences between coaching and on-the-job instruction are more a matter of degree than of substance. Theoretically, both include the same steps as those listed for management of learning above.

Coaching, On-the-Job Instruction, and Authority

In most of their work, managers have authority that can represent the potential of negative implications to a staff member. When coaching, a manager/leader must, therefore, do something to blunt the implied risk or threat, and make it very clear to the staff member that they are acting in a different role, a helping role.

To establish the open communications climate and the mutual trust that is important for fully effective coaching, staff members must feel secure that the coach's sole purpose is to help them gain the specific competence that is the objective of the coaching.

In short, no matter how compassionate managers are, and no matter how much trust they have established, it is likely that they are always seen as someone who provides many carrots but also carries a stick. Even if used only on the rarest of occasions, the

2   Insights G2 Continued

stick is always there. If at no other time it shows itself at performance appraisals, even when they are favorable.

There is nothing wrong with managers/leaders being authority figures. Most of the time it is good that staff members are aware of it. This is particularly true during counseling and even during performance evaluation.

On the other hand, for coaching purposes, the very existence of the authority can be damaging to the coach's capacity to help. For that reason, everything possible must be done to convince the staff member that it is safe to share knowledge of a competence weakness so that it can be addressed openly, and directly, without concerns or wasted effort.

Even though there are great similarities in the skills which managers must apply when coaching and when counseling staff members, there are significant differences in the purposes of these two functions and the managerial actions which are appropriate for them. These two managerial responsibilities are therefore covered in separate Additional Insights sections, together with related topics. Briefly, however, as far as your coaching function is concerned, counseling comes in only if coaching has run into obstacles related to resistance to learning.

First and foremost, the coach is a helper; he or she helps the person being coached to acquire knowledge and skills. Secondly, the coach is a manager of learning, and sometimes an instructor who provides on-the-job training (OJT). The coach is also a guide who suggests direction and advice for reaching learning goals which are defined primarily by the learner. In providing this guidance the coach performs all the management of learning functions:

- Analyzing
- Helping to select study/practice assignments
- Helping to establish priorities and the setting of target dates in an action plan
- Communicating
- OJT

2 Insights G2 Continued

On-the-Job Training (OJT)

On-the-job training, also called one-on-one training, applies the management of learning steps in a slightly modified way. It is used primarily for repetitious, relatively technical tasks. In one-on-one training, the trainer first prepares the learner by ensuring that any apprehension he or she may feel has been calmed as much as possible. Then the trainer uses the following specific steps:

1. Explains what has to be learned or has to be done. This is done carefully, step-by-step if possible.

2. Shows how that knowledge would be applied immediately and demonstrates how that could be done, with a specific example.

3. Asks the learner to articulate what he or she will do, before doing it. (This substep should *not* be neglected.)

4. Asks the learner to do it and commends for any achievement during this step, including any improvement over the previous tries.

5. Discusses any shortcomings that need to be corrected and asks the learner to try again.

6. Whenever possible, the learner is provided an opportunity to apply the new knowledge or skill in his or her work as soon as possible.

The trainer then repeats steps 1 through 5 as often as is advisable, but avoids doing it frequently at any one time. Practice that is too extensive at any one time is not nearly as effective as if some time is allowed to pass between practice. This time helps to allow the new knowledge to become integrated into the learner's knowledge and skill base. Whenever possible, a follow-up several days or weeks later will assure that the new competence has been fully mastered.

2   Additional Insights H

Communications Theories, Techniques, and Skills

Introduction

After the introduction, the following topics will be discussed in this section:

Two theoretical concepts

1. Transactional analysis

2. The Johari window

Knowledge, skills and abilities (KSAs) for effective communications:

1. Conduct of effective meetings

2. Writing and speaking

    a. Communicating information to groups

    b. Communicating information to individuals

3. Listening

    a. Active listening

    b. Passive listening

A self-analysis questionnaire

4. Probing

    a. Probing with closed questions

    b. Probing with open questions

    c. Probing with information-seeking statements

    d. Probing with moments of silence

    e. A Word of caution about probing

    f. Practicing empathy

5. Communicating with nonverbals

6. Seeking and providing feedback

> The Most Important Obstacle to Effective
> Communications Is the Illusion
> That It Has Been Achieved
>
> *Anonymous*

This little saying clearly articulates the reason why a section devoted solely to communications concepts, techniques and skills is included in this book. Communications affect every aspect of ensuring Control, Competence, and a favorable Climate. They involve so many facets that to fully understand and appreciate thorough, open, two-way communications in all managerial and leadership activities takes many years or exceptional concentration on the subject.

Even the best communications do not necessarily bring agreement. Achieving agreement requires much more than good communications. Mutual understanding, which communications can bring, can be a necessary condition for preventing serious conflict. In a conflict, even when mutual understanding has been achieved, agreement may still be impossible if one or both of the parties to the conflict stand fast on unreasonable or irrational positions. It wouldn't matter that both parties are skilled in the techniques—good at asking questions, experienced in observing and interpreting nonverbals, and skillful listeners. The harshness of the conflict is likely to be gone.

Beyond avoiding serious conflict, sound communications can bring many benefits in more satisfying relationships and possibly even greater mutual trust.

After a brief discussion of two theoretical concepts and of policies for thorough communications, this section outlines the knowledge, skills, and abilities (KSAs) that staff members, and especially those with managerial and leadership responsibilities, should sharpen so they can better establish and maintain comprehensive, open two-way communications in their units and with other stakeholders. These include conduct of effective meetings, writing, speaking, listening, probing, and seeking and providing feedback and sensing of nonverbal communications—all tools that can help managers/leaders strengthen the 3Cs.

Two Theoretical Concepts

1. Transactional Analysis

Transactional analysis is a psychological theory that has practical applications in communications. It became a management development fad during the 1970s, with two best-selling books (Berne 1967; Harris 1976), but faded rather quickly, in part because of the excesses of the programs of the time. These explored issues far beyond communications, and placed emphasis on the psychological foundations, on games which people play (on—not with—each other), and on life scripts. With that, useful focus was lost. Still, many people have retained an understanding of the three ego states of the individual, and apply them effectively when communicating.

Briefly, *transactional analysis*, gets its name from the idea that every set of messages between two people is a *transaction*. In transactional theory, everyone can speak from three different levels—as a *parent*, as a *child*, and as an *adult*. These levels (*ego states*) exist in everyone, together, no matter what the person's actual age is.

- As *parent* we preach, moralize, and act as though we are superior. The *parent* in us is the stuffy know-it-all, the self-righteous part that has an answer for everything.

- As *child* we show emotions easily, we like to play and have fun, explore, rush into things. Our *child* is insecure, relatively weak, and unsure. Sometimes it is rebellious.

- As *adult* we are rational. We recognize our emotions but we channel them so they will not interfere with what we are

2 Insights H Continued

trying to say or do. In a communication we think of the other person's needs. We ask appropriate questions, listen carefully, obtain clarification, observe the nonverbals, seek and provide feedback; in short, we are the consummate communicator.

There is an appropriate time to let each of these three levels dominate our behavior. In serious communications, whether at home, in social interactions, or at work, the *adult* should have the upper hand, most of the time. When we are playing, we will have most fun when we give the *child* a wide leash. There are even times when the *parent* is entitled to the upper hand—when we are expected to teach or preach, or when we are commiserating with another *parent* about how terrible it is that there is so much crime or so little free time.

Communications is a series of transactions. Recognizing the other person's ego state allows us to communicate more effectively. Berne's *Games People Play—The Psychology of Human Relationships* (1967), and even more Harris's *I'm OK, You're OK—A Practical Guide to Transactional Analysis* (1976), can provide ideas on how to use TA for better communications. A didactic simulation game (Clary, Lieberman, and Rausch 1974) is even more specific on management/staff member communications.

2. The Johari Window

The Johari window diagram can be useful, even for people who are not too keen on diagrams. It shows how all the communications techniques interact to achieve fully open communications. It's title comes from the names of the two men who developed it—Joseph Luft and Harry Ingham (Luft 1970).

The Johari window was also popular during the 1970s. It was often presented as an intensely personal device for achieving self-awareness through self-disclosure and seeking feedback. That may be the reason why it first gained great popularity in management development programs, when self-analysis was a major theme and then quickly lost favor. It has, however, much broader

2   Insights H Continued

application when used to create a climate of open communications between two people or two groups. It is explained in this light in Rausch's book on the linking elements concept (1978) and in the didactic simulation exercise (Clary, Lieberman, and Rausch 1974).

The diagram is a square, resembling a window because it is separated into four squares, like the old-fashioned, double-hung windows. At the start of every conversation or discussion, these four squares are all the same size as shown in Figure 2.1.

1. The first square is the *open communications* area. Both sides to the discussion, whether it be an interview, a coaching or a counseling session, a conflict, or just an exploratory conversation have the same amount of information about the topics that are in this window, at the beginning.

2. The second square is the *blind* area, which represents the information that the person who seeks to open communications does not know about the matter under discussion.

3. The third square is the *hidden* area, which represents what the other person or persons do not know—what you have not yet disclosed, or do not want to disclose.

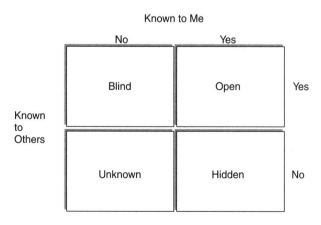

Figure 2.1 The Johari Window.

4. Finally, the fourth area, the *unknown*, represents relevant information that neither party has but that would be useful.

Your objective is to enlarge the *open communications* square as much as possible, at the expense of the other three squares. Strictly speaking, during any one discussion, the unknown area cannot be shrunk (but the desired information may be available at the next discussion), and enlargement of the open communications square has to come from the blind and hidden areas.

The point of the diagram is that open communications can best be achieved by

- Seeking information, including information about what the other person does not yet know on the matter under discussion, requesting feedback, asking questions, and listening effectively. These activities will help to enlarge the *open communications* square at the expense of the blind area (the relevant things that are not yet known to you).

- Providing information and feedback, and self-disclosure about feelings will help to enlarge the *open communications* square at the expense of the hidden area (which represents what the other person or persons do not yet know).

The Johari window applies to both parties—each side has its own. Each discussion also starts with a new diagram because often some time has passed, the parties may be more knowledgeable than they were the first time around, and each area therefore has different content.

Knowledge, Skills, and Abilities (KSA) for Effective Communications

The KSAs for effective communications, which are discussed in this Additional Insights section and which could be used for developmental sessions, are:

2 Insights H Continued

1. Conduct of effective meetings
2. Writing and speaking
3. Listening
4. Probing
5. Communicating with nonverbals
6. Seeking and providing feedback

1. Conduct of Effective Meetings

It is necessary to keep only a few minor rules in mind to avoid most of the problems with meetings, including the dissatisfaction of participants who are frustrated by a waste of their time. To hold meetings that are both productive and satisfying, these rules may help. First, though, two tongue-in-cheek thoughts:

1. Rausch's Laws of Meetings

    a. More meetings are held than are needed

    b. Most meetings take longer than necessary to bring the desired result

    c. More people are asked to attend most meetings than are needed

    d. Few meetings are adequately prepared

2. Are You Lonely? Work On Your Own? Hate Making Decisions?

    HOLD A MEETING; You Can: * SEE People * DRAW Flowcharts * FEEL Important * IMPRESS Your Colleagues * EAT Donuts

    ALL on company time

    MEETINGS . . . The Practical Alternative To Work
    Anonymous

Insights H Continued

Rules for meetings:

a. If something can be addressed without a meeting, don't call a meeting, but handle it the alternate way—by phone, via the network, with memos, and so on (participation in decisions does not require face-to-face discussion).

b. If you do call a meeting, prepare for it carefully. If complex decisions have to be made, it is usually more efficient and satisfying to participants at meetings if they do not have to start defining alternatives. It is usually preferable to present one or two alternatives and ask the meeting to revise them and choose the better one. Sometimes an entirely new alternative emerges.

c. Call only the minimum number of people to the meeting necessary for the technical and acceptance requirements (see Chapter 1, Additional Insights D, Participation in Decision-Making and Planning, and Norman Maier's technical and acceptance quality criteria for effective leadership decisions, in Chapter 3, Additional Insights I, Decision-Making Procedures and Theories).

d. It may not be necessary to postpone an urgent meeting because a critical person is unavailable, especially if it is difficult to get everyone together soon. It is often possible for you to consult with that person after the meeting, make whatever adjustments may come from such a discussion, and inform everyone affected. Occasionally it may be possible and desirable to call a follow-up meeting, but that meeting is likely to be short. In the meantime, useful steps on the challenge may have proceeded.

e. State the objective of the meeting at the beginning, and then keep the meeting focused on that outcome. Do not allow yourself to get sidetracked, and deal effectively with difficult people (Bramson 1981; Rausch and Wohlking 1969; Rausch 1971).

2 | Insights H Continued

f. Make sure that there is as clear a plan for proceeding as possible at the conclusion of the meeting. At that time, the plan should be understood by all participants, and each one who walks away with an assignment knows it and has accepted it willingly.

g. Ensure that those who are invited or expected to attend the meeting are reminded of it on the day before it is to take place.

2. *Writing and Speaking*

This obviously is not the place to discuss the arts of writing or persuasive public speaking. Being talented or skilled in either will certainly not hurt. However, these are both functional competencies and only tangentially relevant to effective management/leadership. Furthermore, since local colleges and even adult education programs provide courses in writing and possibly also in public speaking, a manager/leader can easily suggest ways for staff members to improve these competencies.

Nor is this the place for discussions of communications that are functional in nature, such as preparations of promotional materials, technical procedure manuals, communications with clients or customers, or formal oral presentations. What is important, however, is that managers/leaders are competent in the decisions on *what* to communicate, verbally and in writing, that pertains to the 3Cs.

Two types of written and verbal communications have to be considered:

- Communicating information to groups
- Communicating information to individuals

a. Communicating information to groups

When deciding what and how to communicate to groups, their needs are the foremost consideration. A manager/leader who

2 Insights H Continued

regularly thinks of the 3Cs guidelines to stimulate decisions on issues that might otherwise be ignored will have little difficulty realizing when information about new procedures and policies have to be communicated, and to whom. Equally important is the need to keep staff members informed about events that they consider useful or interesting. In reinforcing mutual trust, sharing of such information can be very helpful.

Still, few clear guidelines are possible in this area. Two opposing forces shape each individual decision. On the one hand, the more that can be communicated to the staff, and to other groups, the greater the trust and confidence of that group in the leader. On the other hand, it is almost impossible to share confidential information with a group and expect it to remain confidential. Case by case review is therefore necessary, with the bias as much as possible in favor of sharing information as early as possible.

Whether to communicate in writing or orally is primarily a matter of logistics—whichever is more convenient or more useful to the audience. For instance, for procedures and policies, writing, or both writing and verbal announcements and explanations, may be most appropriate.

b. Communicating information to individuals

When communicating with individuals, their needs go beyond the needs of the group and more skills are needed. In addition to what they want as members of the group, individuals want information on how their performance is seen, and they want signs that their efforts are noticed and appreciated. These needs are also in addition to any that arise as a consequence of conflicts, negotiations (a form of conflict), counseling, and coaching.

Though most managers/leaders are aware that written signs of appreciation are more powerful and satisfying than verbal thanks or commendations, recognition in writing is not as widely used as would be beneficial (see Scenario 2.3). In fact, few managers are highly competent in providing psychological rewards as frequently, and as effectively, as would be desirable.

2 ### Insights H Continued

3. *Listening*

The anonymous quote that introduced this section can even more aptly be paraphrased for this topic, considering the widespread complaints by staff members that "management does not listen to us":

> The most important obstacle to effective listening is the belief that it has been achieved.

Few programs are available on listening, unless the organization offers one. Staff members with managerial/leadership responsibilities need to be aware of a number of facets of the listening competence, and be given opportunities to practice, reflect, assess their strengths and weaknesses, and develop improved habits. They also need to be keenly aware that staff members have a broader view of *listening* than the act of hearing and even understanding. They include the action that results from hearing and understanding— some form of action, even if it is no more than a follow-up that explains what is being done, or why more is not being done.

a. Active listening

Everyone should be aware that listening involves not only the hearing of words but an active search for their meaning and their relationship to what is already known. It provides the basis for questions that help to clarify what has been said. It is the key to uncovering needs or to get cues that hidden objections or conflicts may exist. Listening is needed when the other person is speaking, of course. It is also necessary while speaking to pick up the other person's reaction (primarily from nonverbals).

There is also a need for clear awareness that there are two levels of effective listening: passive and active listening. *Passive listening* is paying attention to what the speaker is saying. *Active listening* includes the need for empathy and the responsibility for ensuring that, in addition to hearing the words, the speaker's full thought has been understood. That requires two-way communications and the ideas expressed by the Johari window.

b. Passive listening

Passive listening occurs when we fall victim to our own listening faults. For example, Nichols (1962) has identified 10 bad listening habits:

- Calling the subject uninteresting
- Criticizing the delivery
- Getting overstimulated
- Listening only for facts
- Outlining everything
- Faking attention
- Tolerating or creating distractions
- Evading the difficult
- Submitting to emotional words
- Wasting thought power

To break these bad habits, he suggested using the power of the mind through three mental manipulations to promote active, effective listening: (1) anticipating the speaker's next point, (2) identifying elements, and (3) making mental summaries.

How effectively do you listen? The following self-assessment questionnaire, or a commercially available program on listening, followed by coaching, may be adequate for sharpening staff member listening competencies to adequate levels.

Listening—A Self-Analysis Questionnaire

How effectively do you believe you listen?

Please answer this question with a percentage between 0% and 100%: _____ %

After you have entered the percentage, please place check marks in the appropriate columns on the following page.

2 Insights H Continued

	Always	Usually	Sometimes	Rarely
1. Do you look the speaker in the eye?				
2. Do you look for nonverbal signs with which the speaker communicates?				
3. Do you concentrate on ideas when you listen?				
4. Do you determine, while you are listening, whether you agree or disagree?				
5. Do you begin to phrase your responses while you are listening?				
6. Do you accept the responsibility for making certain that you have received a message correctly and completely?				
7. Do you listen while you are speaking?				
8. Do you try to summarize, in your mind, what the speaker has said before you shape your response?				
9. Do you concentrate on feelings when you listen?				
10. Are you affected in the way you listen by your relationship with the speaker?				

When you finish, check whether your marks are consistent with the percentage you wrote down.

4. *Probing*

Probing is another technique that can clear the way to better communications. It is not widely understood, even though it can usually bring the information we need so we can hear where the other person is coming from, or determine whether our message was understood. Probing may also be necessary so we can be sure we understood a message that came our way.

Most people are not aware that asking appropriate questions is a skill. Asking good questions, at the right moment, is not easy at all. In fact, it requires conscious awareness and practice. A wide range of professionals to whom communications is of paramount importance spend considerable effort to learn and sharpen probing skills. These include psychologists, trainers, mediators, case workers, detectives, and technical sales representatives, as well as all others whose work revolves around exchanging information. In interpersonal skill-development programs, managers asked to probe effectively usually do not display great skill.

Since programs are not readily available, the development of the probing skill will probably require setting aside some time for it in staff meetings. Concepts to cover, and practice, in such sessions include all four ways to probe: closed questions, open questions, information-seeking statements, and moments of silence. In addition, communicating with nonverbals, cautions about probing, and empathy could be included. Expectations for probing also need to be clarified—that even the most competent probing cannot get other people to talk about matters which they simply do not want to share. Nevertheless, good questions can be expected to produce far more information than inappropriate questions; sometimes they can even bring surprising, unexpected disclosures.

a. Probing with closed questions

Closed questions can be answered with a single word or brief phrases like *yes, no, 8:30, Monday, I think so,* or *that's true.* Closed questions are not very useful for obtaining information, but an occasional question such as *When was that?* or *Where was it?* are much better than grunts to show you are listening, and to show that you are trying to fully understand. Closed questions can also help you set the stage for further probing, or for the continuation of your explanation: *Do you mind if I ask another question?, Am I correct in saying that . . . ?, Alright if I continue?,* or, *Do you agree that . . . ?*

Closed questions such as *Do you like . . . ?, Do you agree that . . . ?* can be good as bridges between different thoughts. Other types of closed questions are good for obtaining confirmation. *It was three o'clock when we got there, wasn't it?* or There were about twenty of us, right?

Sometimes there are unique situations when a closed question can help obtain significant information. That happens when the question is used to gain a foothold by searching for areas to explore: *Where do you think the problem could be, with your inventory records or with your schedules?* or *Did you go to the library?*

This type of closed question begs for a very specific answer that is at the core of the information being sought. If the person answering the question can be honest and forthright, the question will be answered with a few words at most. When trying to hide something, the person answering it is on the spot.

Finally, closed questions can sometimes be better than direct statements for carrying some messages. This is especially true when you suspect that the other person may have tried to make you believe something that is not true. In this situation it may be desirable to let that person know, politely, that you are aware of the truth. *Wasn't the price you quoted $249?* That's so much less threatening or challenging than the direct statement: *The price you quoted me was $249.*

Closed questions can also be a polite way to ask someone to do something. *Should we add a few words of thanks to the letter?* is such a question.

Closed questions have a negative side, however. They can shut you out and make it difficult to continue. The trick is to avoid questions such as *Do you want to tell me . . . ?, Would you like*

2 Insights H Continued

to . . . ?, *Shall we talk about . . . ?*, or *Do you know why?*, if the other person might end the discussion by replying with a cryptic *no*. Even two of the questions mentioned, *Do you mind if I ask another question?*, and *Alright if I continue?* have to be used with care.

Questions that often lead to trouble include: *Do you understand? Was that clear?*, and even sometimes *Do you have any questions?* These are likely to bring misleading replies because the other person may be reluctant to admit lack of understanding, not being able to think of a *smart* question, or, heaven forbid, having failed to pay attention. The worst one of these questions is *Do I make myself clear?* because too often it sounds almost like a threat.

Closed questions, then, can be useful to test for receipt of a message, and for agreement or disagreement; they can obtain a specific item of factual information, or convey it, and they can sometimes be used to search for areas to explore.

If your purpose is to obtain information, closed questions must be used with care, and sparingly.

b. Probing with open questions

Open questions are much better than closed questions for obtaining information that the other person is willing to share. They draw people out, stimulating them to tell what they know and what is on their minds. In a group setting, they promote participation in the discussion. For instance, instead of asking *Do you understand?*, you could ask *How do you feel about . . . ?*

Most open questions specifically ask for an explanation. They usually start with *what, how,* or *why*. *What happened?*, *What is that all about?*, *What did you do then?*, *What are your reasons?*, *What would you do . . . ? How would you approach this situation?*, *How do you feel about . . . , Why do you think that happened?*, *Why were you there?* All these questions must be used tactfully, especially the *why* questions. *Why did you . . . ?* and *Why didn't you . . . ?* may sound more like accusations than questions. When phrased and asked properly, *why* questions can be perfectly good open questions.

Much, of course, depends on the relationship between the people involved in the discussion. If there is much mutual trust and

2 **Insights H Continued**

confidence, questions are not likely to be misinterpreted. If there is only casual contact, or if there is doubt about motives, question phrasing can be crucial.

Where questions can be either open or closed. *Where did you go?* is mainly closed, since it can be answered with *Out* or *To the doctor*. On the other hand *Where could we go?*, *Where might we hold the meeting?*, or *Where could he have gone?*, are questions that beg for information.

Another way to obtain more information is by rephrasing something that another person has said into a question. *You don't agree, then, that it would be a good statement to add?* is likely to bring an extensive response. If the other person is reluctant to speak, it might be better to rephrase into information-seeking statements.

c. Probing with information-seeking statements

Some kinds of statements effectively ask questions. Instead of *You don't agree, then, that it would be a good statement to add?*, you could say: *Please tell me why you feel that way.* The same way, *Tell me more about . . . .* is really not very different from *What is this all about?* Sentences like *Let's talk about that a little more, I believe you said that . . . , I was wondering what . . . , If you don't mind, I'd like to . . . ,* or *Then you agree that . . . .* are similar kinds of information-seeking statements.

d. Probing with moments of silence

After someone has responded to an open question you asked, you may feel that more could or should have been said. You may be tempted to ask another question. However, it is often better to hold such a follow-up question for a while. Sometimes a brief silence will bring amplification, or another thought that a premature follow-up question might have aborted.

Moments of silence should not be overdone; they should neither be too long nor too frequent. They should be natural, or they will raise doubts about your motives.

2   Insights H Continued

e. A word of caution about probing

Several questions, information-seeking statements, and moments of silence in a row can easily give the other person the feeling of being *pumped* for information or of being in an *interrogation*. Sharing information is, therefore, an essential companion to effective probing and should be provided between questions or short series of questions.

f. Practicing empathy

Communications without empathy are shallow. Especially when a delicate topic is involved, nothing is more important than empathy, *tuning in,* putting yourself into the shoes of the other person. Then your questions become more relevant and are less likely to be threatening. Empathy can also help you to sense when you are in danger of stepping across that vague line that separates prying from probing.

Empathy is not sympathy. When you are empathetic you understand the other person's situation and position. You need not agree with it or even share the feelings. Sympathy adds feelings to understanding.

Thorough communications do not need sympathy, but empathy is essential. Sympathy with the joys and sorrows of others cannot be learned, like a skill. It is a feeling. You've either got it or you don't. Sympathy does, however, grow with age and life experience.

It's different with empathy. All you have to do is ask yourself, *What is the other person thinking?* If you listen carefully, you will either confirm what you thought or you will learn more about the needs, concerns, and feelings of the other person. Doing this often will help you acquire higher and higher levels of empathy.

5. Communicating with Nonverbals

Much has been written about interpretation of nonverbal (nonvocal) signs—about the voluntary and involuntary messages carried by them and about what they can reveal. Listeners send messages

2 Insights H Continued

via these nonverbals, and senders reinforce or contradict their words with them. Nonverbals include

- eye contact and expression
- other eye movements
- head movements
- facial expression like smile, smirk, seriousness, sternness, pensiveness
- gestures and other body movements, including those of the fingers, hands, limbs, and shoulder
- poise and posture
- voice strength and emphasis
- other overtones like questioning, relaxed, sarcastic, sharp, harsh, happy, cynical, laughing, smooth
- hesitant speech, careful choice of words, long (possibly pregnant) pauses

If we could only read these as well as we can read spoken and written words—imperfect though that would be—it still would be much better than what we can do now.

Feelings and lack of interest when not expressed in words, can be detected by observing nonverbals. Some are easy to recognize in most people; anger, joy, apprehension, lack of interest, or sadness, especially when strong, reveal themselves readily.

There are experts, such as Julius Fast (1970), who write as though they can interpret nonverbal messages quite accurately. They may read eye movements or other facial expressions, leg positions, or specific body movements like looking away, finger tapping, arms crossing, and leaning forward. Because there probably is a fair amount of similarity in the way people reveal their emotions, these experts can offer some useful insights.

A healthy dose of skepticism about the interpretation of most nonverbals is always advisable. While the similarities between people may be greater than the differences, nonverbals are not reliable indicators, unless or until confirmed through adroit probing.

6. Seeking and Providing Feedback

With feedback you give your reaction to a message, or obtain reaction to what you have said. Verbal feedback usually comes in the form of questions or statements in response to a message. Nonverbal feedback can be especially valuable because it is usually spontaneous, sometimes involuntarily. Often the person sending the nonverbal message is not even aware of it.

Feedback can confuse, be misunderstood, intimidate, or hurt the person to whom it is directed. All that can happen even when feedback was solicited.

While most nonverbal feedback comes naturally, seeking and giving verbal feedback requires skill.

When *seeking* feedback you have to be willing to accept it without becoming defensive. You also have to keep in mind that the other person may not be fully candid out of concern that the feedback may have a negative impact on you.

When *giving* feedback, obviously you should not interrupt at the wrong time, be too abrupt, too blunt, unclear, or untimely.

A few useful rules for providing feedback are:

- Feedback to statements should be factual, based on what the sender has said, and not on how the *receiver* interpreted it. Interpretations and other assumptions should be clarified with probing questions, before being used in feedback.

- Feedback should be given calmly. When given in an excited manner it can be perceived as disagreement or criticism.

- Feedback should be as timely as possible. It should refer to something the speaker has just said, not to something that was said several minutes ago.

Insights H Continued

• Feedback should concern only things that are currently under the control of the speaker. Telling someone that he or she does not know enough, or can't comprehend, will not bring better two-way communications.

Useful ideas for feedback and empathy can be found in Tannen *You Just Don't Understand* (1990) and Gray *Men are from Mars, Women are from Venus* (1992), both of which make for enjoyable reading.

The 3Cs Guidelines at the Comprehensive Level

Introduction

This chapter begins with the three comprehensive 3Cs guideline questions. Because there is now considerable detail behind each one, this chapter may have more long-term use as a reference, when important decisions have to be made, or plans have to be prepared.

Like Chapter 2, this chapter illustrates its version of the guidelines with three scenario examples. The examples will be examined more rigorously, because the extensive structure of the comprehensive guidelines lists all the issues covered by the 3Cs model. At the same time, however, there will be less depth, especially where there has been detailed discussion previously. References are provided to the Additional Insights.

Comprehensive Guideline Questions

1. Comprehensive Control Guideline Question

What else needs to be done to ensure effective Control and coordination, so that the decision which we are considering will lead toward the outcome we seek, and so we'll know when we have to modify our implementation, or plan, because we are not getting the results we want? More specifically:

a. When setting a goal, what else can be done to ensure that:

- strategies and timelines for achieving and communicating it are considered, as well as

- the importance/urgency status of the goal,

- the distinction between goals and action steps,

- the workload on teams and individuals,

- the achievability and challenging aspects of the goal,

- progress reviews, and

- the respective responsibilities of managers and staff members? (See Chapter 2, Additional Insights E, Making a Goals Program Work.)

b. What else can be done so that participation in decision making and planning, including goal setting, will bring the highest level of success in all aspects, including:

- whom to involve,

- for what purpose,

- with how much authority,

- at what time, and

- considering all relevant situational factors? (See Chapter 1, Additional Insights D, Participation in Decision Making and Planning.)

c. What else can be done to improve the thoroughness, openness, and honesty of the communications, and communications systems, between the organization's units, within units, and with other stakeholders? (See Chapter 2, Additional Insights H, Communications Theories, Techniques, and Skills.)

d. When ensuring coordination and cooperation, what else can be done so that:

- procedures are appropriate and effectively communicated to all stakeholders,

- so there is early identification of coordination or cooperation problems, and

- so that all potentially damaging conflicts are either prevented or effectively resolved?

e. When ensuring positive discipline, what else can be done so that appropriate norms, including norms pertaining to morality and diversity, are established and maintained, and so that every staff member, at all levels of the organization, respects and follows them?

f. What else can be done to ensure that overall performance, and individual staff member performance, are reviewed continually so that potential challenges and problems are identified, and so that evaluations are as factual, fair, and meaningful as possible?

g. With respect to counseling, what else should be done to ensure that all staff members with managerial/leadership responsibilities competently counsel for performance problems and other problems which do, or may, affect performance? (See Chapter 3, Additional Insights J, Interviewing.)

2. Comprehensive Competence Guideline Question

What else needs to be done so that all those who will be involved in implementing the decision, and those who will otherwise be affected, have the necessary competencies to ensure effective progress and satisfying use of the product or service? More specifically:

a. What else can be done in recruiting and selection so the processes are efficient and effective in filling vacant positions with highly qualified, flexible candidates whose norms are reasonably in line with those of the organization?

b. What else can be done to help staff members, including those in managerial positions, accept greater responsibility for their own competence development, and provide all necessary and desirable support and development opportunities to members of their staffs?

c. What else can be done to identify competence strengths and weaknesses accurately, to take advantage of the strengths, when delegating and assigning projects and in career advancements, and to apply management of learning concepts, including coaching, effectively, where weaknesses exist? (See Chapter 2, Additional Insights G1, Learning Theories and Management of Learning, and G2, Coaching and On-the-Job Instruction.)

d. With respect to communications, what else can be done to ensure that all staff members are skilled in meeting conduct and are effective:

- as listeners (with ears *and* eyes);

- in probing and asking of questions;

- in providing useful feedback during conversations, discussions, and meetings;

- in written communications; and

- in providing information? (See Chapter 2, Additional Insights H, Communications Theories, Techniques, and Skills.)

e. With respect to counseling, what else should be done to ensure that all staff members with managerial/leadership responsibilities competently counsel for all four purposes: performance problems, self development and learning issues, career development, and personal problems?

3. Comprehensive Climate Guideline Question

What else needs to be done so that the reaction of the various groups and individuals who have to implement the decision or plan, and those who will be affected by it, will be in favor of it or at least have as positive a view as possible so there will be a favorable Climate? More specifically:

a. What else needs to be done to ensure that all staff members with managerial/leadership responsibilities are alert to opportunities for providing positive feedback and other psychological rewards to all deserving staff members (even those who rarely do something outstanding), and that they use the many possible ways for taking advantage of such opportunities?

b. What else needs to be done to ensure that all staff members with managerial/leadership responsibilities provide appropriate and fair work assignments, and delegate effectively?

c. What else needs to be done to ensure that all staff members feel little work-related stress, feel as secure as possible, and have trust and confidence in the organization and its managers?

d. What else can be done to ensure that the organization offers appropriate tangible rewards, and that all staff members with managerial/leadership responsibilities provide deserved tangible rewards effectively to stimulate the strongest possible motivational climate (for those who receive the tangible rewards, and those who do not receive any at the moment)?

e. What else can be done so the users of products or services will be fully satisfied?

Please keep in mind that the specific issues added to the guidelines discussed here, though they add depth, will not greatly enhance the benefits that you will derive from regular use *of a system of management/ leadership decision guidelines, even if you use only basic ones. What the more comprehensive list of issues can do is to trigger ideas that may not come to mind when you think of the respective basic or* more detailed *guideline. They can also help you develop a thought process that automatically expands each guideline into the kinds of issues that you may want to consider. However, and this is the key point, the detailed questions suggested here, like those in Chapter 2, can be used as presented here, but can also serve to stimulate ideas for development of a system of guidelines with which you may be more comfortable, or which may better fit your style.*

THE SCENARIOS

SCENARIO 3.1

Mary's New Position: A Challenge of Coordination and Cooperation

Focus: The control guideline, emphasis on coordination and cooperation

Abstract: Mary is the new Director of Operations for a large, fairly modern printer with about 150 employees. Mary's challenge, to forge a cohesive, high-quality and highly productive team, would not be a simple one. As a first step she wants to develop an open communications climate, leading to mutual trust and effective prevention and resolution of potentially damaging conflict.

❖ ❖ ❖ ❖ ❖ ❖

The Scenario

Mary's predecessor had been dismissed suddenly, after about six months as Director of Operations. Not only had he been regarded as a poor manager/leader, but during his last week he had overruled the quality assurance manager on an expediency issue. It was an unwise decision which resulted in immediate problems with an important customer.

As part of the interviewing process, Mary had met with the Directors of Personnel, Marketing and Sales, and Finance, who apparently had input into the selection.

---

*This story is adapted from one published in *TQM Magazine* V8/5, Sept./Oct. 1996, pp. 69–70, MCB University Press.

Then, when the choice had narrowed on her and one other candidate, the personnel director called a meeting of the six department managers who report to the Director of Operations and introduced her, so he could obtain their input, too. Some of these managers have multiple responsibilities with supervisors. Susan has prepress and typesetting, Tim is in printing and shipping, Eric has responsibility for purchasing and maintenance, Ida is in quality assurance, Laura has both customer relations and scheduling, and Mike is in information/production systems. During that meeting Mary answered questions about the resume she had submitted, and then was briefed on their work.

On Monday morning, when she reported to work, each of the directors introduced her to the members of their staffs.

Then Mary met again with her management group. She announced that she would like to hold operations review meetings, with a goal of one hour maximum, each Tuesday morning to discuss urgent issues and to bring everyone up-to-date on general progress. During the first meeting of each month she would like to allow considerably more time so they could more leisurely share information on company news, operations improvement goals, and progress on other major matters of common interest.

She asked for comments, all of which were basically positive. There was the suggestion that meetings be convened just before lunch rather than first thing in the morning, so that the start-of-the-day activities could first be taken care of. There were also questions about being late or excused from meetings and Mary offered to brief anyone who could not make a meeting afterward. She did ask, however, that they all be as punctual as possible and that absences be held to a minimum. Then she offered another opportunity for questions—none were asked. Before closing the meeting she explained that she planned to meet with them individually that afternoon and all day Tuesday.

With each one she toured the respective department, met supervisors, shook hands with all members of the staff, and became more specifically acquainted with equipment and procedures.

In the process she concluded that the managers were all competent professionals. With one exception, they said that they looked forward to someone taking on the job of operations director, after more than three months of reporting to the President who had little time for them.

The one person who did not seem to welcome Mary was Mike, who frankly admitted that he was disappointed. He had hoped to be selected for the operations manager position himself, because of the critical importance of his department, not only for management information, but also to production systems.

During the following two weeks, in conversations with individual managers, Mary came to sense that, under the surface of a smooth working team, there were stresses caused by conflicting needs of department performance. For instance, Susan from prepress and typesetting, and Tim from printing, both felt that Ida, who was responsible for quality assurance, had a tendency to be a purist and would not adequately consider overall business interests when she insisted on extensive rework. At the same time, when part of a print-run was rejected, there was a tendency for prepress and printing to blame the other. When there was an equipment breakdown, maintenance rarely fixed it fast enough to satisfy the affected department. When an order did not go out as planned, there might be recriminations between scheduling, shipping, and printing, and when a shipment of supplies was late, there sometimes was finger-pointing between purchasing and printing.

Mary realized that forging a truly cohesive, high-quality, and highly productive team would not be a simple challenge. As she saw it, her first step would have to be to develop an open communications climate, leading to mutual trust and effective prevention and resolution of potentially damaging conflict. If, at the same time, she could ensure solid decision-making competence, she might be able to tap the potential of the team and move the operations department to higher levels of performance.

From her previous position, where she reported to an exceptionally competent manager, she had gained a keen appreciation of the need to move very cautiously on cooperation, and even on coordination issues. He had advised her to always first assess the potential conflicts that may be just under the surface.

Mary also understood that coordination depends on sound procedures, which could be sharpened and made more useful with time. Cooperation, on the other hand, she realized, was much more a matter of norms and people's perceptions, views, and actions.

As a rule she liked to plan carefully for meetings. Still, for the first extended one, she decided to play it by ear. The issues of coordination and cooperation were going to be her first priority, right after the operations review portion of the meeting.

"Well, that does if for operations review, it seems. Anything else to talk about?"

There were no responses. Everyone looked at her, expectantly, to see how she was going to handle the remainder of this, and the other first-Tuesday-of-the-month meetings.

Mary smiled: "Looks like you're all wondering what I hope to use this time for. I really don't know myself, yet. I just know that, if we are going to forge an even better team than you had before I arrived, we need some quality time together. We need to learn how we can best become a close team and how we should plan to make things better for the company and for us. Now, it seems to me that there are a number of topics we could talk about today. But, first I think I would like to see whether anyone has any suggestions."

There was a brief silence and then Ida from quality assurance spoke up: "As everybody here knows and agrees, quality is so important today. Still, often I feel like my department has to carry all the burden. When one of my inspectors, or I, see something we believe is a problem, and that happens only when it's a close call, because the more obvious things are corrected right away, we have to make the tough decisions. And then we are usually at odds with the respective departments. As I told you, Mary, we are responsible not only for the product that goes out, but also for the quality of incoming materials, monitoring customer relations and scheduling, ensuring that printing receives quality work from prepress, and so on. These decisions should be more structured, or more of a joint responsibility, but I often feel as though I have to make the decision, which is tough enough, and then fight with people about it. Can we do something . . . ?"

"I think I know what can be done. You and your people should get a better feel of what it's like to be in our shoes." Tim interrupted her. "We are constantly under pressure to meet schedules, and to bring lower costs. When you make us rerun part of a job, especially after it's already off the press, it hurts us. The schedules get fouled up and so do our costs."

It looked as though others wanted to say something, but then thought better of it. Instead, all eyes were on Mary. She waited a moment and, when no one spoke up, she asked: "Any ideas on what we could do to make sure we maintain at least as high a quality level as our competition, without hurting ourselves unnecessarily?"

"We've gone round and round on this thing, like forever." Eric, the purchasing manager, responded. "At one time I suggested that we set up a little committee that would resolve the issue, whenever there was a difference of opinion with Ida. But while it wasn't shot down, it never got off the ground, either."

"Does anyone know what happened to Eric's suggestion? How do you feel about it, anyhow?" Even though she was surprised at the sharpness of Tim's response to Ida, Mary liked the way the discussion had started. This was not only about quality standards, a tough issue, admittedly. More important, though, she could see how it would allow her to get right to the core of coordination and cooperation.

"I don't blame Ida for wanting others to share responsibility in case a decision backfires and the customer complains, but that's not going to do it." Tim did not think a committee would make things better for him. "What we need, I think, are clear standards that everyone can understand. Then the decision in a specific instance is easy. That's how I see it."

"Tim, maybe we should give the committee idea a try." Laura, as Mary had noticed before, likes to satisfy all sides. "We haven't got much to lose. Maybe the committee could be asked to see whether it can set a standard, whenever it is asked to make a decision. That would gradually build a book or a history of standards, if they are possible—I personally think they need to be somewhat flexible to adapt to the type and need of the customer. Still, we may make it easier, and fairer for Ida, and at the same time, ensure that production needs are satisfied as much as possible."

"OK, for the sake of getting this thing off center, I'll agree. Who should be on the committee? It's probably best if Mary appoints two or three of us." Tim wanted to be on the constructive side of the issue.

"I can, if you all want me to," Mary responded, "but that's not the way I think we should work. Don't get me wrong, when a decision which affects all of us has to be made, and that you find it difficult to make as a group, or when there is high risk, I don't mind making it. But when you can agree on a course of action, I prefer that—that is, of course, if you have the information for making such a decision. With respect to the committee composition, I think there should be two or three members, preferably volunteers. If we have to appoint them, I'd appreciate nominations and then I'll select. OK, any volunteers?

Laura raised her hand. "Not that I like the assignment. But I have more contact with customers than anyone else, so I think that I have the obligation to provide input from that perspective."

"Thanks Laura. Anyone else?" Mary looked around and then straight at Ida, who spoke up a little hesitantly. "Well I guess I might as well be on the committee since they would call me anyhow, to present the quality assurance side of the picture."

"Sounds good, thanks, Ida. Looks like we need one more, preferably someone who is rarely involved in a quality problem." Mary looked around again, this time primarily at Eric and Mike.

Eric spoke up first. "I think Mike is our best choice and I nominate him. He is level-headed, in touch with the entire situation from a broad perspective, and rarely directly involved in a quality problem."

Mike answered, with a light smile, looking at Eric: "Thanks Eric, I'll do the same for you sometime." Then: "Seriously, I think Eric is right, though I hate to have to agree with him. Yes, I'll accept the third spot."

"That was great. Thanks, Eric." Mary gladly expressed her enthusiasm. "You gave a beautiful example of good coordination and cooperation. More coordination will come from the record of decisions of the committee. It will be called on only if either or both parties to a quality issue want it to make the decision. I would like to request that whenever a pass-or-reject decision was difficult, and the committee was not asked to get involved, that you remember to tell Mike about it." Looking at Mike. "Are you willing to set up a database for the standards—is that OK?" Mike nodded agreement.

"That'll give us the procedures that should make for smooth coordination on an issue. If anyone sees another area where you think that there is need for better or clearer procedures, please let me know—I'll put it on the agenda for the next extended meeting. After all, nothing will help us more with coordination than useful procedures—not big books of procedures, but only those that we really need."

"Is there anything else that someone wants to bring up?"

It was close to lunch time and heads shook slightly.

"OK then, before we close I want to congratulate you on the way you handled this little conflict. You know, I'm sure that conflict, of one sort or another, is the most important, if not the only obstacle to good cooperation. If we'll always nick it in the bud, the way you did with this one, I can only say that I'll be most grateful."

"If there's nothing else, I think we can go to lunch. Let's go out together, if you want, and the company will pick up the tab—this time."

Before reading the analysis below, and those for the other scenarios, always take a few minutes to jot down your own comments based on your approaches to similar challenges in the past, or based on your interpretation of the comprehensive control guideline question. That way you will gain most from the points in the analysis, the conclusions, and in the conceptual summary at the end of the chapter.

❖ ❖ ❖ ❖ ❖ ❖

Analysis: Mary's New Position:
A Challenge of Coordination and Cooperation

As with the other scenarios, there are many perspectives from which to comment on Mary's situation. All, in one way or another, relate to the 3Cs guideline questions which pertain to Control, Competence, and Climate.

1. Control

Emphasis in this review of the first scenario of the chapter is on the comprehensive Control guideline question. The basic guideline is restated, below, followed by the specific issues, each with their analyses, one by one.

> What else needs to be done to ensure effective Control and coordination, so that the decision which we are considering will lead toward the outcome we seek, and so we'll know when we have to modify our implementation, or plan, because we are not getting the results we want? More specifically:

a. When setting a goal, what else can be done to ensure that strategies and timelines for achieving and communicating it are considered, as well as the importance/urgency status of the goal, the distinction between goals and action steps, the workload on teams and individuals, the achievability and challenging aspects of the goal, progress reviews, and the respective responsibilities of managers and staff members?

No goals were specifically discussed, except Mary's tacit goals to establish procedures for coordination and set the foundation for norms that would ensure cooperation and early identification, and competent resolution, of potentially damaging conflicts (see Chapter 2, Additional Insights E, Making a Goals Program Work).

Still, if Mary had been aware of this aspect of the guideline, she might have asked herself whether explicit goals should be set. If she did, she would have quickly reviewed, in her mind, the subissues of the question:

- What strategies would best help to ensure achievement of the goal? (Mary could have discussed these with the team, or just noted them for herself.)

- Whether the goals are indeed important, but not urgent, so that milestones could be set which would ensure that the goal does not fade in the sea of urgent matters to be done

- Whether a specific goal could be assigned as a task, if it were fully under the control of the person assuming responsibility for its achievement

- Whether it is appropriate to set a formal goal, in light of other goals in existence, and the workload being added by the goal

- How the goal should be stated so that it would be both achievable and challenging

- How, to whom, and when it should be communicated

- What responsibilities and accountability she would have to retain if one of her staff members were to assume responsibility for leading toward achievement of the goal, what she should communicate on this issue, and what role the staff member should have in the decisions

b. What else can be done so that participation in decision making and planning, including goal setting, will bring the highest level of success in all aspects, including whom to involve, for what purpose, with how much authority, at what time, and considering all relevant situational factors?

Even though Mary involved all managers in her discussion, she still might have asked herself either question b. or one or more questions such as those following in conjunction with any thoughts she might have on these issues, if she were aware of this specific aspect of the Control guideline and had used it. For each of these questions it would be useful for her to consider the aspects of participation alluded to by the guideline segment above, and explained in Chapter 1, Additional Insights D, Participation in Decision Making and Planning.

- When and how should the supervisors (those who report to the department managers) become involved in the issues discussed at the meeting?

- Should supervisors be considered for one or more spots on the committee, in addition to or instead of the managers assigned at the meeting?

- To what extent should department employees be involved in the issues, and what, when, how, and how much will be communicated to them?

She might also have asked the specific questions that are in the guidelines segment itself (whom to involve, for what purpose, and so on), with respect to decisions and plans other than those discussed at the meeting.

c. What else can be done to improve the thoroughness, openness, and honesty of the communications, and communications systems, between the organization's units, within units, and with other stakeholders?

Mary is new on the job, so she may still have to become acquainted with the way her departments normally communicate with other departments and with stakeholders. She probably was not fully aware of the thoroughness and openness of communications between the departments reporting to her, or within each department. However, even if she were established in the position, it might still be worthwhile for her to assess communications from time to time. Because they are so much a part of daily activities, communications rarely get the review they deserve, even require. If Mary had been aware of this aspect of the guideline question, she might have asked herself some questions such as question c. or the following:

- Are there any changes that should be considered in the formal reports that are issued from the departments to improve them in content, frequency, and distribution?

- Are there open two-way communications in each department and each section, and do the department managers and the supervisors have the competencies for improving and maintaining a highly open communications climate? (See Chapter 2, Additional Insights H, Communications Theories, Techniques, and Skills.)

- Are there open two-way communications between departments and sections? (See Chapter 2, Additional Insights H, Communications Theories, Techniques, and Skills.)

- What communications training may be needed or desirable?

  d. When ensuring coordination and cooperation, what else can be done so that procedures are appropriate and effectively communicated to all stakeholders, so there is early identification of coordination or cooperation problems, and so all potentially damaging conflicts are either prevented or effectively resolved?

Mary realized (as was discussed in the analysis of Scenario 2.1 in Chapter 2, where there is a fairly detailed discussion of this issue) good coordination is primarily dependent on sound procedures, thoroughly communicated and understood. It does, of course, require willingness to follow the procedures. That could be considered as cooperating with the coordination procedures, and that's probably why these two topics are so closely linked.

Cooperation, on the other hand, depends on attitudes toward the people with whom to cooperate, and on the matter in which cooperation is required or desired.

Mary had become involved in a situation that was full of potential obstacles to effective coordination and cooperation. If she had been aware of this aspect of the guideline question (question d.), she might have asked herself some questions such as the following:

- How well are procedures, and especially quality standards, established and communicated to all staff members who need to be aware of them?

- How well are quality standards communicated to customers who need to be aware of them?

- How can potentially damaging conflicts be detected early and addressed? (See Chapter 2, Additional Insights F, Managing Potentially Damaging Conflict.)

- What competencies do the department managers, supervisors, and staff members need so that potentially damaging conflict does not arise or is quickly resolved? (See Chapter 2, Additional Insights F, Managing Potentially Damaging Conflict.)

- What can be done to ensure the types of open communications and widespread communications skills that will help with early identification and resolution of conflicts? (See Chapter 2, Additional Insights H, Communications Theories, Techniques, and Skills.)

e. When ensuring positive discipline, what else can be done so that appropriate norms, including norms pertaining to morality and diversity, are established and maintained, and so that every staff member, at all levels of the organization, respects and follows them?

The only norms openly discussed in the scenario are the quality standards. However, under the surface, there are many norms that will slowly become apparent as Mary gains greater acquaintance with her staff.

To speed the process, she might ask herself question e. or questions such as:

- What types of norms are important for operations?

- What norms can I identify as a result of the meeting and from my contacts with the departments?

- How can I identify other norms, including norms pertaining to morality and diversity, that are shared by members of the different departments, and those that are not shared?

- What should be done to clarify norms for staff members and encourage discussion of differences of opinion so they can be resolved rather than exist as potential sources of conflict?

In addition to norms, other questions pertaining to positive discipline deserve consideration. They concern the strategies that Mary and the department managers might want to pursue to strengthen the acceptance of behavior norms which contribute to the effectiveness of the teams. These strategies apply to norms (including rules and standards) and also to privileges that can and should be granted. In a way, however, all procedures and rules, including those that guide management/leadership behavior, are norms, and positive discipline depends on the quality of these norms and on the way that adherence to them is stimulated (see Additional Insights L, Positive Discipline and Counseling, Chapter 4).

f. What else can be done to ensure that overall performance, and individual staff member performance, are reviewed continually so that potential challenges and problems are identified, and so that evaluations are as factual, fair, and meaningful as possible?

The scenario did not touch on performance evaluation (see Additional Insights K1, this chapter) and it certainly would not be wise for Mary to discuss this topic so soon after assuming her new position. Unfortunately, performance evaluation, as critical as it is to organization performance as well as to job satisfaction, is one of the least understood management/leadership techniques. It is likely that, claims to the contrary notwithstanding, there is no performance evaluation system which fully achieves its purpose—to help distribute compensation and other rewards fairly in relation to staff member contributions.

Still, if she had been aware of this aspect of the guideline, Mary might have asked herself question f. or some questions such as those following, even if there is a formal, organization-wide performance evaluation system in effect.

- Should there be a fairly formal procedure for reviewing performance of each department and subdepartment? If so, what should it include and how often should it be done?

- Should there be a fairly formal procedure for reviewing performance with each staff member? If so, what should it include and how often should it be done?

g. With respect to counseling, what else should be done to ensure that all staff members with managerial/leadership responsibilities competently counsel for performance problems and other problems which do, or may, affect performance? (See Chapter 4, Additional Insights L, Positive Discipline.)

The scenario did not involve counseling directly, but there appear to be potential opportunities for counseling on performance and on self-development.

Here too, if she had been aware of this aspect of the guideline question, Mary might have asked herself some questions such as the following:

- Are the managers and supervisors effective in identifying situations where performance, self-development, or personal problem counseling would be appropriate?

- Are the managers and supervisors effective in identifying situations where career-planning counseling would be appropriate to strengthen back-ups for critical positions and to help staff members for whom this way of showing appreciation for their contributions would be appropriate?

- Do the managers and supervisors have the competence to conduct effective counseling sessions?

In addition to the Control guideline question, which was the focus of this analysis so far, Competence and Climate guidelines have to be considered. Since the other two scenarios in this chapter will emphasize those guidelines, a few comments may be adequate.

Please keep in mind the intense interrelationships between the 3Cs requirements for an effective organization: that actions taken to strengthen Control affect the strength of Competence and Climate, for better or for worse. The same comprehensive impact is true of actions to improve Competence, or Climate, respectively.

Some of this interrelationship is highlighted in Chapter 4, where there is a list of the most important linking elements for each of the 3Cs. That list also provides a view of the guideline segments that are useful for that respective area.

2. Competence

Competence involves hiring the right people, using sound training strategies, and making effective use of coaching. Mary had no need to consider hiring of staff members. However, with respect to training and coaching, there is the counseling competence mentioned above which she might have considered. In addition, as she proceeds to develop her role as competent manager/leader, she would undoubtedly come to grips with identification of competence strengths and weaknesses of the managers reporting to her. She will also have to develop, probably jointly with the managers, methods for identifying competence strengths and weaknesses of staff members, so the teams can take advantage of the strengths through job and project assignments and even promotions. The teams will also have to develop strategies for reducing or eliminating any weaknesses that were identified.

3. Climate

Climate is off to a good start since Mary has clearly shown herself as a competent leader and manager. Still, as she continues to establish herself, she will have to develop strategies for ensuring that work-related stress is kept in check, that more appreciation is expressed for contributions of staff members, and that maximum benefit is obtained from compensation and promotion policies.

❖ ❖ ❖ ❖ ❖ ❖

**Conclusions: Mary's New Position:
A Challenge of Coordination and Cooperation**

Mary certainly is off to a good start in her new position. From the perspective of Control, Competence, and Climate she seems to approach each of the areas appropriately. Still, if she wants to forge a powerful, achievement-oriented team, with high-level competence for the present and the future, she will have her hands full.

All the tools, new and old, that are at the disposal of the fully competent manager/leader will be needed. Critically important is a clear view of a sound, cohesive, management/leadership model, in addition to high-level technical/functional competence, so the *pieces will fit.*

Using the 3Cs guideline questions (and the linking elements model from Chapter 4) and developing the competence to apply the full meaning of the comprehensive guidelines is probably the shortest and easiest route to take. This does not mean that Mary should accept the guidelines as suggested here. It does mean that she should either adapt them or gradually develop her own set of coordinated, comprehensive guidelines that fit her personal management/leadership style and then work on sharpening it until it is fully satisfactory for all challenges she might face.

SCENARIO 3.2

─────────────────────────

The Challenges of Exceptional
Technician Competence

Focus: The Competence guideline, emphasis on the need for high knowledge and skill levels of all staff members

Abstract: Lieutenant Junior Grade Joe Smith, a fairly new Auxiliaries Division Officer on a large Navy vessel, has allowed Tom Brennan, an exceptionally competent Chief Machinist Mate in the air conditioning and refrigeration division, to do most of the major repairs, with the other members of the Division providing only helper-type support. When Brennan was transferred, serious trouble developed.

❖ ❖ ❖ ❖ ❖ ❖

The Scenario

Lieutenant Junior Grade Joe Smith sat in stunned silence at his desk in the A Division (Auxiliaries Division) office. He had just been severely reprimanded by his boss, Lieutenant Commander Sam Brown, the Chief Engineer. Brown was a stern, no-nonsense type of person, who had worked his way up through the ranks, without formal education, strictly through hard work and innate intelligence. He was from the "old school" when officers considered tight discipline as the key to effective leadership.

While he had criticized Smith on previous occasions, he had never before attacked him personally, as he did on this occasion. This time he called Smith a complete failure as a division officer, because there had been a sudden drop in quality of repairs of air conditioning and refrigeration (AC&R) equipment. This affected a variety of equipment and seriously jeopardized the operational capabilities of the ship, not to mention the comfort of the crew. Brown said he was shocked, would not tolerate such performance, and told Smith to get things "fixed" by the time the ship was scheduled to leave port, in about one week. The threat of an unsatisfactory fitness report, while not directly mentioned, clearly was overhead. Smith hardly said a word as he was being dressed down, but stated that he would find some way to fix the problems.

As he pondered his situation, Smith realized that his old friend and mentor, Matt Simons, was in port. Matt, a Chief Engineer himself, would find a way to help.

Matt was on board when Smith called, and fortunately he could do just what Smith had hoped for—send some very competent mechanics over to help the AC&R group get on top of the situation.

During the phone call Smith brought Simons up to date on what had happened since he had become the Auxiliaries Division officer.

As Simons knew, Smith had come aboard about a year ago having completed his surface warfare officer qualifications and was immediately assigned to the Engineering Department. During his first meeting with Lieutenant Commander Brown, Brown quickly got to the point, as he invariably did in their subsequent meetings. "Smith, I see that you have completed your qualifications and had some experience in the Engineering Department of your last ship. I need an Auxiliaries Division Officer now, and you're it. In this job, you will be responsible for air compressors and compressed air distribution systems, laundry equipment, hydraulic systems, the machine shop, the air conditioning and refrigeration equipment, and so on."

"Yes, Sir, I understand," is all that Smith could say, before Brown continued.

"You know how important the many types of equipment are that are operated and maintained by A Division. This ship and this department prides itself on readiness and capability. I expect you to keep the equipment operating. If something breaks down, I expect it to be fixed quickly, and you should take whatever actions are necessary to make that happen. You've got some good people in that division. Don't get in their way. I don't want to hear any excuses. Keep me informed of any problems that come up and what you are doing about it. Then get the job done! Any questions?"

Smith had heard of officers like Brown, but he had never met one before. The best he could do was blurt out, "No, Sir!"

Brown's "Dismissed," was the end of that initial meeting.

Since then, Smith had tried to make sure that he lived up to Brown's expectations. For the most part he did.

Probably the most critical equipment operated and maintained by A Division was the ship's AC&R equipment. This complex air conditioning and refrigeration equipment chilled drinking water, made ice, kept food frozen and chilled, made living conditions bearable, and, most importantly, helped keep the ship's vital electronic equipment operating properly. In A Division, a group of five enlisted people was assigned responsibility for operating and repair of this complex and diverse equipment. There were two junior enlisted men working toward becoming machinist mates, a Machinist Mate 3/c (MM3), a Machinist Mate 2/c (MM2), and the group's star, a newly appointed Chief Machinist Mate (MMC), Tom Brennan.

Brennan had reported on board four years ago as an MM2. Because he had worked in AC&R, he was assigned to A Division and the AC&R group. He clearly loved the challenges of working with this diverse array of equipment, and almost always took the lead in trouble-shooting and even with the repairs. With an intuitive sense for the intricacies and sophistication of the physics of pressure-temperature relationships and for the complexities of the equipment, he was outstanding in his ability to make repairs quickly and effectively. After his arrival, the operating performance of this group's equipment, and especially repair downtime, had improved dramatically.

Because replacement parts availability is often so important to rapid repairs, he even became an expert in the intricacies of Navy supply systems and procedures and was generally more knowledgeable in the AC&R supply arena than were the ship's supply personnel.

Brennan so impressed his superiors that, as soon as he was eligible, they recommended him for the MM1 exam, which he passed with a high score. As a new MM1, he continued to perform in the same ways as before, as lead-mechanic with the others serving primarily as helpers.

At first Smith thought that it was wonderful to have such a competent man in the division. Gradually he came to see a dark cloud in that clear sky. The others in the AC&R group, although they operated equipment reasonably well and were on hand to assist during repairs, did not seem to be interested in what was being done. On several informal occasions, when speaking with them, Smith sensed that at one time they had wanted to get more involved and to learn more about how to make repairs quickly and effectively. As time passed, and Brennan did not give them the necessary opportunities, they had lost interest and become apathetic. Smith wondered whether the problem was only Brennan's forceful personality or whether these technicians might be lazy or inept.

Such thoughts were easy to ignore, because there were so many more pressing matters on Smith's mind. After all, in addition to the AC&R crews he had six other groups to supervise, some of whom needed more attention than the smoothly operating AC&R group. With these groups he often had to help by exercising very close supervision over a wide variety of operating and maintenance issues.

Trouble started when Brennan was recommended for promotion to Chief Petty Officer (CPO), with strong endorsement from Lieutenant Commander Brown, who often told Smith that he considered Brennan the ideal enlisted man. Sure enough, Brennan "got the hat" (was promoted to Chief Petty Officer—CPO) on his first try.

Smith noted, with some concern, that although Brennan had become a (supposedly) senior enlisted supervisor, he didn't change his behavior as the lead man in his group. When anything broke, there he was, up to his elbows in parts and lubricants, despite his newly purchased khaki uniforms. Smith knew that his division did not rate a CPO in the AC&R group and that he would therefore lose Brennan in the not-too-distant future.

He approached Brennan and said to him, "Chief, don't you think you should become more of a supervisor now and less of a worker?" Brennan responded, "Don't worry about it Lieutenant Smith. My guys are first rate people, and they learn real well by observing. Besides, I love working with this stuff." Smith accepted this argument, but not without some doubt. He decided to talk to Brown about the situation, but the Chief Engineer told him not to worry about it, even suggesting a degree of surprise that Smith would raise such an issue. Results were all that mattered, and the results were outstanding.

About one month ago, Smith's concerns were realized. Orders arrived, transferring Brennan on short notice. Smith, on Brown's specific directions, appointed the most senior man in the AC&R group to be its head. Almost immediately, equipment reliability started to drop and repair downtime began to lengthen. The new group head seemed to lack confidence in all aspects of his new responsibilities. While he was generally adequate in repairing equipment, he did not understand or have experience working with Navy supply procedures. His approach to maintenance and repair actions was haphazard, as Smith discovered. As a first step in providing help, Smith had him work with a supply officer for a few hours when that officer was following up on orders for AC&R parts.

It turned out that the members of the AC&R group were indeed excited at the opportunity to finally have significant roles in the work. They were well intentioned and understood that they faced significant new challenges which they clearly wanted to handle well. They tried hard, but just were not up to the size of the task. The crisis came with the failure of equipment that cooled vital ship's electronics. Lieutenant Commander Brown was informed of the breakdown and had inquired about its repair status after two days. Smith had been assured by his AC&R group head that they were on top of the situation, but still the equipment was not operating at the end of a week. That's when Brown had summoned Smith for the severe criticism.

At the conclusion of this story, to which he had patiently listened, Matt Simons said he not only had some excellent people who would make a "consulting visit," but that he had an excellent spare parts inventory and could probably help get the critical equipment operating in short order. They would work out the problem of "reimbursement" later. He then closed the conversation with a bit of advice, telling Smith that he believed that one of the most important duties of a naval officer was to insure effective technical *and* supervisory development of his people. Simons suggested that Smith needed to give this matter a high priority and said he would be glad to offer comments and advice.

Fortunately Simons did have a critical replacement part in his inventory. Thanks to that, and the help and recommendations which Simons' people provided, the major equipment problem and a number of other important repairs were completed within two days. Smith happily reported this to Brown, minutes after the equipment went back into operation. Brown's only response was "It's about time! Don't let that happen again!" But this time, there was a light smile on his lips.

With the crisis behind him, Smith began to think about Matt Simons' words from the end of their phone conversation. It was time to think about the future. Clearly, he had to come up with a proactive, forward-looking program.

What should he do, Smith wondered, to really prevent such incidents? It was clear to him that he would have to get the divisions' groups working together to find ways to ensure effective team development, improve supervisory competence, and enhance the knowledge, skills, and abilities of all members of A Division.

Smith decided to call a meeting of the senior members of each of his division's groups to develop a plan.

During the meeting it turned out that some of the sailors were quite sharp. The suggestion was made to create a cooperative development program during which members of the division would define what they needed to learn and that an effort would be made to coach them and to schedule them to work with others who were good at the respective work whenever a relevant repair project came up.

With respect to competence in supervisory skills, the group heads suggested that they hold regular meetings. Smith would select one or two references and assign specific readings. On a rotating basis, each group head would make a presentation on an assigned reading and lead a discussion. Coaching was to be given high priority so there would be maximum support for the development of all division personnel.

Before closing the meeting, Smith asked the group heads to hold meetings with their own people to discuss this project and ask for suggestions. These suggestions would then be taken up at the first supervisory development meeting.

Smith was anxious to get started with this new effort. He made a mental note to discuss this project with Simons after it had been up and running for a couple of months.

❖ ❖ ❖ ❖ ❖

Analysis: The Challenges of Exceptional Technician Competence

Emphasis in this analysis is on the comprehensive Competence guideline question.

1. Competence

The basic Competence guideline is restated, followed by the specific issues and their analyses, one by one.

> What needs to be done, if anything, so that all those who will be involved in implementing the decision, and those who will otherwise be affected (all the stakeholders), have the necessary competencies to ensure effective progress and satisfying use of the product or service if they do not have them already? More specifically:

a. What else can be done in recruiting and selection, so the processes are efficient and effective in filling vacant positions with highly qualified, flexible candidates from within or without the organization whose norms are reasonably in line with those of the organization?

While there is little active shipboard recruiting for position vacancies, officers have to be as concerned about the levels of knowledge, ability, and skill of candidates for vacant positions under their purview as their counterparts outside the armed forces. This is especially important because personnel transfers are facts of life in the military and are rarely within the control of the individual command.

Though Smith is not a very seasoned officer, he did seem to have a feel for this need. One has to empathize with a young man who has to gain competence while reporting to an officer who clings to autocratic techniques that never were as effective as managers thought they were, but which have become woefully inadequate in light of today's demands for technical knowledge and enlightened leadership.

Still, had Smith learned about this guideline, and specifically about this component, he would certainly have asked himself either question a. or questions such as:

- Who could be considered for the key position or positions in each group if a vacancy should occur?

- What can be done to lay the foundation for approval of these individuals if and when a vacancy actually occurs?

- What training steps need to be offered, or arranged, with these technicians and others who might feel that they, too, could qualify for consideration?

Had he given these issues greater priority by possibly delegating some tasks that others could perform for him, he might have prevented the crisis.

b. What else can be done to help staff members, including those in managerial positions, accept greater responsibility for their own competence development and provide all necessary and desirable support and development opportunities to members of their staffs?

The first part of the issue raised by this question is possibly the most important aspect of competency development. If staff members, sailors in this scenario, accept responsibility for their own development, the daunting task of assuring competence becomes an almost routine one. It reduces itself to helping—with identifying learning needs, by providing learning opportunities through classes and with materials, by arranging for developmental assignments, and arranging for coaching when these other, less resource-intensive support options are inadequate. The challenge for the officer/leader is to stimulate this desire on the part of staff members to *manage* their own competence development.

If Smith had been aware of this guideline component, he might have asked himself question b. or questions such as:

- What do I have to do to be effective in accepting responsibility for my own competence development, specifically as a manager/leader?

- How can I stimulate the group leaders to do the same?

- What skills do we need to be effective in motivating others toward self-development?

- What resources do I have currently available for providing learning opportunities to the sailors in the various groups?

- How can I best make use of these resources?

c. What else can be done to identify competence strengths and weaknesses effectively, to take advantage of the strengths, when delegating, assigning projects, and in career advancements, and to apply management of learning concepts, including coaching, effectively where weaknesses exist?

If Smith had been aware of this guideline component, he might have asked himself this question c., or a few questions such as:

- What tools do we need to help those who report to us identify what they need to learn?

- What do we have to do to identify learning needs where individuals do not accept responsibility for self-development?

- What do we have to do so we can make best use of competence strengths of individuals, to enhance performance of the groups, and to help others gain similar strengths?

- What do we have to do to become effective as managers of learning and as coaches so we can bring competence weaknesses down to their irreducible minimum?

d. With respect to communications, what else can be done to ensure that all staff members are skilled in meeting conduct and are effective as listeners (with ears *and* eyes); in probing and asking of questions; in providing useful feedback during conversations, discussions, and meetings; in written communications; and in providing information?

With respect to meetings, Smith appears to have handled himself well. At least he saw to it that the meeting ended with specific decisions and that follow-up was arranged.

If Smith had been aware of this guideline component and realized the critical importance of communications to all aspects of the Competence guideline, he might have asked himself question d. or questions such as:

- How can I become more proficient in written and verbal communications?

- Where can I find written, recorded, or live resources for including sections on communications in all training programs and in staff meetings?

e. With respect to counseling, what else should be done to ensure that all staff members with managerial/ leadership responsibilities competently counsel for all four purposes: performance problems, self-development, and learning issues, career development, and personal problems?

Had Smith been more concerned about Brennan's behavior, counseling would have been the appropriate step to take. In a way this scenario demonstrates the need for vigilance in spotting when counseling should be considered, and for ensuring that all managers/leaders in an organizational unit are skilled in, and comfortable with, counseling.

2. Control and Climate

a. Control

It is clear that Lieutenant Commander Brown has only one vague goal in mind, which is really more of a *vision* than a specific goal. He has clearly communicated that to Smith, and undoubtedly to all others on board. Not clearly spelled out, though continuously implied, is a second, more precise, ongoing goal—continued readiness. Participation in decision making, including the setting of goals, does not fit into Brown's autocratic leadership style. Consequently, there was no participation in the scenario. Brown apparently is not a young man so career advancement is probably a secondary issue with him. Younger officers who might be tempted to emulate his style would do so at great risk to advancement, and possibly even continuation in the Navy. Similarly, even if Brown were able to develop a sense of managing with the aid of goals, and be inclined to communicate them, it appears doubtful that he would have been able to do so competently. Finally, with respect to positive discipline, it does not appear that Brown would be able to comprehend the concept. Like it or not, the ship's norms are to be the Navy's, as he interprets them, and as he assumes everyone knows. These norms are to be honored or else.

Smith has painfully come to realize that he must develop and communicate, to all groups reporting to him, a broader set of relevant goals that provide more adequately for the uncertainties of the future without compromising the goal of readiness. In fact, a sound set of goals would undoubtedly ensure against crises that might jeopardize readiness. He has also begun to appreciate the importance of participation in the process. The excellent ideas that came up in the first planning (informal goal setting) meeting strongly reinforced that awareness. Smith might also gradually try to bring about a more participative relationship with Brown after the dust settles.

The steps he started to take to bring improved competence will undoubtedly also lead to improved coordination and cooperation. If he gains an understanding of the elements of positive discipline, it appears that his temperament would allow him to easily adapt that concept into his leadership style.

Brennan would also benefit from learning how to use goals and how to apply them to his situation. He became a CPO based on technical competence and performance. As a Chief, he must make the transition to supervisor if his career is to flourish in the changing Navy.

b. Climate

Helping staff members reduce work-related stress, and using psychological rewards effectively, are the two principal skills which officers can apply to bring a satisfying climate.

With respect to stress, Lieutenant Commander Brown is no help. He actively generates stress with his I-talk-and-you-listen behavior. At the same time he, himself, does not appear to have high tolerance for stress. Anything that might have even minor impact on readiness causes him immediate concern. Still, he cannot translate that personal need to a leadership style that empathizes with the same need by the members of his crew. None of the players in the drama seem to understand that an ongoing pattern of, and commitment to cooperative dialogue, brings stress reduction. Smith might not be able to say to Brown that stress reduction can help with readiness, but he seems to now have an understanding that, in his approach to the AC&R group, the stress issue should receive fairly high priority. The members of that group have been poorly trained and are now overwhelmed by the situation. Helping them to survive this ordeal is vital. Helping them find ways to avoid similar disasters is necessary. Building an atmosphere of openness, cooperation, mutual support, and concern will have great stress-reduction potential, and undoubtedly a highly favorable impact on Smith's image as an effective leader.

With respect to psychological rewards, Brown seems to know only negative ones. He typically reacts to problems with a barrage of implied and actual threats. Clearly, for most players in this drama, including Smith, satisfaction of higher-level needs and rewards are missing from the equation.

The only one enjoying psychological rewards was Brennan, who found them in the most powerful sources, the work and the positive strokes from many people. On the other side of the coin, the other technicians in the AC&R group were severely short-changed, and received little in the way of positive strokes from the work or from people. While this situation is bleak at the moment, if Smith learns how to become a more effective leader, as he seems capable of doing, the situation may change, and he might develop the habits for providing regular psychological rewards to his people (see Scenario 2.3).

With respect to tangible rewards, the scenario speaks only of the promotions for Brennan. Curiously, these tangible rewards placed him at an organizational level at which he would soon be expected to be a competent supervisor. Unless he becomes aware of the need to gain the necessary competencies, his promotions may become an example of the good-news-is-bad-news syndrome.

Navy regulations severely restrict the ability of officers to provide minor tangible rewards. Furthermore, Brown holds the key and he is inclined to recognize only outstanding behavior. Steady contributors to the mission cannot expect letters of commendation, decorations, superior or special performance reports, or boosts toward promotion. Brown would have to realize need, and that is not likely to happen. He might, of course, be relieved and replaced by a more enlightened officer.

❖ ❖ ❖ ❖ ❖

Conclusions: The Challenges of Exceptional Technician Competence

This case demonstrates, albeit with a fairly extreme example, the significant contributions that explicit goals can make to the performance of an organization or unit.

It should be obvious that even crudely set and poorly communicated goals can sharply reduce the incidence and severity of operational, and even strategic, crises.

Goals on competence were especially highlighted by Smith's situation. In addition, specific goals for each group, and even for each individual, if competently set and administered (see Chapter 2, Additional Insights E, Making a Goals Program Work), can have a great impact, not only on performance but also on competence and on the feeling of confidence and pride that individuals would feel.

The scenario dramatized, with equal clarity, the need to consider communications policies and competence development as critical elements of successful performance. Less obvious, but still glaring, were the shortcomings of the ship's leadership system, in:

- Effective policies for filling vacancies with the candidates who meet not only technical, but also flexibility standards
- Potential for establishing positive discipline
- Communicating specific norms, in policies to foster coordination and cooperation
- Ensuring a Climate that would be highly motivational to satisfy division members' needs

SCENARIO 3.3

The Hazards of Performance Evaluation*

Focus: The Climate guideline, emphasis on performance evaluation

Abstract: Bernice, a new department manager, has been told not to give ratings as high as her predecessor because they caused problems with other departments. Craig is the first staff member with whom she holds the performance assessment review. Her rating of *Good* greatly upsets him and Bernice reviews her options so that she will not face serious obstacles in relations with her staff.

❖ ❖ ❖ ❖ ❖ ❖

The Scenario

As in past years, Craig had completed the self-appraisal required by company policy, listing his accomplishments and his disappointments. In the *Additional Comments* sec-

---

*This story is adapted from one published in *TQM Magazine* V8/4, July/August 1996, pp. 71–72, MCB University Press.

tion he proudly pointed to the Master's degree he had just received after three years of evening classes. He also wrote that he had stayed late more frequently than in the past to keep up with an increasing workload.

About two weeks ago, he had turned it in to Bernice, his new manager for about eight months. When she called him into her office to discuss his performance evaluation, he expected an *Excellent* or even an *Outstanding* rating, the same as he used to receive during the last few years while George was in charge of the department. Craig had gone far out of his way to pitch in whenever he could be of help, even though Bernice was more difficult to work with because she was not as outgoing as George had been. It made him confident that she appreciated his efforts.

Bernice started the discussion by pointing out to Craig that her meeting with him was the first in the department. She complimented him on the thoroughness of the self-appraisal, and went over her notes and his report. Throughout she confirmed his views and had nothing negative to say, except that it seemed as though she considered the disappointments somewhat more avoidable than he saw them.

Then came the surprise. She told Craig that she had carefully reviewed his record, taken note of the high ratings he had received in the past, and considered the possibility to give him an *Excellent* rating. However, there were several others in the department who had also received *Excellent* and *Outstanding* ratings in the past. One reason why it had taken so long to get to the performance reviews is that she had consulted with other managers on how they assigned ratings and found that they give *Excellent* and *Outstanding* ratings only very sparingly. *Excellent* was reserved for exceptionally strong accomplishments and *Outstanding* for the very rare, truly unique situations, where someone clearly performed at a level above job requirements, indicating that a promotion should be considered as soon as an appropriate vacancy occurred. For these reasons she had decided on a rating of *Good.*

Craig was shocked. She must dislike him for some reason, he thought, because the quantity and quality of his work, he was certain, was better than the work of those others to whom she had referred. How could she give him a rating that was considered by everyone in the department as just average?

He tried to hide his disappointment, but the two questions he asked gave him away, immediately. What else would he have to do to earn an *Excellent* rating, he wondered? Bernice could not give him any specifics on that—"Just do what you have been doing," she advised, "and look at the areas where you could sharpen your skill and knowledge. Soon we will start a competence improvement program to further improve the department's performance. That'll help you identify were you can possibly enhance your competence and your career."

Craig also wanted to know how many of the 15 professionals in the department had received higher ratings and who they were. Bernice told him that there was one staff member who she thought deserved an *Excellent* rating, and one to whom she would give the *Outstanding*. She would not identify the two, nor did she feel that it would be appropriate to discuss the reasons for their ratings. She said that she had gone over the ratings with Henry, her manager, and that he had concurred.

He sensed who they were. One, he thought, was Mac, an exceptionally competent person and Craig felt that the higher rating was justified in his case. The other one who he thought would receive a high rating was Laurie. Laurie was an unusually charming young woman with average competence who was not working any harder than most others. She had gained a high regard by management because she was able to get others to help her with difficult tasks. Occasionally she took credit for ideas, and even accomplishments, of others who were on a team with her. Still, rarely did anyone become upset with her, partly because she did small favors and showed great interest in personal problems of her colleagues.

Craig wondered whether he should challenge Bernice and demand that she reveal to him, and to others, who the highest rated staff members were, but decided to think about that first. George had not made a big secret of who received high ratings. In fact, he had used those ratings to stimulate the others to higher accomplishments. It had worked with Craig. He devoted more effort and, he thought, worked smarter, in large part as a result of the friendly competition in which, it seemed, everyone could win.

Should he tell Bernice about his guesses and challenge Laurie's rating by comparing himself with her?

Just before leaving, he thought of another, possibly even more important question. He asked what impact the rating would have on his annual merit increase. Here, too, Bernice's response was vague—she had not yet received word from Henry on the budget for increases, though she had asked, because she had hoped to inform staff members at the time of the performance evaluation discussion.

After leaving Bernice's office, as his head cooled, Craig realized that Bernice had not been all wrong. He remembered that he had heard a number of complaints from members of other departments about their "strict" rating system. He had even been teased about how easy it was to get an *Excellent* rating from George. Still, he began to wonder about his options and the impact of the situation on his future. The lower-than-previous rating certainly would not help him when the next opportunity for a promotion came along.

He could discuss the situation with others who also had received high ratings in the past; or, he could start fresh with another company. He was still young enough for that. Maybe he should start looking.

Craig's stronger-than-expected reaction concerned Bernice. She had thought about telling him that Henry had cautioned her not to follow in George's footsteps by being overly generous with performance evaluations. They had caused considerable problems in other departments. But she decided against saying something that might sound as though she was hiding behind Henry or blaming him.

Still, this first interview had opened her eyes to the severity of the challenges she faced in trying to make a smooth transition from George's generous appraisals to the more restrictive ones which would satisfy Henry's expectations.

She thought it would be best to talk with Henry before meeting with the next staff member.

First Bernice asked about the merit increase budget. Henry thought that he would be able to get word in about two weeks. Then they discussed various options, including:

- Sharing the appraisals, or all the *Good* and better ones, openly with anyone who inquired, or with all staff members.

- Providing an explanation of the problems which George's high ratings had caused, and why Henry and the next levels of management could not allow the situation to continue.

- How such an explanation should be provided—by Bernice in her one-on-ones or in a meeting, by Henry in a meeting, or by Bernice with Henry present to answer questions.

- Whether Bernice should wait until after the budget was available so she could first apportion it among her team, and know where each individual stood in relation to their last increases. She did not think that she should be specific during the interviews, just in case something came up that might lead to a change in the plan.

They agreed that it would be advisable to hold off for two weeks in the hope that the budget would be available by then, and to be more open with the staff members on explaining the reasons for less generous ratings. Henry left it up to her to select from the options. He did think that the only ratings that should be communicated were those that were *Good* or better.

Because Bernice felt that the responsibility for informing her staff was primarily hers, she opted to provide the explanation, and to make the ratings of *Good* or better public in a meeting. She did ask Henry to attend the meeting since he knew much more about the background of the problems which George's ratings caused and because his clarification of the relationship between budget, merit increases, and ratings, if needed, would have more credibility.

❖ ❖ ❖ ❖ ❖ ❖

Analysis: The Hazards of Performance Evaluation

Emphasis in this analysis is on the comprehensive Climate guideline question.

1. Climate

The basic Climate guideline is restated, followed by the specific issues and their analyses one by one.

What needs to be done so that the reaction of the various groups and individuals who have to implement the decision or plan, and those who will be affected by it, will be in favor of it or at least have as positive a view as possible so there will be a favorable Climate? More specifically:

a. What else needs to be done to ensure that all staff members with managerial/leadership responsibilities are alert to opportunities for providing positive feedback, and other psychological rewards, to all deserving staff members, even those who rarely do something outstanding, and that they use the many possible ways for taking advantage of such opportunities?

If Bernice had been aware of this, and the other aspects of the guideline question, she might have asked herself question a. (above), questions b. through e. (following), or some questions such as those listed after each segment of the guideline, in conjunction with any thoughts she might have had on the issue.

- What kind of psychological rewards did Craig receive when I told him about his rating? Was the explanation, and the confirmation of his self-appraisal, which I gave him, adequate?

- Since I do not have the merit-increase budget yet, should I discuss the procedure for deciding on merit increases, and the impact of ratings?

- What should I do to avoid the negative impact of lower-than-expected ratings now and in the future?

- How can I balance the negative impact of disappointing performance ratings with positive, satisfying moments, before and after the rating, or even during the entire period between ratings?

- How frequently should I review overall performance, and performance on projects, with individual staff members?

- What can I do to improve my competence in administering the organization's performance appraisal system?

- Craig is the only member of my staff whom I had informed about his rating. He asked who the people are who received higher ratings and I did not answer. Should I speak with him before the meeting with the staff, and what should I say?

b. What else needs to be done to ensure that all staff members with managerial/leadership responsibilities provide appropriate and fair work assignments and delegate effectively?

Here she might have asked:

- How can I make more effective use of work assignments and delegation of selected tasks to provide satisfying experiences to staff members?

- What do I need to know about the interests and aspirations of staff members, and about their competence strengths and weaknesses, so I can best make such assignments and delegations?

- What else do I need to know about how to delegate effectively so I can be certain to leave the staff member as much decision freedom as possible, yet not take significant and avoidable risks?

c. What else needs to be done to ensure that all staff members feel little work-related stress and as secure as possible and have trust and confidence in the organization and its managers?

Here she might have asked:

- Are we keeping staff members adequately informed on company developments?

- Do I listen to them adequately so they know that I am aware of their contributions?

- Do I provide adequate evidence that I appreciate their efforts and accomplishments even if they are not outstanding?

- Am I honest with them when I discuss their performance on a delegated project or assigned task by giving them the positives and also the negatives in a constructive way?

- Do I provide adequate support when my "listening" uncovers the need for my involvement or assistance?

d. What else can be done to ensure that the organization offers appropriate tangible rewards, and that all staff members with managerial/leadership responsibilities provide deserved tangible rewards effectively to stimulate the strongest possible motivational climate (for those who receive the tangible rewards and those who do not receive any at the moment)?

Bernice will soon be faced with the challenge to apportion the merit increase budget available to her in such a way that as many staff members as possible, and preferably all, will feel that she has done right by them. Depending on past experiences and the organization's culture, she may even have to convince her staff that she has fought hard for the largest possible budget. In some organizations, where the system works differently so there is more mystique to the distribution of compensation increases, she may even have to satisfy the perception of each staff member that she has done all she could, and done it well, to obtain for him or her the highest possible increase. The critical point is that the amount itself, though important, is not the primary issue. The perception of fairness is. Fairness in relation to others, fairness in relation to other organizations, fairness in relation to perceived effort and contribution (see Chapter 3, Additional Insights K, Performance Evaluation; and equity theory in Chapter 1, Additional Insights C, Motivational Theories).

e. What else can be done so the users of products or services will be fully satisfied?

- In this scenario there was no point of contact with product or service users. Hence, with respect to the issues involved, Bernice had no need to consider those stakeholders.

- In a different situation, she would have to ask what the expectations of those stakeholders were, and how well they were being satisfied by the different options under consideration to meet the challenges in that situation; or, what else could be done to bring higher levels of satisfaction.

2. Control

Effective performance appraisals strongly support an organization's control over its activities. They stimulate attention to areas where improvement in performance is desirable and achievable. Progress reviews, integral to a sound program, bring ideas which can be explored and implemented if useful. These ideas can apply to all aspects of control, including setting new goals, working toward goals, coordination, cooperation, adherence to norms, and conflict management. The reviews may also point to areas where it would be beneficial for staff members to change the way they do things.

3. Competence

Even more strongly than control, performance appraisals, when performed competently, foster improvement in competence. In fact, suggestions for competence improvement, within the procedures of performance appraisals, have a strong impact on staff members because they point the way toward higher ratings and, more importantly, to foundations for career progress, as was illustrated in the scenario.

The primary objective of enlightened performance evaluation programs is competence development. When an organization sees the evaluations from that perspective, most obstacles to open communications and performance improvement do not arise.

❖ ❖ ❖ ❖ ❖ ❖

Conclusions: The Hazards of Performance Evaluation

What had happened here? Are disappointments such as Craig's inevitable? Are they part of the reality that managers rate differently and that only very few people really deserve exceptionally high ratings? Or, can they be anticipated, and prevented?

Performance evaluations are among the most challenging of all managerial/leadership tasks. Sound and fair assessments, while not critical to the satisfaction of the Competence guideline, are vital to the need for Control and they are equally important to a positive Climate. In part, the purpose of this scenario, which emphasizes Climate issues (where performance appraisal is not specifically mentioned) was to dramatize the interrelationship of the guideline questions and the need to consider a decision or plan's impact on two or, more likely, all 3Cs requirements for top-level organizational performance.

Considerable mutual trust, built on honest and open communication, is needed to protect against serious conflict of perceptions and basic interests. Unfortunately, trust is not easy to achieve, especially for a new manager who does not have exceptional talent for communicating (nor possesses the rare quality of charisma).

What then are some of the guidelines that a manager/leader can consider to lay the groundwork for full acceptance of his or her performance evaluations?

1. Performance evaluations should not be a once-a-year thing, to do when the policy calls for turning in evaluations. They should be part of the continuous process of keeping staff members informed about their performance, in comparison to standards that have been mutually agreed on. That takes a lot of honest, open talk, frequently, throughout the year. Progress discussions should occur at least monthly, in which expectations of both sides are laid on the table and where differences are hammered out amicably. Managers/leaders should frequently ask themselves whether the priority they give to communicating on performance is high enough.

2. Dissatisfactions about a staff member's performance cannot be treated lightly but should be brought out in the open. When communicating on performance, managers/leaders should regularly ask themselves whether they are being honest in bringing up and discussing performance problems. Do they take the initiative to call it as, and when, they see it, or do they keep quiet and hope the problem will go away? Are they then offering or providing the support that staff members may need? Do they know what staff members think they need? Most important, do they ask these questions of themselves?

3. What are you doing about staff member expectations for performance ratings that may be unrealistically high? What if a manager in another department rates too leniently? What if a large proportion of the staff members really perform well, above what the organization has a reasonable right to expect? These are not easy questions. They need to be raised and addressed in honest and open communications with higher levels of management and with members of your staff.

4. What should you do to change the climate if it has taken on a negative edge because several staff members are unhappy with their performance ratings or other issues? What can you do to forestall the problem or make it less serious? This is a key question and the answer lies in understanding the many complex factors that shape trust. Thorough understanding of all 3Cs guidelines can be of great help.

3 — Additional Insights I

Decision Making and Problem Solving

Decided only to be undecided,
resolved to be irresolute,
adamant for drift,
solid for fluidity,
all powerful to be impotent.

While England Slept, Winston Churchill, 1936

In this section, after the introduction, the following topics will be discussed:

Decision-Making Concepts

- *Common sense* and rationality
- Significance of assumptions
- Outcome preferences
- Postponing a decision
- Reversibility

Decision-Making and Problem-Solving Procedures

- Decision-making procedure (in the form of questions)
- Problem-solving procedure
- Another approach

Introduction

Of all the competencies, decision making, including problem solving and plan development, is probably the one with greatest influence on success or failure. Managers/leaders would be well advised to ensure that all professional and managerial staff members, and possibly all staff members, are highly competent in these

3   **Insights I Continued**

activities. If no formal, ongoing program exists to ensure continuing development, it might be wise to devote a few minutes at relevant meetings on sharpening and honing these skills. That may require that some structure is provided to managers who conduct such meetings, so decision-making competence development will be an easy task for them and will not require significant preparation time.

Much has been written on decision-making theories and procedures, naturally, since it is such an important topic. This is not the place to summarize all the theories and techniques. One can look at them as being in two segments: functional and managerial/leadership.

Decision making, as a science with branches in mathematics, logic, and even charting, is a functional activity. Most managers, except those with specific relevant knowledge or education, can obtain professional help for these functional considerations when faced with decisions that require application of these techniques.

Identifying practical possible alternatives, including their components, is, of course, the core of sound decision making. Tied to that is the competent selection of the one that appears to be best. We increase the chances for successful outcomes of our decisions as we sharpen the skills for finding and evaluating various choices. The better we get, the more likely that we will do that instinctively in minor decisions, and that we will do it effectively in decisions with greater potential impact. Guidelines can play an important role by ensuring that more bases are covered—by providing a quality check and by serving as comprehensive reminders for using all appropriate resources and looking at all issues.

For the purposes here, the managerial/leadership considerations in decisions, the issue boils down to the use of the 3Cs guideline questions, a few relatively simple concepts, and an understanding of a sound decision-making procedure. These all require development of stop-and-think-before-you-act habits, until they become so much a part of one's nature that they engage, automatically, together with intuitive judgments about people, the business environment, the future, and so on.

Decision-Making Concepts

Common sense and rationality

When thinking about the decisions we make, we have to recognize, first of all, that they rarely come alone; instead, they are usually in lengthy series, such as plans. Going out for lunch, for instance, may involve several decisions such as where to eat, what to order, how to pay for it, when to return, and so on. More complicated decisions invariably involve not only what should be done, but also how, when, and by whom. These subsidiary decisions, in effect, become the plans for implementing the initial decision that triggered them. When we ask ourselves about these related decisions early on, we can often save a lot of grief, like: "Why didn't I/you/we think of that, then . . .?"

Sound decisions have a common theme: rationality. Still, in many, intuition and emotions are involved. Intuition and emotions need not be barriers to rational reasoning.

Making either the initial or subsidiary decisions on the basis of what "comes naturally" is called *using our common sense*. We believe that we know how to make that particular decision correctly, whatever *correctly* means. The trouble is that often we are wrong. There are no quality standards against which we can measure our decisions as we make them. Only with hindsight do we know whether the decision was a *good* one, and often not even then. When we consider a decision as having been *good,* we apply a judgment to the outcome, not to the quality of the thinking and decision making. Sometimes decisions that are carefully considered and sound, based on the available information, may not bring the desired results. In another situation it can be that we made a *poor* decision by not adequately considering the facts and possible alternatives, but fortuitous, unforeseeable circumstances rescued us. Though our decision might have gotten us into trouble, we came out smelling like a rose.

Clearly, if we want to develop a better record of sound decisions, what we need are some quality standards that can help to give us some guidance as we make decisions.

3 Insights I Continued

Common sense is a quality standard of sorts, but for most of us it is a very unreliable one. What is common sense to me is not necessarily common sense to you. That alone tells us that common sense can be a slippery slope. *Common sense* decision-making is an *intuitive* process that relies heavily on accumulated learning, including some baggage we brought with us from childhood. It is based on the lessons we believe, rightly or wrongly, to have learned from what has happened to us.

Beyond trust in our common sense, there are good reasons why we rely heavily on our intuition:

- We often don't know any better. We are simply not aware that we are making intuitive decisions because we have not trained ourselves to distinguish our inclinations from factual analysis, nor have we learned to question our assumptions.

- We also like the easy reliance on intuition and we tend to shy away from the meticulous approach that more careful decision making may require.

- We believe, with some justification, that the experiences and perspectives that we have gained have made our intuition quite reliable.

- Most important, though, we often just cannot get the information necessary to make thoroughly evaluated decisions. The outcomes of many of our decisions depend on what will happen at some time in the future. A certain amount of intuitive judgment therefore has a place, even in very important decisions. Obviously, we should do whatever we can to carefully evaluate the pros and cons of the reasonable ways we could go.

We are biased in favor of making a decision intuitively and we may have a tendency not to listen carefully enough to the more silent intellectual voice within us. We therefore have to adjust for that natural bias when we make important decisions, by developing the habit of asking ourselves whether we have considered at least a few alternatives. Once that habit has developed, the flag goes up intuitively and a voice within us says: stop—look at your choices.

Significance of assumptions

Assumptions can be silent Pied Pipers. If we assume, for instance, that it was human error that created a specific problem, then we will look for a mistake or for a person who might have committed the error. Most of the time, we'll find something, or someone. On the other hand, if we assume that it was a systems or procedure problem, our search will take us in a somewhat different direction.

The point is that as we start on a decision, whether it is to solve a problem or to exploit an opportunity, it pays to first question what assumptions may affect our thinking.

Outcome preferences

Another hidden obstacle to sound decisions lies with our skipping an important step that feels redundant. It concerns clarifying what we want to get from the decision. In a way this is related to the assumption—we have a tendency to feel that it is obvious— that we think we know what we want from a decision. The trouble is that sometimes what we know just isn't so. Giving a few moments of thought to what the outcome should be can pay large dividends.

For instance, do we want to satisfy all of a series of needs, or *satisfice*—strike a good balance between full satisfaction and cost, or full satisfaction of one group of stakeholders versus partial satisfaction of several? Do we want to devote all the resources which the best outcome would probably need, or get the best we can with a fixed bundle of resources?

Even before we identify alternatives, we will gain if we ask: What do we expect from the best alternative? How well should it satisfy all 3Cs guidelines and the functional aspects of the desired outcome, including financial results, for the *short term* as well as the *long term?* The choice that seems most attractive for the short

3 Insights I Continued

term might not be the best one for the long term, or vice versa. Most people have a natural, and partially justified, bias toward short-term benefits and will often favor smaller short-term benefits at the expense of more significant long-term benefits. It is important to help staff members become more aware of their own inclinations and of the need to consider the short-term versus long-term trade-off.

Postponing a decision

One intuitive decision which we make frequently is to postpone a decision. Sometimes that's pure procrastination. Sometimes there is good reason for the postponement. There may be a lot on our plate at the moment and we have consciously assigned a low priority to the decision. Or, we may feel that we may be in a better position to make a sound decision at a later time, possibly because we do not yet have enough information and have good reason to think that we can get more.

We do have to watch, however, that the reasons we give ourselves are valid and not just rationalizations for our failure to tackle the situation. For instance, some people never are satisfied that they have enough information. That's hardly a surprise, since we rarely have all the information we would like. Still, the benefits of a timely decision often outweigh what we could gain by waiting. In some situations, such as in emergencies and in investment decisions, good timing can be more important than any other aspect of the decision.

On many occasions we do not have any reasons—good, bad, or indifferent—to postpone. As the Churchill quote at the beginning of this section dramatized, we just do it as individuals, in groups, and even as a nation, unconcerned by the fact that *not* making a positive decision is also a decision. Postponement is usually more than one decision. It can be a continuous repetition of the decision not to interfere with what is happening.

Intuitive decision making, including postponement, is certainly OK for decisions with inconsequential outcomes and for decisions which we have made so often that we are certain about

3 | **Insights I Continued**

the outcomes. For other decisions, however, it is usually better to take the time to think through the choices that are open to us.

Reversibility

A decision is reversible if the selected alternative can be abandoned if it does not work out well, and another one substituted. When there is no clearly preferable choice, a reversible one is better than an irreversible one, because it is possible to start all over again with relatively little loss.

Decision-Making and Problem-Solving Procedures

As part of a decision-making competence improvement program, it might be useful to practice a step-by-step procedure. Such a procedure would best be reviewed first, and revised on the basis of suggestions by the staff members. They can then be asked to apply it formally to their decisions until they have developed the habits to apply it *intuitively.*

Decision-making procedure (in the form of questions)

- What are the elements of the most desirable outcome of the decision? (Here the 3Cs requirements can provide a check for completeness.)

- Who, if anyone, should be involved in this decision? When and how should they be involved (see Chapter 1, Additional Insights D, Participation in Decision Making and Planning).

- What alternatives should be considered? (At this point it is often useful to consider all alternatives, even outrageous ones. Keeping an open mind may bring the useful adaptation of some other alternative from a feature of a seemingly useless one. The very act of enumerating possible choices [insisting on at least one or two more than the obvious ones] can generate better solutions. One

3 Insights I Continued

alternative which always deserves consideration is the deliberate postponement of the decision.)

- What information is essential for determining other alternatives and for evaluating alternatives? What information is not essential but desirable (including the "data" about the likely emotional reactions of stakeholders)?

- How should the alternatives be evaluated?

- Which alternative is the most desirable one—the one that should be implemented? (Sometimes even with careful evaluation it is difficult to determine which possible choice is best. Still, the process of evaluation helps sharpen views on which alternatives are clearly *not* likely to achieve the desired outcomes, and which appear to be among the best available.) In seeking to identify the best alternative, evaluation on the basis of the 3Cs guidelines and the four decision-making concepts can be useful.

- Unfortunately, there are often so many uncertainties that even the most careful evaluation will not be able to clearly identify a *best* alternative. That's when personal, intuitive, and emotional preferences and crystal balls have to take up the slack.

Problem-solving procedure

Most steps in problem solving are the same as in other decision making. However, when tackling a problem—a situation where something is not as it should be—a few questions about the problem should precede the decision-making steps. These questions concern:

- What is the problem?

- What are possible causes of the problem?

- Who has knowledge about the development of the problem?

Insights I Continued

Another approach

The educational philosopher John Dewey has suggested an eight-step approach similar to the one suggested here, but omits the step of involving others in the process. It may, however, be useful since it captures, rather neatly, a very effective series of steps. They are:

- Felt difficulty (what motivates concern)
- Diagnosis
- Problem statement
- Specification of alternatives and criteria
- Evaluation of alternatives
- Selection of alternatives
- Implementation
- Evaluation

3 **Additional Insights J**

Interviewing

Be careful of the words you speak
Make them soft and sweet.
You'll never know, from day to day
Which ones you'll have to eat.

Anonymous

After the introduction, this section covers:

- Job and competency requirements
- Information to be obtained
- Applying the 3Cs in interviews
- Communicating during interviews
- Empathy
- In-depth probing
- Applicable laws
- Selecting

Introduction

There are two components to ensuring high-level competence, the second of the 3Cs: ensuring that competent people are selected for open positions and competence development.

Interviewing and selection based on the interviews are key activities in seeing to it that the organizational unit will have the raw material on which to build new competencies which the ever-changing situation may require. Interviewing is covered in this section. Competence development is covered in Chapter 2, Additional Insights G1, Learning Theories and Management of Learning; and G2, Coaching and On-the-Job Instruction.

3   Insights J Continued

While a large share of interviewing and selecting may be performed by the organization's Human Resource department, individual managers/leaders have an important role in the selection process. Unfortunately, most managers have had little, if any, training in obtaining the necessary information during interviews and have to rely heavily on their common sense, on the conclusions of the Human Resources staff, and on the exchange of views with other managers who may also have interviewed a specific candidate.

Interviewing is the information-searching and evaluation process in which the qualifications of each candidate are assessed against the job and competency requirements of the position to:

- Screen for candidates who are qualified to fill the position

- Select from the candidates those who are best qualified

Interviewing is primarily an art. Considerable practice is necessary for mastery. As a general guideline you will undoubtedly keep in mind that a candidate's past behavior can be an important predictor of future behavior. However, focusing and getting an accurate handle on past behavior may not be easy.

As with some of the other competencies for which seminars or courses may not be readily available, brief sessions in staff meetings with managers present good opportunities for discussion and possibly for some practice of this important skill. Concepts that would be useful to cover include the importance of job and competency requirements, information to be obtained, specific fine points about communications during interviews, empathy, in-depth probing, applicable laws, and selecting.

Job and Competency Requirements

Most organizations use the job requirements as outlined in formal existing job descriptions (or as they are in the mind of the interviewer) as the primary guides for interviewing. These descriptions usually list the functions to be performed, the major technical skills, and the reporting relationships.

3 | **Insights J Continued**

More important can be the competency requirements which may be implied by the functions, but which are rarely specifically listed and often not obvious.

Information to Be Obtained

Effective interviews seek information in four major areas of inquiry, with emphasis on these unlisted competencies in addition to specifics about education and functions performed in previous positions. These areas concern both will-do and can-do competencies. They include:

- Ability and willingness related to acquiring new skills and knowledge—how quickly and thoroughly candidates can learn something new and how willing they are to do so. Information about candidates' abilities to learn can be determined from performance in previous learning situations, including college grades and in part from brief learning assignments that can be given to candidates to evaluate their relative abilities to learn.

- Hard data on candidate desire to learn is more difficult to come by, since it is a will-do rather than a can-do matter. Candidates' backgrounds, however, can yield considerable information about the degree to which they have displayed inquisitiveness and the desire for study and for self-improvement.

- Information about ability and willingness to apply what has been learned can be gleaned from the extent to which candidates made use of new information on the job. Probing for topics which candidates did not like in previous training programs may provide clues to the extent to which they were unable or unwilling to accept and apply new ideas and knowledge.

- Personal characteristics—those attributes of candidates, including connecting and cooperating with others, which are so deeply imbedded in their personality that it is unlikely that training and coaching will bring change within a reasonable amount of time. To a large extent, these personal characteristics are the determinants of the will-do competencies. They should be thought of in job-related terms and should concern behaviors that can be observed.

When searching for information about personal characteristics, an interviewer has to observe applicable federal and state laws and regulations by being careful not to extend the list of personal characteristics beyond those which are necessary for successful performance of job responsibilities.

- Thinking in terms of knowledge and skills which transfer easily from past experience is important but not crucial, especially if the candidate can learn fast. Previously acquired competence merely provides a headstart for training. (Here a knowledge/skill profile of the position, as discussed in Chapter 2, Additional Insights G1, Learning Theories and Management of Learning, may be useful.)

Applying the 3Cs in Interviews

The 3Cs guidelines can help by providing structure to an interview.

1. When thinking of the way candidates exercise Control, it is useful to ask questions that show what participation means to them and how they practice it when making decisions. This applies to candidates for nonmanagerial positions, too. Similarly it is worthwhile to ask questions that provide insights into how focused the candidates were on the goals they strove for in previous positions, at what they consider their career direction, and what steps they are taking in supporting the direction.

Information about the work habits and values of the candidates should also be obtained and evaluated in light of their career plans and performance in previous positions. The way they coped

3 Insights J Continued

with conflicts of ideas, and with people, is another element that might be worthwhile to explore with candidates.

2. Competence in skills needed for the vacant position is easier to measure and evaluate. However, ability and willingness to learn, and to apply what has been learned, is likely to be more important than specific knowledge or skills. These attributes support the organization's and the individual's need for competence more so than immediately useful capabilities. This is especially true in organizations where significant change is part of the environment.

3. Finally, Climate is also important. It is highly desirable to attempt to determine the expectations of candidates for psychological and tangible rewards, their work-related stress tolerance level, and their willingness to contribute to the general climate of the organization.

Communicating during Interviews

In addition to a good procedure and effective plans to obtain accurate and complete information, success in interviews rests on competent interpersonal skills to gain the candidate's confidence. These skills include:

- Creating a positive climate which will reduce stress on candidates

- Effective use of questions and silence for general and in-depth probing

During all contacts with applicants it is desirable to create a professional atmosphere that puts them at ease so that questions will be answered truthfully, without apprehension.

Interviews are highly stressful situations for applicants. An interviewer can help reduce the stress level for them by giving the interview a conversational tone rather than making it seem like an interrogation. By being relaxed and by probing competently, an interviewer will help to put the interviewee at ease.

3 Insights J Continued

Empathy

Conveying honest empathy with the candidates' situations and needs is an even more effective way to reduce the tension for interviewees and will help to enhance mutual understanding and trust. Allowing candidates to first ask questions about the position can show such interest.

In-Depth Probing

Probing (as discussed in Chapter 2, Additional Insights H, Communications Theories, Techniques, and Skills) can be used to conduct an in-depth examination of subjects in which candidates claim to be knowledgeable. Even an interviewer who is not familiar with the subject under examination can use such in-depth probing to evaluate:

- Depth of knowledge of the specific subject
- Candidate's perception of their depth of knowledge
- Credibility of explanations
- Ability to organize
- Ability to verbalize

In-depth probing is primarily useful to gain information on depth of knowledge of a topic. An equally thorough approach, probing on details of job history or personal characteristics, could quickly become overly inquisitive and be resented by applicants. When the technique is used skillfully to gain information on a technical topic, an interviewer can make applicants feel that they are providing information of interest to the interviewer.

The technique consists of first asking general questions and then increasingly more specific questions on smaller and smaller segments of the topic, until the limits of the candidate's knowledge have been reached.

Even if such a series of questions is softened through careful choice of words, if too many are asked while using the discovery

3   Insights J Continued

probing process, without intervening discussion, candidates may perceive probing as an interrogation and feel increasing stress. However, if interviewers show genuine interest, this interest will be reflected in the nonverbals and the candidate will not perceive a large number of questions as an interrogation, but rather as evidence of real interest in the subject.

Applicable Laws

Interviewers should be aware of the relevant specifics of federal and state EEO laws and regulations to ensure compliance with them.

Selecting

Beyond interviews, competent analysis and evaluation of the information obtained during interviews is necessary for deciding which candidates satisfy requirements, and who is the most desirable candidate for a specific vacancy. This selection process, if based on competent interview data obtained by more than one interviewer, can assure successful selection.

Performance Evaluation

Organizations can ill afford
To let injustice be ignored,
Though it may cause them some surprise
To find where fairness really lies.

Principles of Economic Policy, Chapter 4
Kenneth Boulding (Adapted)

After the introduction, this section will cover:

- Benefits of performance evaluation

- Obstacles to performance evaluation

- Requirements for effective performance evaluation

- Performance evaluations and trust

Introduction

Performance evaluation and recognition share the designation of *Additional Insights K* because effective performance evaluation requires fairly frequent performance feedback. Competent actions in showing appreciation for staff member contributions (recognition) provide such frequent feedback and add greatly to another aspect of sound performance evaluation: they bring some practical outcome—satisfying moments for the staff member (see Additional Insights K2, Providing Recognition).

Benefits of Performance Evaluation

Effective performance evaluation improves performance and quality of work life. In addition, it promotes:

- Better control, though not necessarily tighter control, over the organizational unit's activities

3 Insights K1 Continued

- More competent staff members because performance evaluation provides a sound platform for their development

- More appropriate personnel actions

- Compliance with regulations pertaining to equal employment opportunity

Improved performance and higher quality of work life

Performance evaluation can improve quality of work life if it brings to staff members:

- More recognition for their accomplishments

- More information about how their performance is seen by their managers

- More help with improving their performance

- Guidance on how they can gain greater competence for their current jobs, and to further their careers

- Greater knowledge of the criteria by which they are judged

Performance evaluation achieves improved performance for many of the same reasons and because it ensures that staff members understand clearly what needs to be done and how it is to their benefit to strive for superior performance. In some organizations, it also ensures that thorough documentation of performance deficiencies is available when needed, for developmental purposes and to prevent continuation of performance problems.

Better control

Many managers often equate tighter controls with better control. Still, they are aware that their ability to keep tabs on everything that happens is sharply limited by the available time. Managers who think that way and try to achieve tight personal control often overlook the fact that close supervision is resented, especially by the more capable people, and does very little to encourage development of greater competence by the others.

Soundly administered performance evaluation helps to achieve better control by relying on a system of reviews and by providing regular feedback. It gives staff members freedom, but it clearly identifies limits within which this freedom may be exercised. Experienced and competent staff members are given wider limits than those who are new or less competent (see Chapter 1, Additional Insights D, Participation in Decision Making and Planning).

By establishing and revising limits, and by setting project review periods, managers/leaders are adequately involved in the control process. At the same time, they can provide recognition and positive feedback but also exercise discipline when necessary. Better control, when understood and practiced as a joint activity, will lead to higher levels of competence and performance, and greater work satisfaction for staff members.

More competent staff members and a sound foundation for competence development

A performance evaluation system will provide greatest benefits if it is clear that its primary emphasis is on competence development. A major step in performance evaluation should therefore be the development of a competence-enhancement plan for each staff member. When appropriate, this plan might reinforce steps considered during performance and career counseling activities.

The improvement plan may also include additional coaching. Performance evaluation thus serves to encourage staff members to enhance their skills for their current positions, and to prepare themselves for other desired positions which might become available.

More appropriate personnel actions

Effective performance evaluation can be relied on to provide valid information about the performance and capabilities of staff members. It thus establishes a more solid foundation for personnel actions on compensation and promotion.

3 Insights K1 Continued

Competently administered performance evaluations can also reduce staff member complaints by uncovering dissatisfactions when they are still relatively easy to resolve. At the same time a suggestion system might be enlivened, and open communications are strengthened.

Compliance with regulations

There are many federal and state laws and regulations that affect personnel actions. They are intended to ensure equal employment opportunities, prevent discrimination, and provide the employee with protection against harsh and arbitrary personnel actions.

Thorough performance evaluation practically ensures compliance with laws and regulations. Discrimination is nearly impossible if personnel actions are based primarily on factual performance data, collected over time.

Obstacles to Performance Evaluation

Despite the compelling case in favor of thorough performance evaluation, there are voices recommending their complete abolishment (Deming 1986). The reason lies with some significant obstacles to competent and fair administration which frequently lead to problems that more than offset the benefits (Meyer et al. 1965; Rausch 1985). By taking these obstacles into account, you can minimize their effect:

- Few organizations have soundly designed performance evaluation systems that satisfy all the requirements listed under "Requirements for Effective Performance Evaluation" on page 223. Many impose counterproductive complex procedures and documentation. They emphasize ratings rather than competence development. They fail to rely primarily on relatively lean procedures and thorough development of management/leadership skills for implementing fair, meaningful performance assessments. You can compensate for these by staying focused on competence development and on opportunities for providing recognition.

- When ratings are required, it is difficult to prevent differences in ratings between different departments. Here, too, you can minimize the problem through communications with the other department managers and your own staff.

- Managers/leaders need very high evaluation skills. These are difficult to establish and maintain on an organization-wide basis. This is especially true since serious, compassionate, but tough-minded implementation of performance evaluation makes it necessary to cope with touchy situations and difficult decisions. From your perspective it would be best to work on enhancing your own competence, and to use your influence to seek consideration for organization-wide development programs.

- It is easy to be generous when trying to be as fair as possible. However, generosity toward one staff member may result in unfairness or be perceived as unfair or as favoritism by others. It is difficult to maintain balance. You can, however, achieve a fine batting average if you keep in mind how important perceptions are. It is not good enough that you know that you are fair. It is equally important to ensure that you are perceived as fair. To do your best, you must devote the thought, and effort, to ensure that your actions are fully justified, and that you can explain them to any staff members who compare, or appear to compare, their ratings to those of others.

- Because results are so important, it would, theoretically, be most desirable to base performance evaluation almost solely on results—on goal achievement or on goals and on the quality and quantity of effort devoted to achieve the goals.

  Rating solely on the basis of goal achievement could be unfair, however, because staff members might be evaluated

3 **Insights K1 Continued**

on matters not fully under their control. Hence a sound evaluation system will use goals as guidelines, but place emphasis on the staff member actions to achieve goals and on other important activities on which goals have not been set. Thus the process evaluates the quality and quantity of the effort that staff members devote to goal achievement and to performing *all* other functions of the job. (Understanding and following the approach suggested in Chapter 2, Additional Insights E, Making a Goals Program Work, will minimize this problem or avoid it entirely.)

- Few organizations have taken the tough step of setting up formal appeals procedures that are thoroughly understood by all staff members. If there is no such procedure in your organization, you might be able to set up an informal one in your organizational unit, using competent members of your staff (see Chapter 2, Additional Insights F, Managing Potentially Damaging Conflict).

- Independent reviews of evaluations by other managers are often very difficult to arrange because it may not be easy to find a manager who has sufficient independent, detailed knowledge of the evaluated staff member's work to provide a fair review of the primary evaluation.

Requirements for Effective Performance Evaluation

Requirements of effective performance evaluation (adapted from Rausch, Erwin. 1985. *Win-Win Performance Management/Appraisal.* New York: John Wiley & Sons and Challenge: Performance Evaluations, *The TQM Magazine.* Vol. 8, No. 4, July/August 1996, pp. 71–72).

Fairness

The system is fair, overall, by being thorough, accurate, factual, and meaningful; by satisfying needs; and by offering an opportunity for appeals. To be fair, it should satisfy the requirements following:

3   Insights K1 Continued

Thoroughness

- Performance of all staff members is measured similarly

- Evaluations measure all responsibilities

- Evaluations measure performance for the entire period

Accuracy and factualness

- Standards cover all responsibilities

- Standards are accurate and factual

- There is little or no ambiguity

- Evaluations are comparable between evaluators

- Evaluations are reviewed by at least one manager who has detailed independent knowledge of the evaluated staff member's work, or by an equivalently independent source

- An appeals procedure exists

Meaningfulness

- Standards and evaluations consider the importance of each function

- Standards and evaluations attempt to measure primarily matters under the control of the staff member

- Evaluations occur at regular intervals or at appropriate moments

- Managers/leaders continue to improve skills in applying the requirements for effective evaluation

- Evaluation results are used for important personnel decisions, especially those that pertain to consideration during selection of candidates for vacant positions that might be of interest to staff members

3   Insights K1 Continued

Satisfaction of needs

- Standards are communicated in advance
- Staff members are kept informed about their performance
- Communications are factual, open, and honest
- Standards are challenging but realistic
- Staff members are directly or indirectly involved in the setting of standards and in the evaluations
- Evaluations consider the adequacy of the manager's support
- Evaluations emphasize competence development

Performance Evaluations and Trust

Performance evaluations are probably the most difficult of all managerial/leadership tasks. Sound and fair assessments, while not critical to Competence, do stimulate motivation for specific learning and skill development, and thus impact Competence. Much more important, however, are their critical roles in Control and coordination, and their vital roles in helping to shape a positive Climate.

Only considerable mutual trust built on honest and open communications will bridge the many potentials for serious conflict of perceptions and basic interests. Unfortunately, trust is not easy to achieve, especially for a manager/leader who does not have exceptional talent for communicating (and thus cannot demonstrate the rare quality of charismatic leadership.)

What then are some of the thoughts that you can consider to lay the groundwork for full acceptance of performance evaluations?

1. Performance evaluations are not a once-a-year thing, to do when the policy calls for turning in evaluations. They are part of the continuous process of keeping staff members informed about their performance, in comparison to standards that have been mutually agreed on. That takes a lot of honest, open talk frequently throughout the year. It takes the willingness to hold at least monthly progress discussions in which expectations, of both sides, are laid on the table and where differences are hammered out amicably, the way any conflict should be resolved. So, you might frequently ask yourself whether the priority you give to communicating on performance is high enough.

2. Dissatisfactions about a staff member's performance need to be brought out in the open. You might ask yourself regularly whether you are being honest in bringing up and discussing performance problems. Do you take the initiative to call it as, and when, you see it, or do you keep quiet and hope the problem will go away? Do you then offer and/or provide the support the staff member may need? Do you know what the staff member thinks he or she needs?

3. What is being done, and what are you doing about expectations for performance ratings that may be unrealistically high? What if a manager in another department rates too leniently? What if a large proportion of the staff members really perform well above what the organization has a reasonable right to expect? These are not easy questions. They need to be raised and addressed in honest, open, sound communications with the people above, as well as with the members of the staff.

4. What is being done, and what are you doing to see to it that performance evaluations, especially favorable ones, are used for personnel decisions, including those pertaining to compensation and to consideration for vacant positions of interest to the respective staff member?

3 Additional Insights K2

Providing Recognition*

Blow, blow, thou winter wind
Thou art not so unkind
As man's ingratitude.

As You Like It, Act II, William Shakespeare

After the introduction, this section will cover:

- Noticing achievements
- Types of achievements
- Showing appreciation for staff member contributions and accomplishments
- Manager concerns about showing appreciation
- Ideas for providing signs of appreciation and awards

Introduction

As was pointed out in the beginning of Additional Insights K1, Performance Evaluation, competent actions in showing appreciation for staff member contributions (recognition) provide frequent feedback and add greatly to sound performance evaluation: they bring some practical outcome—satisfying moments for the staff member. These moments, at least partially, balance the many negatives in the workplace—the dissatisfying moments that come

---

*Recognition, though it is a popular word and will be used here for lack of a fully meaningful one, is not really appropriate because it implies an audience and hints at an outstanding accomplishment. There is no single word that conveys the expression of appreciation for all contributions, including the nonspectacular but consistent ones, which are so important to staff member satisfaction.

3 | **Insights K2 Continued**

from monotonous or disliked tasks, errors, new restrictions, tight budgets, and conflicts.

Expressing appreciation for the contributions of staff members is the primary way for most managers/leaders to work toward achieving the Climate requirement for an effective, successful organizational unit. Two skills and abilities are required:

• Recognizing opportunities for showing appreciation

• Using appropriate techniques for showing appreciation

Both were discussed fairly thoroughly in Scenario 2.3, The Case of an Insufficiently Appreciated Staff Member.

Rewarding the members of your team for both their visible and their less-obvious accomplishments is one important road to greater mutual trust and confidence. Show your people that you appreciate what they are doing, that you recognize the effort and thought they are devoting to making your team successful, and they will have greater confidence in you. Your work life will be enriched by the pleasure you will gain from showing appreciation and giving out awards, from better mutual understanding, and by helping them grow.

As manager/leader you can reward the members of your team with more than just competitive incomes and benefits. You can help them enjoy a richer, more rewarding work life by providing more frequent satisfying moments which balance the negative feelings resulting from the avalanche of problems, conflicts, challenges, and frustrations inherent in everyday work life. To accomplish that goal, you have to:

• Identify achievements

• Use the many ways available to you for showing your appreciation

First, a word of caution: providing evidence of appreciation for staff member contributions should not be attempted as a device to manipulate them to work harder. Many staff members are skepti-

3   **Insights K2 Continued**

cal of *recognition* programs. Though they are inevitably pleased when appreciation is shown for one of their contributions, they can easily become cynical if they suspect that the purpose of showing appreciation is to manipulate them to greater effort.

Sincere, competently directed evidence of appreciation will, nevertheless, undoubtedly lead to a more efficient team. Additional achievement may come in improved teamwork, better quality, greater attention to detail, better methods (smarter ways of doing the work), and widespread willingness by staff members to overlook, or downplay, the many annoyances that are unavoidable.

If you are perceived as insincere or as using superficial signs of appreciation to manipulate people, then relatively little is gained from showing appreciation. That is why competence in identifying staff member contributions and in applying the many possible ways to recognize staff members is so important.

Noticing Achievements

Anybody can notice the outstanding, unusual contribution. Managers rarely have a tough time identifying the best performers in any activity and let those staff members know (at least once in a while) that they consider them tops in that respect.

What about the second best, or even the third best? What if they are all good, even though not as good as the best? How likely is it that managers will notice them and show some outward signs that they appreciate the contributions?

Managers need to identify the areas where each staff member's unique contributions are. Following is a partial list of functions, activities, and staff member characteristics that can help. It is by no means complete and you should be able to extend the list to make it appropriate for your people. Moreover, during any one time period, you can emphasize those items which focus on one or more activities that you want to stress; for example, quality, safety, attendance, or customer relations.

3   Insights K2 Continued

*Types of Achievements**

1. Activities applicable to most work environments include:
   - Planning
   - Meeting deadlines
   - Safety and use of safe practices
   - Quantity of work
   - Accuracy and quality of work
   - Suggestions to improve the way work is done
   - Skill in handling stressful situations
   - Skill in handling routine tasks and nonroutine assignments
   - Avoidance of waste and spoilage
   - Activities involved in housekeeping and maintaining appropriate work-area appearance
   - Caring for equipment
   - Use of space
   - Accuracy in record keeping
   - Factualness and accuracy in communicating information

2. Secretarial and administrative activities
   - Typing, filing, transmitting messages, scheduling meetings, keeping logs and records

3. Retail activities
   - Greeting customers, identifying customer interests and needs, politeness, appropriateness of suggestions when a specific item is not in stock

---

*See also Didactic Systems, 1977, *Providing Recognition: A Handbook.*

3 Insights K2 Continued

- Communicating with customers
- Knowledge of stock and prices
- Stocking
- Pricing
- Cash register competence
- Administrative activities

4. Financial and information systems activities

- Recording, arranging, and analyzing data
- Activities related to budgets, financial and data recording systems
- Modifying or recommending a modification in a system
- Preparation of reports
- Computer programming and troubleshooting

5. Manufacturing, processing, and service activities

- Use of equipment and materials
- Use of techniques and methods
- Greeting customers, identifying their interests and needs, politeness, appropriateness of suggestions when a specific item is not in stock or a specific service not available
- Communicating with customers
- Knowledge of services, products, stock, and prices
- Handling customer complaints
- Administrative activities
- Budget development and implementation
- Preparation of reports

6. Research and development activities
   - Design of experiments and studies
   - Collecting, recording, and analyzing data
   - Use of equipment and materials
   - Budget development and implementation
   - Preparation of reports and papers

7. Health care activities
   - Empathy with pain, loneliness, apprehension, and fear
   - Sensitivity to patient needs
   - Ability to reassure patients
   - Ability to accept unreasonable requests or behavior from patient or patient's family
   - Ability to relate to patient's family members
   - Care in various aspects of physical handling of patient
   - Accuracy in maintaining patient records

8. Activities in interpersonal relations
   - Cooperation and teamwork
   - Assisting others
   - Verbal expression
   - Effective use of questions
   - Presentation before a group
   - Serving as a role model
   - Listening
   - Contributing at meetings
   - Conduct in controversies
   - Written communications (memos, letters, proposals)

3 | Insights K2 Continued

9. Personal characteristics

- Attendance and punctuality
- Reliability in achieving results
- Being available
- Meeting commitments
- Sound decision making
- High personal standards (quality, quantity, reliability, dependability)
- Cheerfulness
- Creativity, innovation, and imagination
- Incisiveness
- Acceptance of and ability to cope with pressure
- Empathy
- Helping to prevent and resolve conflict
- Helping to ensure open communications
- Showing the positive when others show dissatisfactions

Showing Appreciation for Staff Member Contributions and Accomplishments

That's the hardest part for most managers/leaders. Most are good at saying *thanks*, paying personal compliments, talking about family matters, and joking about sports. They can say *that's great* when a staff member reports some accomplishment that is pleasant to hear, that is needed for some project, or that they sense the staff member is proud of.

In a more significant vein, some managers show their high regard for the members of their teams in a variety of ways: by taking their suggestions seriously, by asking for their opinions, and by consulting with them on many decisions. Whenever possible,

3 Insights K2 Continued

these managers will share information they obtain about what is going on inside and outside the organization.

By blurring the distinctions between the job of the manager and the jobs of the other team members, competent managers create a highly positive climate in which each member of the team can feel secure and wanted.

Still, most managers neglect the opportunity to enrich the work day for their people by regularly showing evidence of their appreciation for the positive things the members of their team contribute.

Manager Concerns about Showing Appreciation

There are at least five reasons why so little attention is paid to this important need:

- Managers are not aware of the many benefits such attention could bring.

- Their organizations don't provide the necessary support.

- Managers are concerned that they might be perceived as showing favoritism if they then fail to show appreciation for someone else's contribution.

- Managers think that they don't have the time.

- Managers haven't developed the skills and habits needed to show appreciation for many of the valuable contributions by team members.

Let's look at these reasons more closely.

The benefits

The benefits can be really significant, both in their immediate and delayed effects. The immediate effect is a pleasant moment for at least one staff member. Pleasant moments can have contagious effects, reinforcing each other throughout an organization, creating a constantly strengthening positive climate.

3 Insights K2 Continued

There are many probable overtones to these multiplying effects that develop when staff members know that their manager appreciates their contributions:

- Staff members are more likely to feel good about their work, and they are then challenged to do at least as well in the future. They will want to continue to deserve high regard, and any extra attention to their work that they may contribute is hardly felt because the sign of appreciation has made the work a little more pleasant.

- Staff members feel more confident in coming forward with suggestions. Action on these suggestions further strengthens the positive bond between staff member and manager, while bringing a direct benefit in effectiveness, quality, safety, or customer relations.

- Staff members develop better understanding of the manager's views and are more comfortable and secure as a result of increased trust.

- When the manager involves other departments by extending the signs of appreciation to the members of these other departments, interdepartmental conflicts are less likely. Reciprocating actions by managers and members of other departments add further positive moments.

- Sometimes, managers can involve clients, customers, a patient's family members, or other "outsiders" with similar results in improved relations.

Even when the climate is healthy, it gradually improves, and better mutual understanding between managers and other staff members strengthens.

Some of these benefits may not come immediately when a manager begins to show more frequent signs of appreciation. They will surely come if the manager is sincere, develops skills for recognizing the wide range of performance and personality strengths, makes full use of the many ways to show appreciation, *and perseveres.*

3 Insights K2 Continued

Organizational support

Organizational support can certainly make it easier to provide meaningful recognition. Still, strong, competent managers can accomplish much, even without organizational support, by making effective use of the many psychological awards that are always available. They cannot, however, do nearly as much alone as they can do with upper management's backing.

When the entire organization is actively involved, top management commitment and full endorsement intensify the value of the recognition. Equally, or possibly more important, it supplies funds for tangible awards, which managers can use in addition to the psychological ones. Organization support also furthers uniform actions in all departments.

Concern about showing favoritism

This concern, though possibly valid, is not a good reason for showing less appreciation for contributions than could be shown. If you show appreciation regularly and sincerely, staff members will give you credit for the effort and are not likely to quibble with what they realize may be an unfair perception of favoritism. Benefits greatly outweigh this possible minor dissatisfaction by one individual. As with most of your actions, it's the batting average that counts.

Not enough time for this additional responsibility

Even if providing signs of appreciation were an additional responsibility and were to require additional time, the benefits would make such time highly productive. That this activity needs significant chunks of time, however, is probably due to some misconception. Award meetings are not the important issue—chances are that they take place already. If they don't, and time is really too tight, they won't be missed much if a manager effectively uses other approaches. Saying something about the work that is pleasant hardly takes any time. Even short handwritten notes take

3 Insights K2 Continued

hardly any time. These two, however, are the place where *the tire meets the road*—this is where the beneficial action is.

Inadequate skills and habits

As Scenario 2.3 has shown, there may be a small investment of time in getting started, but thereafter the sharpening of the two skills—identifying contributions and using many different ways to show appreciation—comes naturally. The following guidelines may help.

*Ideas for Providing Signs of Appreciation and Awards**

There are four groups of ideas for showing appreciation of staff member accomplishments. They involve nontangible (psychological), semitangible, and tangible signs of appreciation and frequency.

Offering nontangible (psychological) signs of appreciation

There are many ways for saying thanks, at several levels of seriousness and emphasis. At one extreme is simply saying *thank you* for a task the staff member completed, possibly with different words like *that's great*. A pleased expression, a friendly wave of the hand, or even a pat on the arm or shoulder or a handshake (if it comes naturally), when added to the words, raises the level of the gesture.

Paying personal compliments, talking about family matters, and joking about sports, TV, or social events are similar, yet less relevant and more general ways of showing that the staff members' contributions are appreciated.

The list of verbal expressions of appreciation on page 238 provides the seeds for many basic ways to show appreciation in nontangible ways. The first items are relatively mild and the last are the strongest. The list is not exhaustive, nor are the items

---

*See also Didactic Systems, 1977, *Providing Recognition: A Handbook.*

mutually exclusive; most can be used in conjunction with one or more of the others.

More important, there are no unique items in the list. You have undoubtedly used every one, either frequently or on occasion. The purpose in providing the list is to supply a reference that will make it easier for you to use these simple means of showing appreciation more frequently, and possibly more consistently.

Verbal expressions of appreciation—either spoken or informal notes (these are also listed in Scenario 2.3, The Case of an Insufficiently Appreciated Staff Member):

- Pointing to the importance of a specific accomplishment

- Indicating awareness of an accomplishment that came to your attention without the staff member's knowledge

- Offering help with an assignment

- Asking for an explanation of how a difficult task was accomplished

- Distinguishing the *thanks* from routine acknowledgements by setting them deliberately into a different place or time, such as your office, in front of other staff members or staff members from other department(s) informally, or even formally in front of some or all members of the team, and so on.

- Asking for ideas and suggestions

- Asking for the staff member's opinion on one of your ideas or of ideas and suggestions from others

- Promptly providing information on occurrences affecting the team

- Arranging for members, or the manager, of another department to provide any of the items above

- Arranging for a higher-level manager to provide any of the items above

3

- Arranging, through verbal or written requests, for customers or members of the public with whom a staff member may be in regular contact to provide any of the items above

- Including a staff member in the list of those to whom management/leadership tasks (that the staff member can perform) are delegated, such as leading a meeting in your absence or taking your place at an interdepartmental meeting you cannot attend

- Initiating career counseling and responding effectively to questions on career opportunities

- Giving full consideration to staff members during the selection of candidates for vacant positions

- Helping staff members acquire skills that might be useful for positions up the career ladder (through developmental assignments or a training program)

- Taking the staff member into your confidence on an event or a decision not yet public knowledge

- Promptly implementing a suggestion or idea

- Consulting regularly with a staff member who has the knowledge or experience to contribute effectively

These techniques blur the line between the work of the manager and the functions of other team members. They create a highly positive work climate that adds many pleasant moments to the work day for team members and for the manager.

You have full control over your nontangible signs of appreciation. You also have considerable control over those that come from higher-level managers since they are not likely to refuse a request from you to say something positive to one or several members of your team.

Help from other departments should also not be difficult to obtain, especially if you are willing to reciprocate. All it might take is for you and for some members of your team to show appreciation for achievements of members of the other departments when these accomplishments favorably impact your team. If you want to be even more certain of cooperation, you can reach an informal agreement with the manager of the other department.

Gaining help from customers and/or other members of the public is not as easy, of course, but it can sometimes be stimulated, especially when your staff member has performed a service that is appreciated by the person. You can directly ask that person to send a note, thanking the staff member. Word can also go out that says, in effect: "When something is not what you expected, let me know; when everything is OK, let the person know with whom you have been in contact." If sent frequently, a message like this might bring some results.

Providing semitangible signs of appreciation

Semitangible signs are of three main types

- Memos and letters
- Certificates and plaques
- Trophies

Memos and letters can stem from the same sources as non-tangible signs of appreciation. You have full control over the memos and letters that come from you. You also have considerable control over those that come from the higher-level managers, and you can make arrangements with other departments to ensure their cooperation. Memos and letters from outsiders can also be stimulated.

Certificates and plaques are most appropriate for departmental accomplishments on formal programs such as *Most Days without Accident, Most Days without Absences,* or *Most Units without Defects* or other team awards on various goals like quality, service, or safety.

For individual accomplishments they are appropriate for programs such as *Staff Member of the Week/Month/Year* and for more

3 Insights K2 Continued

specific accomplishments, in some environments, especially those where customers or members of the public can see them.

Certificates and plaques are best for staff members who have their own offices or private spaces where they could be displayed. They can sometimes be mounted in a central, highly visible area together with all other recent ones.

Even more important is the climate. In all likelihood, certificates will only be appreciated in an environment where staff members are proud of them and actually want to display them.

Trophies are similar to plaques. They lend themselves best to departmental accomplishments. For presentations to individuals, the environment must be one in which staff members are proud of such evidence of appreciation and will actually display them.

Providing tangible signs of appreciation

There are many types of tangible signs of appreciation in each of these major groups:

- Salary increases

- Bonuses

- Monetary awards

- Merchandise and travel awards

Decisions on the compensation structure that controls the salary increases and bonuses must balance many factors (Rausch 1978, 240–242). These considerations are primarily functional issues for managers in human resources management compensation departments.

Your involvement in tangible rewards is in two areas:

- In your role in allocating any salary and bonus budgets to your staff members. Here is where you face the difficult task of tying performance evaluation to personnel actions. Unfortunately there are few guidelines that you can follow, beyond those that are discussed under performance evaluation in this section. However, these tangible rewards are usually communicated only to the recipients, or are given as checks, without fanfare.

- The situation is different with monetary, and monetary equivalent, achievement awards (merchandise and travel, or points which can be collected and then exchanged for these). These are usually presented at staff meetings and how you conduct such meetings can make a difference to the climate.

Awards meetings are for giving out awards, of course. That can be: "We are gathered here to honor . . .," and so on. Your meeting will be better, though, if you make it fun for everyone—for those who get the awards and for those who don't.

In order for your meetings to strengthen team spirit, add to the motivational climate, and enhance your image among the employees, there are two things you can do. The first one is the most important:

- Communicate your appreciation to the recipients and to those who are not getting awards
- Mix some fun with the serious stuff

The second one is not easy, of course, except if you happen to be a great entertainer or if some members of your staff have such talent and are willing to display it. Most likely, you will have to scratch a little harder, and possibly use budget for entertainment and refreshments.

The first one can be easier, especially if you keep in mind that those in attendance who are not receiving an award are your more important audience—the others are probably happy anyhow. Here are some suggestions to ensure a satisfying experience for the former:

- Carefully explain the reasons for the awards. That will add value for the recipients. At the same time it will go a long

3 Insights K2 Continued

way to reduce or eliminate the "why not me—why never me?" feeling that you can be sure is shared by some of the people at the meeting.

- Have a higher-level manager open the meeting with a few words of thanks to the entire group. If the manager does not plan to stay for the actual distribution of the awards, he or she should express special thanks to the award recipients.

- If you did not recently cover them in other departmental meetings, briefly report on progress, departmental accomplishments, and challenges.

- Explain carefully why and how the recipients were chosen. The more you can say about the *why* the better. If others have performed almost as well as the recipients, acknowledge them. Express the hope that they will be recipients in the future.

- Acknowledge that the accomplishments being rewarded are only some of the contributions that members of your team have made during the past period.

- Try to give credit for other, less-visible contributions.

Ensuring that neither too few nor too many instances of the various types of evidence of appreciation for achievements are shown

Numbers are important for both nontangible and tangible rewards. Too few is obviously not desirable. Too many of either, or both, can lessen their impact and value.

There are no hard and fast rules to follow in showing nontangible appreciation for achievements. One instance, once a week on average or even more is OK, while once every other month is undoubtedly too little.

3 Insights K2 Continued

Summary

Ten Steps for Showing Appreciation of Accomplishments

1. Provide informal acknowledgements as soon as you become aware of a deserving accomplishment.

2. Set aside a few moments each week to write down what accomplishments of staff members deserve notice beyond the oral acknowledgement already provided.

3. Add these to the list from any previous week since the last presentation of awards. List all significant and outstanding acknowledgements and any ongoing important contributions that would go unnoticed without the preparation (and availability) of your list.

   Consider all activities that enhance departmental or organizational performance:

   - General activities

   - Activities specific to the staff member's work

   - Activities in interpersonal relations

   - Personal characteristics

   Do not make the list overly long and review the lists of previous months to avoid duplication.

4. Decide on the level of appreciation you might consider for each specific accomplishment.

5. Act on the verbal and written signs of appreciation that you want to use.

6. Where applicable, enlist the aid of higher-level managers and managers in other departments for oral and written signs of appreciation.

3

7. Where applicable, review what additional steps can be taken to gain cooperation from customers or members of the public, and implement these steps.

8. Prior to each award presentation, make final decisions on specific signs of appreciation to award.

9. Conduct an informal presentation ceremony fairly regularly. Make the annual and semiannual presentations more formal and include the tangible awards.

10. At every ceremony, think of those who do not receive an award and focus your remarks on them in such a way that they, too, will gain satisfaction from the session.

The 3Cs of Management/Leadership and the Linking Elements Concept

Introduction

This chapter elaborates on the brief introduction of the 3Cs model in Chapter 1. The model provides a way to look at how managerial/leadership decisions can be enhanced. It is considerably more promising than management development programs that have preceded it (see Chapter 4, Additional Insights N, Management Development Programs: Hopes, Disappointments, and Status). The guidelines derived from the model permit you to become a more effective leader, even though you continue to live in the culture of your organization. By applying the guidelines to your decisions, supported by an understanding of the 3Cs—Control, Competence, and Climate (and the other aspects of linking elements)—you can strengthen the positives in the organizational culture. At the same time you can insulate your staff members, as well as possible, from the negatives.

The primary purpose of this chapter is to offer the conceptual underpinnings for the guidelines. As has been pointed out in various places, guidelines based on the 3Cs can probably fit your managerial and leadership style quite well. However, if you are not fully comfortable with some, you can gain ideas for developing your own from the model presented here.

You are familiar with the first part of the chapter's title, *The 3Cs of Management/Leadership*. It is descriptive. It emphasizes that, for effective performance, an organization needs *Control* and *Competence,* and it must provide a satisfactory *Climate* for the people who make up the organization.

The second part of the title, *Linking Elements Concept,* is more functional than descriptive. It considers that the individuals in an organization may have strong views about the policies, procedures, and norms which define how the organization exercises *Control* over its activities. It also dramatizes that an organization can be effective only if it possesses the necessary *Competence* for the tasks that have to be performed. This competence is the sum of the competencies of all of its staff members. Finally, an organization needs a *Climate* that is sufficiently satisfying, or motivating, so that the members of the organization will not desert it or rebel against it.

The model thus shines the spotlight on the *linking elements,* the managerial and leadership decision making skills, which can bring closer alignment between:

- The Control needs of the organizational unit and the attitudes of its people toward the policies, procedures, and norms shape the way in which control is exercised

- The Competence needs of a task or of the organizational unit and the knowledge, skills, and abilities (KSAs, or competencies) of the individuals in the unit

- The Climate that the individuals in the unit expect and the Climate that the organizational unit currently supplies

In summary, the 3Cs (Control, Competence, and Climate) are the needs and characteristics of the organization and of its members. The linking elements are the managerial and leadership skills. They are the adhesive that can bind the unit and its members into a powerful, purposeful, and coordinated whole, or can leave them weak and ineffectual in the face of the opportunities, challenges, and problems which they confront.

The idea is not new, of course, that the manager of an organizational unit links the unit to the larger organization of which it is a part. It has been expressed well by Rensis Likert in his widely known *New Patterns of Management* (1961). However, Likert described the situation and the dilemma of the person in the middle, but did not offer any significant suggestions on how to cope with the challenges. In effect, he left the manager with the thought: "You're it—good luck." The guidelines derived from the linking elements model, while not prescriptive, do provide considerable foundations for useful managerial/leadership initiatives.

Linking elements do not suggest complex routines and procedures, such as job enrichment or dramatic changes in the manager's style. Instead they show how decisions, on establishing direction toward greater accomplishment, and satisfying the requirements for getting there, can be made with more thorough consideration of all relevant issues.

In many instances participants in management development programs and consulting clients who were about to make an important decision were asked to first decide on their preferred course of action. They were then shown how to apply 3Cs guideline questions to their individual decisions. In almost every instance, evaluating the impact of the preferred course of action on each of the 3Cs brought a slightly, or significantly better, course of action than originally contemplated.

The Linking Elements Model

Figure 4.1 describes the 3Cs of management/leadership in greater detail than the skeleton diagram in Chapter 1. In a more formal way the diagram is also the *linking elements concept* because it provides guidance on how a manager/leader can best act as a catalyst in shaping a cooperative, smoothly running, effective team from the resources of the organization and those of its members or employees. The term *linking* is used because the manager's job is to *link* the needs and also the characteristics of staff members and of the organization.

The 3Cs of management/leadership and linking elements are based on the fundamental truth that an organizational unit will achieve the highest level of performance that its environment permits if its manager/leader can bring a high level of alignment between the characteristics and needs of the unit and the characteristics and needs of the people in it.

The model is based on an assumption that is probably obvious—an organization or an organizational unit, whether in the public or in the private sector, part of a small or a large organization, wants to achieve a high level of performance, whatever meaning the word *performance* has for the unit. For business organizations, for instance, performance might be in terms of product or service quality; return to stockholders; growth and stability; and quality as an employer, customer, and member of the community and of society at large.

Figure 4.1 identifies the 3Cs on the top half of the diagram. They spell out the characteristics and needs of an effective organization. In effect, they define the arena where your decisions are made.

The bottom half of the diagram details what employees bring to the work scene; in other words, their attitudes toward organization policies and procedures, competencies, and needs. Your job is to merge these disparate elements to bring the characteristics and needs of the organization in line with those of the people in the organization. The goal is to reduce, or eliminate, the gaps between the opposing arrows in the diagram.

It is important to remind you that your implementing decisions all involve two separate sets of considerations, as discussed in Chapter 1. They are:

- The functional considerations which are determined by the position and organization

- The considerations that are common to all management/ leadership positions, regardless of function. They apply even in managerial positions to which no staff members report but where decisions, nevertheless, affect others— the stakeholders.

The 3Cs and the linking elements concepts apply only to guidelines for the latter, the management/leadership considerations.

In fostering alignment you perform the linking elements functions. Some are obvious, such as the requirement to be a role model in your communications, cooperation, adherence to the organization's policies, procedures, norms, and so on.

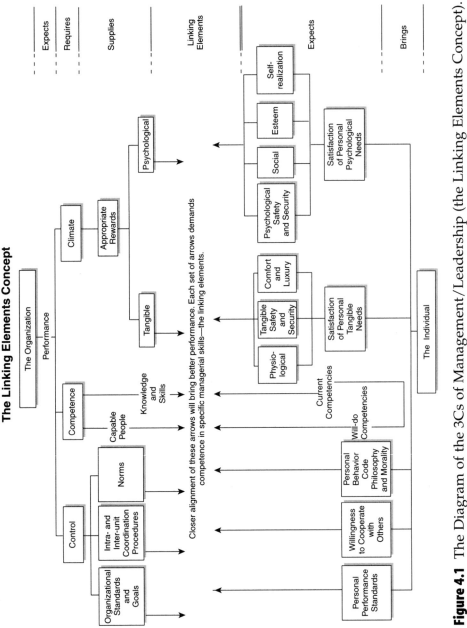

Figure 4.1 The Diagram of the 3Cs of Management/Leadership (the Linking Elements Concept).

251

In addition to being a role model, you need to develop those knowledge, skills, abilities, and traits which help you be a more competent leader. While your knowledge, skills, and abilities (KSAs) are subject to development, the traits such as integrity and honesty, empathy and liking for other people are integral to your personality and not easily changed. The 3Cs guidelines suggests an approach that makes KSA development relatively easy, and encourages the gradual modification of traits.

Figure 4.1 covers some of the specific components of the linking elements concept.

A More Detailed View, from the Perspective of the Organization

From the top of the diagram, on the *Organization* side, the diagram shows that, in order to achieve high-level performance:

1. An organizational unit must have Control to achieve a high level of performance.

    a. First of all, the unit must have direction. It must know where it wants to go and how fast it wants to get there. That is, it must have *goals* that it wants to achieve and must have *standards* of performance so that everyone knows what and how to contribute toward the achievement of these goals.

    b. To achieve Control, an organizational unit needs *coordination* and *cooperation*. Coordination implies sound procedures so that everybody knows what to do. Cooperation means that people want to do it because they have the self-discipline of a team, in which every individual recognizes the needs of the team and voluntarily gives higher priority to achieving the team's goals than to most-personal interests.

    For instance, everybody in an organization can agree with the goal that all output shall be of high quality. If coordination or cooperation are lacking, a lot of wasted motion will stymie the achievement of this goal. A competent team with members who have strong personal discipline will coordinate its actions, and each member will cooperate.

    c. For good Control there must also be policies and norms, arrived at with appropriate participation, which establish and communicate what the unit can expect from the team members, and what they can expect from the organizational unit and the other team members.

2. An organizational unit must have at least adequate functional Competence (and management/leadership competence for all members with such responsibilities) if it expects to achieve high-level performance. In today's changing world, this includes the flexibility to adapt. This means that either each individual on the team has the necessary knowledge, skills, and abilities (KSAs) to perform well, or that the unit can obtain any required skills not currently available. To achieve such competence, the unit must select people who either have most of the internally needed KSAs now or can acquire them readily.

3. An effective unit must have a favorable Climate that satisfies the needs of its members to achieve high-level performance.

   Climate depends on the satisfactions that people get from their work. There are two kinds of satisfaction, tangible and psychological. An organizational unit must provide adequately for both kinds. The psychological satisfactions include an absence of excessive work-related stress.

An organizational unit can achieve Control, technical Competence, and a positive Climate only if the people in the unit have the needed KSAs and are willing to devote them to the goals of the organization. The relationship of the individual to the organization is a critical factor in the achievement of performance goals, and the manager/leader, the person in the middle, can do much to shape that relationship.

A More Detailed View, from the Perspective of the Individual

From the bottom of the diagram, on the *Individual* side, the diagram shows the characteristics and needs of the individual which a manager/leader must balance with the characteristics and needs of the organization.

1. Individuals come to an organization with *personal performance standards and attitudes toward work and the organization's policies and procedures.* All or some of these may or may not match what is necessary to achieve the organizational goals. If willingness to work on required tasks and to accept the norms and assignments is sufficient to meet the unit's needs, then you have

very little to do. If, on the other hand, there are gaps, as frequently is the case, then there are a number of managerial KSAs that you must apply.

2. The coordination an organization needs so that all subunits and individuals can move toward the goals in an organized fashion requires procedures and methods, thoroughly understood by every staff member. In addition, it requires *cooperation* between people and with the procedures. There are many obstacles to cooperation, including differing team and individual objectives, workload demands, other conflicts of interests, and conflicts between people.

3. An individual brings a philosophy of life, norms, or a morality that may be compatible with the organization's norms. Often, though, individuals feel that some norms are inappropriate or that they should not be applied in a certain situation. When this is the case, difficult decisions have to be made. (A concept that might help with these decisions is described in a 1971 article reprinted as Appendix D in *Balancing Need of People and Organizations,* Rausch, 1978.) Sometimes these concern privileges by waiving the requirements of the norms, temporarily. At other times you must demand adherence to the norms. At the same time you must ensure that the norms are still appropriate and valid. You may have to work to bring changes in the norms if it turns out that they are no longer appropriate.

This dual responsibility, incidentally, highlights a major foundation of the diagram. It is not your task to force people into a mold that will bring some ideal arrangement. Rather, you must strive, wherever possible, to adapt the organization's norms and policies to the competencies and capabilities of the people, while at the same time helping people adapt themselves to the way the organization can be most successful.

4. New staff members and newly appointed managers come to their organizations with their own strengths and weaknesses, as well as with views on what they are willing to do. Some people call these will-do and can-do competencies. At the same time, some staff members have the ability to adapt, a certain flexibility that others do not possess. As a matter of fact, throughout their lives most people have deficiencies relative to the needs of the things they do or would like to do, including the tasks on which they work. Also, they often lack knowledge and skills needed for higher-level jobs that they hope will bring greater work satisfaction to their lives.

It is your task to help staff members, including managers who report to you, eliminate these deficiencies and develop KSAs in ways that increase their effectiveness. It is also your duty to help your staff members as they prepare themselves for jobs or assignments from which they will gain greater work satisfaction as they progress in their careers.

5. Finally, every individual expects that the organization will satisfy a complex set of both *tangible and psychological needs.* On the tangible side, there is the need for adequate income to pay for food, clothing, and shelter as well as for insurance and for a certain level of comfort and luxury. On the psychological side, there is the need to feel secure and not be subjected to excessive stress, the need to work for a manager in whom they have confidence and whom they can trust, the need to belong and to be respected, and the need to find a measure of satisfaction in one's work. There is a great deal that you can do to create the Climate that will raise the satisfaction staff members can obtain from their work.

In short, it is your responsibility to create an atmosphere in which your staff members can find the enthusiasm and motivation that will lead to top-level performance, even excellence in every function, not only during exciting and interesting challenges.

The Linking Elements

The linking elements are the *KSAs that you must apply* so that the organization's needs and the climate achieve the greatest possible balance with the characteristics and expectations of staff members. Each set of arrows shown in Figure 4.1 demands attention to the respective linking elements. Management/leadership guidelines can provide the decision considerations that will help you sharpen these skills and competencies.

As you get into the habit of doing the mental check demanded by the guidelines, you will find that more and more of your decision making will be comprehensive. It will become natural to you so that you can move through the linking elements analysis quickly and easily. Eventually, the triple analysis of:

1. How to build competence, while

2. Seeing to it that the unit enhances control, and

3. How to take these actions so they do not harm, but possibly enhance, the climate

will come almost instantaneously.

The linking elements diagram can serve as a guide for self-development in constantly providing a clear guide to the functions you must perform so that the organization or unit will be most effective. In effect, it lists the competencies for highly effective management and leadership, even for managers who do not possess a good measure of natural leadership talents and traits.

Linking elements, of course, do not stand alone. They overlap and support each other in an infinite number of ways.

People like to be members of a successful unit. They get satisfaction from teamwork, from their own high knowledge and skill levels, and from the effectiveness of other members of the team. Thus, good Control and Competence reinforce a good Climate brought on by managers/leaders who know how to satisfy the psychological needs of their people.

A positive Climate in turn reinforces positive attitudes and willingness to devote efforts to enhance personal effectiveness, bringing even higher performance levels and still greater personal motivation.

Specific Linking Elements

Most linking elements help to bring alignment of the characteristics and needs of the organization and those of the people, in all 3Cs. Some are more specifically useful in Control, Competence, or Climate, but there is always some fallout in the others. Sometimes this fallout is so strong that a specific management/leadership activity and the respective guideline, or guideline segment, has to be considered to be in more than one of the 3Cs.

Two linking elements that apply strongly to all 3Cs are sound *communications policies* and *appropriate participation* in decision making and planning.

For Control, the most important linking elements are:

- Goals

- KSAs

- Appropriate participation

- Coordination procedures

- Managerial/leadership actions that stimulate cooperation

- Performance evaluations

- Positive discipline

- Appropriate norms

- Conflict management

- Performance counseling

- Time management and delegation

- Effective meetings

- Effective delegation and task assignment

For Competence, the most important linking elements are:

- Recruiting

- Candidate selection and hiring (including interviewing)

- Management of learning

- Self-development counseling

- Coaching

- Communications policies and KSAs

- Appropriate participation

For Climate, the most important linking elements are:

- Communications policies and KSAs

- Appropriate participation

- Work-related stress control

- Psychological rewards
- Semitangible rewards
- Tangible rewards
- Performance evaluations
- Career and self-development counseling
- Conflict management

4   Additional Insights L

Positive Discipline and Counseling

For the artist, life is always a discipline,
and no discipline can be without pain.

The Dance of Life
Havelock Ellis

Introduction

This section covers:

1. Positive discipline

   - The five foundations
   - Requirements for positive discipline

2. Counseling

   - Performance and self-development/learning problem counseling
   - Counseling on career decisions
   - Counseling on personal issues affecting work performance
   - Counseling on personal issues possibly not affecting work performance

Positive Discipline

Most people are uncomfortable when they hear the word *discipline*. To many, it is almost a synonym for punishment. Some even hear *punishment* when the word is used to describe tight authoritarian controls, criticisms, or penalties for individuals who do not meet standards or adhere to rules and accepted practices.

Yet, discipline also has another, more positive meaning—the discipline that unites a successful ball team as it works in

well-coordinated fashion. This type of discipline is largely self-generated. Each member is aware of the team's objectives, strategies, and tactics and voluntarily, even eagerly, subordinates personal interests to those of the team. In this environment, trust between leader and team is strengthened and discipline is:

- A common understanding of the rules of the game and of the standards of performance (the norms, including those for morality and diversity, for work ethic, for quality, for cooperation and for behavior limits)

- Awareness of the personal and team benefits of the rules and standards

- Willingness, on the part of individual team members, to make personal sacrifices, if necessary, to help the team achieve its goals and to adhere to the norms

The five foundations

Positive discipline rests on five foundations:

1. There is an open two-way communications culture.

2. The same standards and norms apply to all.

3. Staff members who deserve commendation and privileges will receive them.

4. Those who violate accepted rules or fail to adhere to reasonable norms and standards, cooperatively determined, receive help, at first, and then gradually more stringent warnings until their behavior conforms, or disciplinary steps have to be invoked.

5. Counseling is used competently to reduce, to a minimum, the use of the organization's disciplinary procedure.

Positive discipline thus supports all 3Cs—Control, Competence, and Climate—and has no negative implications. It is closely related to coaching and to counseling. Through coaching, members of the team come to thoroughly understand their roles—*what* has to be done and *how* it is to be done. Counseling helps them see *why* something is necessary and to their benefit, so they will be fully motivated to devote maximum effort when needed.

Requirements for positive discipline

Effective positive discipline demands that you:

1. Create, with appropriate participation, fair standards and norms

2. Review standards and norms regularly with your people to ensure that they continue to be fair and equitable

3. Expect adherence to standards and norms, fairly and equitably

4. Demonstrate a willingness to discuss them when there are complaints of inadequate fairness

5. Ensure that you and all staff members with managerial/ leadership responsibilities:

   - Provide coaching where necessary

   - Provide recognition and psychological awards fairly and equitably

   - Communicate the standards and norms clearly during performance evaluations and coaching and counseling sessions

   - Criticize constructively by making sure that suggestions to improve are given in ways that will bring positive reactions

   - Provide counseling when appropriate

   - Are able to explain compensation decisions, including reasons for salary structure and salary differences (the importance of salaries paid in the respective industry for the type of work being done by the staff member, as well as the impact of time on the job, and of individual performance)

- Administer the disciplinary procedure in a consistent equitable way if the other steps do not achieve positive discipline and full cooperation

If you are skillful in establishing an atmosphere of positive discipline you have little need to apply disciplinary procedures. Still, situations will come up from time to time when, no matter how skillful you are, someone will not accept your suggestions and/or instructions to change inappropriate behavior. Under those conditions, after initial counseling rounds have failed, you have to apply the penalties of the organization's disciplinary procedure.

You must be thoroughly familiar with disciplinary procedures. It is equally important to the positive climate in your organizational unit that you apply those procedures with compassion. That means reasonable concern for any personal hardship that a disciplinary step may impose on an individual.

At the same time, avoiding disciplinary procedures is unwise. Ignoring infractions is unfair to all other members of a team and two of the five foundations of positive discipline are violated.

Counseling and discipline, even positive discipline, often involve some form of conflict (see Chapter 2, Additional Insights F, Managing Potentially Damaging Conflict).

Counseling

There are four uses for counseling (see segment e. of the Comprehensive Competence Guideline). The first two concern:

- Work-related opportunities, challenges, or problems

- Self-development and learning challenges

For these, staff members need guidance to become aware of and adopt appropriate behaviors or courses of action.

Counseling is often required for the third use: staff member career decisions where the manager/leader has a distinct, though more limited role.

Finally, counseling applies in personal issues that do or may affect performance. Here the manager's/leader's role is even more sharply limited.

All four uses affect the positive discipline climate. Managers/ leaders therefore need to ensure that counseling is performed competently in each segment of their respective organizational units. This is especially important because counseling is not a comfortable task for most managers. There might be conflict, especially in performance counseling and possibly in self-development and learning issues. In career development and personal problem counseling, there can be significant risks.

Beyond being a difficult task, recognizing when counseling is appropriate, and being adequately proactive without being intrusive, also requires greater knowledge and skills than the average manager possesses. Lack of skills, however, does not signal itself. Even in crisis situations, the problem is often seen to lie with the staff member rather than with counseling competence that might have prevented it. Ensuring ongoing development of counseling competence is, therefore, the type of responsibility that has to be undertaken without any clear symptoms of organizational need.

Developing competence for counseling, and especially for performance counseling, revolves around the need to consider several questions, which also can serve as guidelines for counseling:

- Will counseling intervention in this situation enhance positive discipline?

- If a counseling interview is called for, what steps should be taken prior to the counseling interview and during the counseling interview?

- Should an action plan be developed and formalized?

- Will follow-up be desirable?

Performance and self-development/learning problem counseling

There are three reasons why staff members may fail to do what is appropriate in a situation. They may:

4 **Insights L Continued**

UNAWARE	be not aware that the respective behavior is required or desirable at that point
UNABLE	not have the knowledge and/or the skill to perform the task at the expected level of competence
UNWILLING	have reservations about performing the task at that point, or simply do not want to do it

In the first two instances, staff members fail to do what they should do, either because they are not aware that it is required or desired, or because they do not have the competence to perform the task at the expected level. The third reason is different. Staff members have the skill to perform the task as expected and know that they are expected to do it. Still, they will not do it, because their norms do not match those of the organization.

Different managerial actions are appropriate for these three situations. In the first two, the behavior discrepancies can be remedied through *coaching*, by helping the staff members become aware that certain behavior is appropriate and/or helping them achieve the desired competence level.

In the third reason for the behavior discrepancy, the appropriate first remedy is counseling. Shaking out whether a staff member has the competence to do something, *cannot* do it, or is actually *unwilling* to do it is an essential early step in counseling. The unwillingness may be due to the apprehension about admitting lack of competence. If that apprehension exists, counseling may have to be used to overcome that concern, and possibly to overcome resistance to learning.

With competent counseling, reliance on the disciplinary procedure is held to a minimum and positive discipline is strengthened.

Counseling on career decisions

Effective managers/leaders consider the career aspirations of their staff members. At appropriate times, they share with their staff members the broader perspective which their position and experience is likely to have given them. They thus help each indi-

4 Insights L Continued

vidual gain a more realistic view of the potential career paths that exist within the organization, and sometimes even elsewhere.

Competent career counseling can add to the effectiveness of performance evaluations. There are two major problems that career guidance can relieve:

1. In most organizations, the discretion a manager/leader has for providing compensation increases to staff members is sharply limited. Raises have to be distributed based on factors such as the amounts available for general increases, the compensation range of the job, and the relative position of the staff member's compensation to the top of the range. Hence, there is a need to demonstrate to staff members that the effort to achieve a good performance record can have benefits in addition to the immediate salary increase.

2. At the same time, it appears to staff members that performance evaluations are geared primarily toward improvement of staff member performance. On the surface, advantages to staff members are clear only if there is a visible relationship between the evaluation and tangible rewards. Career counseling can show that the improvement plan, a primary output of a performance evaluation, can help to better prepare a staff member who seeks career advancement or a career change.

Most managers/leaders do not find themselves involved in career counseling situations very frequently. However, performance evaluations can sometimes lead to discussions of career possibilities. There are also occasions when the staff member takes the initiative, seeking advice on how to progress both financially and in position.

Requests for information on opportunities for higher earnings are not necessarily requests for career counseling. They could be introductions to requests for salary increases or for counseling on personal issues. Requests for information on how to advance to higher or better-paying positions, on the other hand, are requests

for career counseling. Managers/leaders need to be aware of the potential and sources of risk-financial and moral, that can accompany discussion about career opportunities:

1. When managers give advice, they assume a certain amount of responsibility over the outcome.

2. Instead of giving advice, it is wiser for managers to point out that:

   • They cannot provide any specific advice, only general guidelines for enhancing the staff member's competitive position in relation to others who may seek a position.

   • There is no assurance that these guidelines will actually lead to finding, and obtaining, a desired position.

3. In career counseling, it is appropriate for managers to clarify what they may be able to do:

   • Provide assistance in clarifying the factual elements that will help staff members evaluate the advantages and disadvantages of the position to which they may aspire

   • Provide information about the competencies that are necessary for success in that position

   • When personally qualified, provide assistance, guidance, or suggestions for acquiring those competencies

   • Possibly arrange for staff members to speak with incumbents in the type of positions to which they aspire, to obtain information on the pluses, minuses, and requirements from that person's point of view

Helping managers in the organizational unit understand their role in providing career planning assistance is not intended to make them career counselors. They need to understand that their objective is limited—to help their staff members gain perspective on the knowledge, skill, and other requirements for

4   Insights L Continued

favorable consideration, as applicants, to those positions in which they may be interested.

Counseling on personal issues affecting work performance

You will sometimes be called on to provide either advice or assistance to staff members with personal problems. In these situations you need to have a clear view of your responsibilities.

Some of the situations directly affect work performance. Acrimonious divorce proceedings, illness of close relatives, overindulgence in alcohol, and drug abuse are examples of personal situations that have considerable potential for affecting performance. These may even first manifest themselves in performance problems requiring counseling. Unfortunately, sometimes they may be so serious that they cannot be resolved that way.

Regulations and laws have to be considered and more than one counseling session may be required before a decision can be made that more than counseling is necessary—whether the disciplinary procedure is applicable or whether the situation is one in which the employee's problems are beyond his or her control and therefore professional help or involvement of social services agencies is called for. In any case, the organization's policy on these matters should, of course, be followed. It is likely that it calls for sending the staff member to the Human Resource department. If there is no such department at the location, or if no policy is in place, all 3Cs guidelines call for serious consideration of developing a policy, even if it applies only to you or to you and the managers/leaders in your organizational unit. Control may suffer, competence is threatened, and various stakeholders might be affected negatively in various ways, creating a disturbance in the climate.

Counseling on personal issues possibly not affecting work performance

There are also personal problems of staff members that do not affect their work. They concern matters of health, interpersonal relationships with other staff members and with family or friends,

or difficulties with offspring. Staff members often look to their manager as an experienced, knowledgeable friend to whom they will turn for advice in difficult situations.

It is important to clarify what the appropriate limits should be for helping in such situations.

Here, too, organizational policy is likely to call for obtaining guidance from the Human Resource department, if one is available.

Policies should also make it clear that managers/leaders need to keep the possible liability in mind that could lead to problems for the organization if well-meaning suggestions or advice do not work out well.

Counseling in personal problem situations should therefore be totally nondirective, intended solely to help the staff member see issues in better perspective. Even explaining what the manager might do, if he or she were in that situation, might be risky if the exposure is large.

4   Additional Insights M

Time Management and Delegation

Art is long and time is fleeting
And our hearts, though stout and brave
Still, like muted drums, are beating
Funeral marches to the grave.

A Psalm of Life
Henry W. Longfellow

Introduction

While much has been written and said about time management, it boils down to two things: set priorities, and do not do what you can delegate or assign to others if it does not fit your priorities.

Time Management

Time management is another skill that was on the top of the lists for management development programs during the 1970s and has since then almost disappeared. Still, there is something of importance involved.

Alan Lakein, the top guru on the subject (Lakein 1973), covered all the bases for effective time management. High in his list were setting of priorities and avoidance of time wasters.

Little needs to be said about time wasters. We are all aware what they are: unimportant phone calls, interruptions, uninvited visitors, unnecessary or poorly conducted meetings, and so on.

More important, however, are priorities. They determine what work managers do themselves and what they delegate or assign.

Here Lakein suggested three groupings: priority 1 items are done by the manager, those in priority 2 are delegated, and (tongue in cheek) those in priority 3 are placed in the bottom drawer of the desk—if they don't rear their "ugly" heads within a month, they are thrown away.

4 Insights M Continued

Not bad. However, not much guidance, either. The importance/urgency separation suggested in a diagram first published in a simulation exercise (Didactic Systems 1977), then in other publications, and made famous in two of Stephen Covey's books (1989, 1994), can shed some light.

The diagram below considers all four possible combinations of importance and urgency.

- Matters that are low importance/low urgency can be postponed until there is some spare time available, or they can be given to anyone who has, or will have, time and the necessary competence.

- Matters that are high importance/low urgency should be assigned to someone who has the necessary competence and preferably is not busy with tasks that are more important and at least equally urgent.

- Matters that are low importance/high urgency should be delegated (often with goals—see Chapter 2, Additional Insights E, Making a Goals Program Work).*

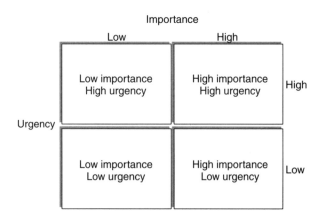

*The importance of considering the conclusions from this diagram for goal setting cannot be overstated. There is no limit to the number of goals that could be set if goals were set on all the things an organizational unit and its people do. Careful analysis of the importance/urgency considerations are therefore critical in making goals an effective management/leadership tool.

4 | **Insights M Continued**

- Matters that are high urgency/high importance should be done, with portions delegated.

With these four categories in mind, managers/leaders can concentrate on those things that most deserve personal attention. At the same time, the added impetus to delegate can bring developmental assignments that will strengthen the organizational unit's competence.

Developing the discipline necessary to avoid time-wasters, though not high urgency, is also among the important matters to which managers/leaders must attend themselves.

Time management thus is a primary reason for delegating projects and responsibilities. That is why delegation has been combined with time management in this section.

Delegation

It is worthwhile to think of delegation and task assignment in a similar vein as participation in decision making and even, to some extent, as goals and action steps (see Chapter 1, Additional Insights D, Participation in Decision Making and Planning, and Chapter 2, Additional Insights E, Making a Goals Program Work).

In delegation, as in setting of goals, the manager/leader and the delegatee jointly set goals on what is to be achieved, and the delegatee has wide authority to make the necessary decisions, with the manager providing all needed and requested support. Both parties understand that it is the delegatee's responsibility to achieve the delegated results or, if obstacles develop that may prevent such achievement, to give the manager/leader adequate notice and information so timely intervention with additional resources is possible. In effect, this defines the responsibility that remains with the manager/leader: to intervene and accept responsibility for the outcome when the results are threatened.

Task assignment, on the other hand, applies to action steps. Here the manager/leader and the assignee agree on the definition of the task and on the resources that may be required. Then the assignee can be expected to complete it.

4 Insights M Continued

Clear definition and communication of the limits of authority and the way responsibilities are shared is of great importance in delegation and even in task assignment.

When a delegated assignment requires the efforts of several staff members at the same organizational level, and especially when staff members from different departments are involved, it is even more important, than with delegated projects, to clearly define these limits and to reach thorough mutual understanding on when the manager has to be asked for support and/or involvement.

4 | Additional Insights N

Management Development Programs:
Hopes, Disappointments, and Status

> Let us then be up and doing,
> With a heart for any fate
> Still achieving, still pursuing,
> Learn to labor and to wait.

> *A Psalm of Life, Longfellow*

Introduction

This section traces the search for truly effective management development approaches, from the time when such programs first became popular to the present. There have been many such attempts to help managers become more effective. All have contributed extensively to the knowledge that management development professionals can use to develop programs for their organizations or offer publicly.

Some, like Blake and Srygley-Mouton's Managerial Grid (Blake and Srygley-Mouton 1964, 1968), have been adapted into the theories taught in management eduction courses (see Chapter 1, Additional Insights B, Leadership Theories). Most started in management development, based on ideas presented in the books of the original authors or their disciples.

The Programs

Some of the earliest programs during the 1950s, on predetermined time standards, and a few minor components of the programs on goals and objectives, covered topics which dealt extensively with functional issues (Barnard 1938; Batten 1966; Drucker 1954, 1974; Hughes 1965; Odiorne 1961, 1968; Odiorne 1987).

Then, for many years, the primary thrust of programs was on the managerial/leadership aspects of managerial work, including

4 Insights N Continued

interpersonal skills and self-awareness. Programs involved sensitivity training or T-groups (Marrow 1964), communications skills (Luft 1970; Berne 1967; Harris 1976), decision making (Kepner and Tregoe 1965, 1981), time management (Lakein 1973), managerial grid (Blake and Srygley-Mouton 1964, 1968), and life-cycle theory of leadership/situational leadership (Hersey and Blanchard 1969, 1982).

Gradually self-motivational, almost inspirational overtones crept into the picture. Examples are the highly popular books *The One-Minute Manager* (Blanchard and Spencer 1982), *In Search of Excellence* (Peters and Waterman 1982), *A Passion for Excellence: The Leadership Difference* (Peters and Austin 1985), *Thriving on Chaos* (Peters 1987), and *The Seven Habits of Highly Effective People* (Covey 1989).

During the 1960s, there was great hope that programs, considered comprehensive at that time, would bring significant improvement in the quality of managerial decision making and behavior. That hope gradually faded as it became apparent that no concentrated program, even with several follow-up sessions, would generate long-lasting comprehensive behavior change. It became apparent that for change to take hold the culture of the entire organization needed to undergo transformation, and the dramatic changes that would be required did not seem to have happened anywhere, not even in organizations where there was strong initial commitment.

Then, under the intensifying competitive international pressures of the 1980s and 1990s, emphasis shifted from these attempts to bring change by developing people to approaches that changed the organization.

Human resource development programs were then used to develop competencies for achieving these changes, and to help people cope with the challenges they would have to meet. These included quality circles (Lawler and Mohrman 1985; Wood 1983), quality management and continuous quality improvement (Juran 1964, 1989; Torbert 1992), reengineering (Hammer and Champy

4 Insights N Continued

1993; Hammer and Stanton 1995), self-directed teams (Katzenbach and Smith 1993), the learning organization (Senge 1990).

How the Linking Elements Concept (the 3Cs) Differs from All Others

The linking elements concept is somewhat different from all these programs. It offers the managers/leaders an opportunity to review their decisions so they can become more effective in *all* their activities. It is not prescriptive as most of the earlier widely accepted approaches, yet it is pervasive and unobtrusive. Each manager who wants to improve competencies as manager *and* leader can begin to gradually develop the habits that will sharpen the 3Cs decision-making skills and implement the results, regardless of the culture of the organization. There is no required formula, and even the guidelines suggested by the 3Cs model are subject to modification to better fit the specific manager's style.

As mentioned in Chapter 1, in addition to the basic benefit of better decisions and plans from consideration of appropriate guidelines, there are several other points in favor of decision making with guidelines (the 3Cs guidelines or others):

1. By creating a structure for participation, guidelines can ensure that the special knowledge and the views of several people can be used to enhance any decision in which they are invited to comment. With the spreading use of PC networks, these insights and views can be focused on a specific decision or plan without the need for lengthy meetings or the emergence of conflicts.

2. By providing a framework for easily recording the use of the guidelines, a record and audit trail can allow review of decisions or plans just prior to implementation.

3. Decisions of new managers/leaders can be monitored for coaching purposes.

Insights N Continued

4. If an organization decided on encouraging the regular use of guidelines, it could make that a requirement for consideration in promotion decisions, thus signaling to all staff members that it would be in their interest to develop their decision-making competence with the use of the 3Cs guidelines or their own.

Additional Insights O

Guidelines for Management Functions Other than Leadership

The moving finger writes;
and, having writ, moves on . . .

Rubaiyat, Omar Khayyam

Introduction

Models similar to the 3Cs model for management/leadership can be developed for functional management decisions and for professional development in fields such as marketing, finance, manufacturing or operations, physical distribution, and so on. They can also be useful in health care, institutional and social support functions, and social science fields. Such models would expand on the benefits from use of the guidelines concept by making it applicable to those fields where guidelines are not already the foundation for learning and application. In technical fields, more-or less-specific guidelines are, of course, the foundation for professional practice, and even for regulations. Architects and structural engineers abide by very rigid guidelines, while diagnosis procedures for physicians are less formal. On the other hand, there are no widely accepted guidelines used for many fields such as social services, marketing, fire service, and so on.

The crude examples of models that can serve as foundation for guidelines for marketing and for two fire service activities, outlined in this section, are only initial models. They need considerable refinement since they have not had the benefit of the extensive development and testing that has been devoted to the management/leadership model.

A Foundation for Decision-Making Guidelines for Marketing

It is the function of marketing to:

- Identify prospective users of the products or services

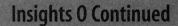

- Determine the needs of prospective and current users relative to the products or services

- Determine how the products or services meet those needs

- Develop messages that will clearly communicate these benefits

- Develop strategies for disseminating the messages

- Obtain the resources to carry out the strategies

- Ensure availability of the products or services in the markets where promoted

These thoughts could be expressed in a fashion similar to the fundamental statements used in the management/leadership model. Initial guidelines could be two or more questions based on each of these statements. Theories, concepts, and even history could be built on that foundation.

A Foundation for Decision-Making Guidelines for Officers in the Fire Service

The examples below pertain to only two functions of fire departments—incident command and fire safety education.

Incident command

The primary objectives of incident command are to ensure that all is done that can be done to protect people, both the civilians at risk and the firefighters and, beyond that, everything is done to preserve and protect property by confining the fire and extinguishing it as quickly as possible.

Here, too, guidelines can be drawn from this statement. As an example, a guideline that could quickly run through a fire officer's mind is:

To protect people, both the civilians at risk and the firefighters and, beyond that, to preserve and protect property, what else do

Insights O Continued

I have to consider in the size-up so that I will use the most appropriate strategy and tactics action plan?

Behind this basic guideline could be a more comprehensive one that involves the specific items to consider, including the situation, the needs, and the resources.

Fire safety education

The primary objective of fire safety education is to increase awareness and to motivate toward changes in behavior of the public through various programs and delivery methods, utilizing all mobilizable community and departmental resources.

Here the guidelines could be:

What else can be done to enlist more community resources to reach more people in the community effectively with the fire safety message?

What else could be done to motivate those who have been exposed to the fire safety message to act on it?

What else could be done to evaluate to what extent fire safety is being practiced in residences, businesses, and institutional occupancies?

Conclusions

These examples show that focus on the most important issues can provide a basis for the development of a set of fundamental guidelines. These, in turn, can help a learner gain sound perspective on the subject. They can then gradually lead to a comprehensive, coordinated picture, which can serve as foundation for the acquisition of more knowledge, for skill development, and most importantly, for decisions.

References

Adams, J. S. 1965. Inequity in social exchange. In *Advances in experimental social psychology.* edited by L. Berkowitz. New York: Academy Press.

Alderfer, Clayton P. 1969. A new theory of human needs. *Organizational Behavior and Human Performance.* (May):142–75.

Associates, Office of Military Leadership. (Ed.) 1976. *A Study of Organizational Leadership.* Harrisburg, Penn.: Stackpole.

Avolio, Bruce J., and Bernard M. Bass. 1995. You can drag a horse to water, but you can't make it drink: Evaluating a full range leadership model for training and development. Unpublished paper, Center for Leadership Studies, Binghampton University, Binghampton, NY.

Barnard, Chester. 1938. *Functions of the executive.* Cambridge, Mass.: Harvard University Press.

Bass, Bernard M., and James A. Vaughn. 1966. *Training in industry: The management of learning.* Belmont, Calif.: Wadsworth.

Batten, J. D. 1966. *Beyond management by objectives.* New York: American Management Associations.

Bennis, Warren, and Burt Nanus. 1985. *Leadership: Strategies for taking charge.* New York: Harper & Row.

Berne, Eric. 1967. *Games people play: The psychology of human relationships.* New York: Grove Press.

Blake, Robert R., and Jane Srygley-Mouton. 1964. *The managerial grid.* Houston: Gulf.

Blake, Robert R., and Jane Srygley-Mouton. 1968. *Corporate excellence through grid organization development.* Houston: Gulf.

Blanchard, Kenneth H., and Spencer Johnson. 1982. *The one-minute manager.* New York: Morrow.

Bloom, Benjamin S., ed. 1956. *Taxonomy of educational objectives, the classification of educational goals, Handbook I: Cognitive domain.* New York: David McKay.

Bowditch, James L., and Anthony F. Buono. 1994. *A primer on organizational behavior.* 3d ed. New York: Wiley.

Bramson, Robert M. 1981. *Coping with difficult people.* Garden City, N.Y.: Anchor Press.

Bruner, J. S. 1966. *Toward a theory of instruction.* Cambridge, Mass.: Harvard University Press.

Burns, J. M. 1978. *Leadership*. New York: Harper & Row.

Clary, Thomas C., Harvey Lieberman, and Erwin Rausch. 1974. *Transactional analysis—Improving communications: A didactic exercise*. Cranford, N.J.: Didactic Systems.

Covey, Stephen R. 1989. *The seven habits of highly effective people: Restoring the character ethics*. New York: Simon & Schuster.

Covey, Stephen R. 1994. *First things first: To live, to love, to learn, to leave a legacy*. New York: Simon & Schuster.

Deci, E. I. 1975. *Intrinsic motivation*. New York: Plenum.

Deming, W. Edwards. 1986. *Out of the crises*. Cambridge, Mass.: MIT Center for Advanced Engineering Study.

Didactic Systems. 1970. *Selecting effective people: A didactic simulation/game*. Cranford, N.J.: Didactic Systems.

Didactic Systems. 1971. *Effective delegation: A didactic simulation/game*. Cranford, N.J.: Didactic Systems.

Didactic Systems. 1974. *Appraising employee performance: A self-study unit*. Cranford, N.J.: Didactic Systems.

Didactic Systems. 1974. *Managing time effectively: A self-study unit*. Cranford, N.J.: Didactic Systems.

Didactic Systems. 1975. *Time management: A didactic exercise*. Cranford, N.J.: Didactic Systems.

Didactic Systems. 1977. *Management in the fire service*, edited by Erwin Rausch. Quincy, Mass.: NFPA.

Didactic Systems. 1977. *Managing and allocating time: A didactic simulation exercise*. Cranford, N.J.: Didactic Systems.

Didactic Systems. 1977. *Positive discipline: A study unit*. Cranford, N.J.: Didactic Systems.

Didactic Systems. 1977. *Providing recognition: A handbook of ideas*. Cranford, N.J.: Didactic Systems.

Didactic Systems. 1996. *ASP—The achievement stimulating process: A handbook for managers/leaders*. Cranford, N.J.: Didactic Systems.

Drucker, Peter F. 1954. *The practice of management*. New York: Harper Brothers.

Drucker, Peter F. 1974. *Management: Tasks, responsibilities, practices*. New York: Harper and Row.

Fast, Julius. 1970. *Body language*. New York: M. Evans and Company.

Fiedler, F. E. 1967. *A theory of leadership effectiveness*. New York: McGraw-Hill.

Fiedler, F. E. 1986. The contribution of cognitive resources and leader behavior to organizational performance. *Journal of Applied Social Psychology* 16:532–548.

Fisher, Roger, and William Ury. 1981. *Getting to yes*. Boston: Houghton Mifflin.

Fleishman, E. A., E. F. Harris, and R. D. Burtt. 1955. *Leadership and supervision in industry*. Columbus, Ohio: Ohio State University Press.

Gagne, Robert M. 1968. Context, isolation and interference effects on the retention of fact. *Journal of Educational Psychology* 60:408–414.

Gagne, Robert M. 1977. *The conditions of learning.* 3d ed. NY: Holt, Rinehart and Winston.

Ghiselli, E. E. 1963. The validity of management traits in relation to occupational level. *Personnel Psychology.* 16:109–113.

Gordon, Myron. 1981. *Making meetings more productive.* New York: Sterling Publishing.

Gray, John. 1992. *Men are from Mars, women are from Venus: A practical guide for improving communications and getting what you want in your relationship.* New York: Harper and Collins.

Hammer, Michael, and James Champy. 1993. *Reengineering the corporation.* New York: Harper Business.

Hammer, Michael, and Steven A. Stanton. 1995. *The reengineering revolution.* New York: Harper Business.

Harris, Thomas A. 1976. *I'm OK, you're OK: A practical guide to transactional analysis.* New York: Avon.

Hersey, Paul, and Kenneth H. Blanchard. 1969. Life cycle theory of leadership. *Training and Development Journal* 32(2 May).

Hersey, Paul, and Kenneth H. Blanchard. 1982. *Management of organizational behavior: Utilizing human resources.* 4th ed. Englewood Cliffs, N.J.: Prentice Hall.

Herzberg, Frederick, B. Mausner, and B. Snyderman. 1959. The motivation to work. New York: Wiley.

Herzberg, Frederick. 1968. One more time: How do you motivate employees? *Harvard Business Review,* Jan/Feb.

Heyel, Carl, ed. 1982. *The encyclopedia of management.* 3d ed. New York: Van Nostrand.

House, R. J. 1971. A path-goal theory of leader effectiveness. *Administrative Science Quarterly* 16 (September):321–338.

Hughes, Charles L. 1965. *Goal setting: Key to individual and organizational effectiveness.* New York: American Management Association.

Jones, Betty, and Harvey Lieberman. 1978. Linking Elements: A comprehensive approach to management training. *Canadian Training Methods* (February):23–25

Juran, Joseph M. 1964. *Managerial breakthrough.* New York: McGraw-Hill.

Juran, Joseph M. 1989. *Juran on leadership for quality: An executive handbook.* New York: The Free Press.

Kahn, R. and D. Katz. 1960. Leadership practices in relation to productivity and morale. In *Group dynamics, research and theory,* eds. D. Cartwright and A. Zander. Elmsford, NY: Row, Paterson.

Katzenbach, Jon R., and Douglas K. Smith. 1993. *The wisdom of teams: Creating the high performance organization.* New York: Harper Business.

Kepner, Charles H., and Benjamin B. Tregoe. 1965. *The rational manager.* Princeton, N.J.: Kepner-Tregoe.

Kepner, Charles H., and Benjamin B. Tregoe. 1981. *The new rational manager.* Princeton, N.J.: Kepner-Tregoe.

Kirkpatrick, Donald L. 1971. *Supervisory training and development.* Reading, Mass: Addison-Wesley.

Kirkpatrick, Donald L. 1994. *Evaluating training programs: The four levels.* San Francisco, Calif.: Berrett-Koehler.

Knowles, Malcolm. 1968. Andragogy, not pedagogy. *Adult Leadership.* April, as discussed in Kirkpatrick, 1971.

Knowles, Malcolm. 1990. *The adult learner: A neglected species.* 4th ed. Houston: Gulf.

Konopacki, Allen. 1987. Eye language: Clues to your prospects' thoughts. *Medical Marketing and Media* (June):66, 70–72.

Koontz, Harold. 1980. The management theory jungle revisited. *Academy of Management Review* 5 (2):175–187.

Lakein, Alan. 1973. *How to get control of your time and your life.* New York: P. H. Wyden.

Lawler, E. E. III, and S. A. Mohrman. 1985. Quality circles after the fad. *Harvard Business Review* (Jan/Feb):65–71.

Lazarus, Sy. 1975. *Loud & clear: A guide to effective communications.* New York: Amacom (American Management Association).

Lefrancois, Guy R. 1995. *Theories of human learning.* 3d. ed. Pacific Grove, Calif.: Brooks/Cole Publishing.

Lieberman, Harvey, and Erwin Rausch, eds. 1977. *Providing recognition: A handbook of ideas.* Cranford, N.J.: Didactic Systems.

Likert, Rensis. 1961. *New patterns of management.* New York: McGraw-Hill.

Locke, Edwin A., and Gary P. Latham. 1984. *Goal setting: A motivational technique that works.* Englewood Cliffs, N.J.: Prentice Hall.

Locke, Edwin A., and Gary P. Latham. 1990. *A theory of goal setting and task performance.* Englewood Cliffs, N.J.: Prentice Hall.

Luft, Joseph. 1970. *Group processes: An introduction to group dynamics.* Mountain View, Calif.: Mayfield.

Mager, Robert F. 1968. *Developing attitude toward learning.* Palo Alto, Calif.: Fearon.

Magoon, Paul M., and John B. Richards. 1966. *Discipline or disaster: Management's only choice; How to fulfill employees' basic emotional job-security needs.* New York: Exposition Press.

Maier, Norman R. F. 1974. Assets and liabilities in group problem solving: The need for an integrative function. *Psychological Review* 74(4):240–241.

Marrow, Alfred J. 1964. *Behind the executive mask.* New York: American Management Association.

Maslow, Abraham H. 1954. *Motivation and personality.* New York: Harper and Row.

Mayo, Elton. 1933, 1946. *The human problems of an industrial civilization.* Boston, Mass.: Division of Research, Harvard Business School.

McClelland, David C. 1961. *The achieving society.* New York: Van Nostrand.

McGregor, Douglas. 1960. *The human side of enterprise.* New York: McGraw-Hill.

McLagan, Patricia A. 1978. *Helping others learn*. Reading, Mass.: Addison-Wesley.

Meyer, Herbert H., Emanuel Kay, and John R. P. French, Jr. 1965. Split roles in performance appraisal. *Harvard Business Review* (Jan/Feb). Reprinted in *Harvard Business Review, Business classics: Fifteen key concepts for managerial success*. Various dates.

Moorhead, Gregory, and Ricky W. Griffin. 1992. *Organizational behavior: Managing people and organizations*. 3d ed. Boston: Houghton Mifflin.

Nelson, Bob. 1994. *1001 ways to reward employees*. New York: Workman Publishing.

Nichols, Ralph. 1962. Listening is good business. *Management of personnel quarterly* 1(2):2–9.

Nirenberg, Jesse S. 1963. *Getting through to people*. Englewood Cliffs, N.J.: Prentice Hall.

Odiorne, George S. 1961. *How managers make things happen*. Englewood Cliffs, N.J.: Prentice-Hall.

Odiorne, George S. 1968. *Management decisions by objectives*. Englewood Cliffs, N.J.: Prentice-Hall.

Odiorne, George S. 1987. Measuring the unmeasurable: Setting standards for management performance. *Business Horizon* 30(4):69–75.

Peters, Tom, and Robert H. Waterman, Jr. 1982. *In search of excellence: Lessons from America's best-run companies*. New York: Harper & Row.

Peters, Tom, and Nancy Austin. 1985. *A passion for excellence: The leadership difference*. New York: Random House.

Peters, Tom. 1987. *Thriving on chaos*. New York: Alfred A. Knopf.

Rausch, Erwin, and Wallace Wohlking. 1969. *Handling conflict in management I, II and III: Business games*. Cranford, N.J.: Didactic Systems.

Rausch, Erwin, ed. 1970. *Interviewing*. In Simulation Series for Business and Industry. Chicago: Science Research Associates.

Rausch, Erwin. 1971. The effective organization: Morale vs. discipline. *Management Review*. New York: American Management Association.

Rausch, Erwin, and George Rausch. 1971. *Leading groups to better decisions: A business game*. Cranford, N.J.: Didactic Systems.

Rausch, Erwin. 1978. *Balancing needs of people and organizations: The linking elements concept*. Washington, DC: Bureau of National Affairs (Cranford, N.J.: Didactic Systems, 1985).

Rausch, Erwin. 1980. How to make a goals program successful. *Training and Development Journal* (March).

Rausch, Erwin. 1985. *Win-win performance management/appraisal*. New York: John Wiley & Sons.

Rausch, Erwin, and Harry Carter. 1989. *Management in the fire service*. 2d ed. Quincy, Mass.: NFPA.

Rausch, Erwin, ed. 1980. *Management in institutions of higher learning*. Lexington, Mass.: Lexington Books.

Rausch, Erwin, and John B. Washbush. 1996. A new pedagogical and management/leadership model—and research opportunities. In

Proceedings of IBAM4, Institute of Behavioral and Applied Management. Annual Conference, October.

Rausch, Erwin, and Harry Carter. 1998. *Management in the fire service.* 3d ed. Quincy, Mass.: NFPA (in development).

Senge, Peter M. 1990. *The fifth discipline: The art and practice of the learning organization.* New York: Currency and Doubleday.

Skinner, B. F. 1968. *The technology of teaching.* New York: Appleton Century Crofts.

Steers, R. M., and Lyman W. Porter. 1979. *Motivation and work behavior.* 2d ed. New York: McGraw-Hill.

Stogdill, Ralph M. 1974. *Handbook of leadership: A survey of theory and research.* New York: Free Press.

Tannen, Deborah. 1990. *You just don't understand.* New York: Ballantine Books.

Tannenbaum, Robert, and Warren H. Schmidt. 1958. How to choose a leadership pattern. *Harvard Business Review* (March/April): revisited May/June 1973.

Torbert, William. 1992. The true challenge of generating continual quality improvement. *Journal of Management Inquiry* 1(4):331–336.

Ury, William. 1991. *Getting past no.* New York: Bantam Books.

Vroom, Victor, and Philip W. Yetton. 1973. *Leadership and decision-making.* Pittsburgh: University of Pittsburgh Press.

Wood, Robert C. 1983. *Beyond quality circles: The path to profits.* Chicago, IL: Blackman, Kallick, Bartelstein.

Yate, Martin J. 1987. *Hiring the best: A manager's guide to effective interviewing.* Boston: Bob Adams.

Index

READER FEEDBACK
Fax to ASQ Quality Press Acquisitions: 414–272–1734

Comments and Areas for Improvement:
High Quality Leadership: Practical Guidelines to Becoming a More Effective Manager (Rausch H0984)

Please give us your comments, feedback, and suggestions for making this book more useful. We believe in the importance of continuous improvement and in meeting your needs. Your comments will help determine what improvements can be made in all ASQ Quality Press books.

Please share your opinion by circling the number below:

Ratings of the Book	Needs Work		Satisfactory	Excellent		Comments
Structure, flow, and logic	1	2	3	4	5	
Content, ideas, and information	1	2	3	4	5	
Style, clarity, ease of reading	1	2	3	4	5	
Held my interest	1	2	3	4	5	
Met my overall expectations	1	2	3	4	5	

I read the book because:

The best part of the book was:

The least satisfactory part of the book was:

Other suggestions for improvement:

General comments:

Name/Address/Phone: (optional)

Thank you for your feedback. If you do not have access to a fax machine, please mail this form to: ASQ Quality Press, 611 East Wisconsin Avenue, P.O. Box 3005, Milwaukee, WI 53201-3005   Phone: 414-272-8575